ANNA ELEANOR ROOSEVELT

THE EVOLUTION
OF A REFORMER

~

ANNA ELEANOR ROOSEVELT

THE EVOLUTION OF A REFORMER

JAMES R. KEARNEY

illustrated with photographs

HOUGHTON MIFFLIN COMPANY BOSTON

1968

First Printing w

To the memory of my father-in-law
JOHN HARDING McNATT

~

CONTENTS

ILLUSTRATIONS

(following page 176)

Eleanor Roosevelt and her father, Elliot, about 1889.

Contributor to a complex: Anna Hall Roosevelt, whom her daughter called "the most beautiful woman I have ever seen."

The diffident young matron with her awesome mother-in-law, Sara Delano Roosevelt.

Mrs. Roosevelt with New York City schoolchildren, and at the Brooklyn Jewish Hospital.

Mrs. Roosevelt with Jack McMichael and William Hinckley, leaders of the Communist-infiltrated American Youth Congress.

Eleanor Roosevelt at a 1920-Democratic conclave, and with the President on a campaign trip.

Mrs. Roosevelt at the Democratic National Convention, 1940.

Mrs. Roosevelt flew wherever she could on her extensive travels.

Mrs. Roosevelt in Puerto Rico and the Virgin Islands, and at the Golden Gate International Exposition in 1939.

Mrs. Roosevelt at the White House, 1940.

(Unless otherwise credited, the photographs are reproduced through the courtesy of the Franklin D. Roosevelt Library, Hyde Park, N. Y.)

INTRODUCTION

THE GREATEST OBSTACLE confronting any study of Eleanor Roosevelt is the fact that the bulk of her papers are currently closed to research. The papers, mountainous in volume, repose in the Franklin D. Roosevelt Library at Hyde Park, New York. They consist of her correspondence with the general public, government officials, and her friends and family, and include diaries and other personal observations as well. It is to be hoped that such a potentially valuable contribution to history will soon be made available to scholars and interested parties generally.

Even without use of these papers, however, it is high time that Mrs. Roosevelt's career be subject to critical appraisal. Her role in United States history since 1933 was a prominent one. Not only were her ideas often influential in the shaping of federal policy, but she also was a leading spokesman for getting these ideas accepted by a large portion of the electorate. Bearing the prestige of the Roosevelt name, she acted as the President's "second self," frequently assuming a stand on public issues which her husband, because of political considerations, could not afford. At the same time her position was entirely unofficial; she could always claim that she was merely acting in the capacity of a private citizen. She thus came to have something of a dual identity, either side of which she could emphasize as the occasion demanded. This flexibility was, as shall be seen, a tremendous political advantage.

Fortunately, an immense amount of material, above and beyond her private papers, awaits the student of Eleanor Roosevelt's activities. Some of her correspondence is available in various private collections; some also is included in the official records of certain of the New Deal agencies. Without question, however, the most valuable source lies in her own enormous output of the spoken and written word. Through the media of speeches, articles, books, press conferences, and her columns she incessantly strived to gain a wider acceptance of her views. This indefatigability has rendered her ideas, in the broad sense, a matter of public record, and it will be surprising if even her private papers clarify them much further.

In addition, there exists the ever-growing accumulation of Rooseveltiana, that vast body of literature dealing with the years when her husband became one of the most influential men on earth. Much of this, as far as it concerns Eleanor Roosevelt, is repetitive or pedestrian; in some cases, however, there are first-hand accounts of certain aspects of her career, citations of letters, and general observations which help greatly to illuminate her role in the events of these years. There are also, of course, an increasing number of scholarly studies dealing with various aspects of twentieth-century American history. These provide helpful insights into the environment in which Eleanor Roosevelt lived and labored.

~

There have been few scholarly works dealing with Mrs. Roosevelt herself. Several dissertations have been written in connection with her speaking style and delivery; these, while of value in their own realm, are ephemeral from the standpoint of her overall career. This writer wrote a Master's thesis on one of Mrs. Roosevelt's interests — that of the Negro — and many of its conclusions have been incorporated into Chapter II of the present work. Benjamin A. Spence also wrote a Master's thesis on Mrs. Roosevelt; it dealt mainly with her work concerning Palestinian refugees, an activity beyond the scope of this study. Considerably broader in treatment is Tamara K. Hareven's Doctoral dissertation, "The Social Thought of Eleanor Roosevelt," which, although useful in certain of its aspects, is yet by no means comprehensive. These, outside of the present work, constitute (as far as this writer is aware) the body of academic studies having a major focus on the life and career of Eleanor Roosevelt.[1]

After this, there is a considerable step downward, in quality if not in quantity. Often the contemporary criticism directed toward Mrs. Roosevelt was querulous and ill-informed, and sometimes, as in the case of Westbrook Pegler's later diatribes, obscene. On the other hand, published books about her, both during her lifetime and afterward, are in the nature of encomiums rather than dispassionate analysis. Ruby Black's biography, though written comparatively early (1940), is probably the least unsatisfactory. While sycophantic, it does attempt to present some supporting evidence, in the form of Mrs. Roosevelt's own words, for the author's position. The tenor of Joseph Lash's book, *Eleanor Roosevelt: A Friend's Memoir*, is aptly summarized in the foreword wherein the author declares (p. ix) that he hopes the subject's admirers will find it "not unworthy of that extraordinary woman." Nevertheless, Lash's account of the youth movements of the thirties (in which he was an active participant) contains much that is enlightening. Of less value are the devout reminiscences of Lorena Hickok and former California Congresswoman Helen Gahagan Douglas. Both are actually lengthy editorial tributes rather than rounded accounts. The fullest biography, Alfred Steinberg's *Mrs. R*, unfortunately not only lacks documentation but also often bespeaks the mood

of a "true confessions" narrative. The characters mentioned in
the book are artificially portrayed — they tend to assume the
proportions of angels or demons merely for purposes of dramatic
effect — and situations purportedly factual all too frequently
occurred only in the author's imagination. These defects do
not enhance the book's reliability or usefulness.[2]

~

When Mrs. Roosevelt died on November 7, 1962, comment
upon her contributions to American life was almost unanimously
favorable. This widespread admiration, it must be remembered,
stemmed in large part from a generation which had come of age
after the days of the New Deal. This group, familiar only by
proxy with earlier aspects of her career, thought of Mrs. Roosevelt in terms of her post-World War II activities, especially those
pertaining to her service with the United Nations. They often
neglected her actions of an earlier day, failing to note that they
had been the subjects of considerable debate and that, with increased maturity and experience, she had modified or even
changed many of her former views. They did not remember
that Mrs. Roosevelt's outlook on various issues was neither
wholly consistent at any given time nor by any means static over
a period of years.

These facts must be kept in mind when reading the account
which follows. We are here concerned with Mrs. Roosevelt
before 1941, and if certain portions of her viewpoint do not
appear to square with what she would come to feel later, it is
because she herself altered her opinions. Thus, all references to
her, unless specifically otherwise indicated, are meant to apply
solely to what she thought and did before 1941. To an extent,
of course, her own and other recollections of earlier years were

Introduction xv

affected by subsequent events, but this is a defect inherent in most reminiscences.

~

In this work there has been no attempt to change the punctuation or spelling in quoted sources; they have been left as in the original, with any necessary corrections inserted in brackets. All emphasis of words or phrases used in quotation is original and not interpolated by this writer. All citations of Mrs. Roosevelt's column "My Day" are, unless otherwise indicated, taken from unedited copies at the Roosevelt Library (FDRL), Hyde Park. The same is true of certain of her articles; when this is the case, it is plainly shown in the citation. The initials "ER" refer, of course, to Mrs. Roosevelt herself.

I should like to acknowledge the gratitude I feel to the staff of the Lincoln University Library at Jefferson City, Missouri; to Miss Jane Smith and her co-workers at the National Archives; to Professor Clarke Chambers and Miss Andrea Hinding of the Social Welfare History Archives Center, University of Minnesota; and to the staff of the University of Wisconsin Historical Society Library, all of whom have been unfailingly helpful both in time and effort. To Bess Furman Armstrong, Marion Dickerman, James A. Farley and Raymond Moley I am much indebted for the cordiality and frankness which characterized their conversations with me. For the gracious Director of the Franklin D. Roosevelt Library, Miss Elizabeth Drewry, and her staff, especially Messrs. Marshall and Deyo and Miss Morris, I retain a particular fondness. No group could do more to make a visitor feel comfortable and welcome. Mrs. Sherry Saunders, Secretary to the Department of History at Montana State University, displayed unfailing patience and good humor during her exhausting task of typing the final manuscript. Finally, my association with Professors E. David Cronon, David A. Shannon and Ralph E. Morrow, all of whom have given me such unstinting aid in preparing this work, has been one of the fine things of my life.

For the interpretations and for any inaccuracies which appear in the following pages, I alone am responsible.

I

MOTHER TO A GENERATION

MOTHER TO A GENERATION

Cynics take note as you come and go.
Youth has a dream and a leader who heeds it.
Hark how the challenging echoes flow —
Hold fast to you[r] dream. America needs it.

From an unidentified correspondent;
reprinted in "My Day," October 26, 1936.

N O PHASE of Eleanor Roosevelt's activities, commented one of her biographers, "brought more criticism upon her, in the newspapers, in Congress, and in her enormous mail . . . in her first seven and a half years in the White House" than her patronage of the American Youth Congress.[1] That organization, now almost completely forgotten except in the nostalgic reminiscences of a few who passed through its ranks and by an occasional Congressman especially hard pressed to dredge up a column or two of newspaper space, was, in the late 1930's, given serious heed in what passed for serious and important circles. Its meetings and their progeny — manifestos, resolutions, declarations, and creeds — were supposed to represent the united aspirations of America's young. Its legislative demands, embodied in the American Youth Bill, were introduced in every Congressional session save one from 1936 through 1940. Columnists like Walter Lippmann and Raymond Moley, unaccustomed to suffer national developments lightly, lent earnest consideration to the significance of its debates. Leading New Deal officials met with its spokesmen at the White House. And, on one occasion, it could feel the strength of its position with assurance sufficient for its members to deride the President of the United States to his face.

The principal reason why the Youth Congress could reach this high estate lay in the prestige given it by Mrs. Eleanor Roosevelt. She, to an extent greater than any other individual or organization, "could [have been] called [youth's] mentor . . . to the Youth Congress she had been sponsor, patron, defender and benefactor." [2] From the first time she spoke to an AYC group in January, 1936, until the fall of 1940 when she began her painful drift away from it, she constantly propagandized its aims, advised its leaders, and acted as its liaison to the Chief Executive. When at last it became evident that its leadership did not embody (and, indeed, never had embodied) ideals close to her own heart, she still could not find it in herself to regret the role she had played. Instead, she could later say that she had experienced an invaluable lesson:

> I learned what communist tactics are. I discovered for myself how infiltration of an organization is accomplished. I was taught how communists get themselves into positions of importance. I understand all their tactics of objection and delay. . . . These tactics are all now familiar to me.[3]

If there is truth in this rationalization, it none the less leaves unsaid the reasons why Mrs. Roosevelt, who had been involved in public life for well over a decade and was herself in her middle fifties, embraced the American Youth Congress in the first place, and why, after she did, she clung to it so tenaciously — and, in the end, so distressingly.

A partial explanation for Mrs. Roosevelt's course of action can be found in her deep interest in other aspects of youth programs during the New Deal. This concern must be examined in order to understand her ultimate gravitation toward the activities of the American Youth Congress. Basic both to her role in the administration's official proposals in behalf of young people and to those of the AYC, however, were certain experiences she herself had undergone or, more properly, those experiences as she was to come to see them. For, ultimately, it was Eleanor Roosevelt's reflections upon them that were to form her intense interest in the youthful problems of others.

~

All her life Mrs. Roosevelt seemed to an unusual degree preoccupied with her early years. The first of her three volumes of autobiography dealt at length with her girlhood;[4] and in speeches, broadcasts, columns and articles she frequently referred to her youthful experiences. Unfortunately, there exists one very formidable obstacle for those wishing to check the accuracy of her recollections; there are virtually no other sources of those years besides her own accounts.* This is in no wise meant to imply that she falsified her own versions, but the paucity of independent corroboration indicates that they should be accepted with some degree of caution. It is difficult, in spite of Mrs. Roosevelt's apparent candor, to be wholly dispassionate about oneself.

This is especially true in light of the fact that Mrs. Roosevelt appears to have viewed her early environment through various lenses. The description most accepted is told in *This Is My Story*, a narrative which appeared in 1937 and which was widely received as "frank," "an unvarnished account," and "engagingly and unassumingly candid." [5] Its sentiments have been incorporated, virtually without change, into the substantial works of Ar-

* This appears to be true even as it pertains to the as yet unopened papers of Mrs. Roosevelt. Miss Elizabeth Drewry, Director of the Franklin D. Roosevelt Library, informed this writer that personal material regarding Eleanor Roosevelt's pre-marriage years is not copious.

thur M. Schlesinger, Jr., and Frank Freidel. Rexford Tugwell has called its subject "the very prototype of the poor little rich girl." [6]

The elements which Mrs. Roosevelt introduced in it are simple. She was physically plain and made to realize it. She was shy and, with the exception of her father, felt herself unloved. She was, after her mother's death, raised in the confined and narrow atmosphere of the homes of her maternal grandmother. She had no friends. Her insecurity, loneliness, lack of intellectual stimulation, and sense of uselessness were to be alleviated only when she was sent abroad to finishing school at the age of fifteen. [7]

This recollection, despite its manifest oversimplifications, contains a considerable amount of truth. Furthermore, it is of vital importance as a clue to seeing how Mrs. Roosevelt regarded her own youth at a time when she was beginning to embark on her greatest interest in the youth of America. Nevertheless, one gains the impression, upon examination of other of her observations, that occasional distortions have crept in, that certain of the more sunny aspects of her childhood have been forgotten; that, in other words, she had arrived at a point where, because of her very different social outlook in the 1930's, her younger years seemed bleaker in retrospect than they perhaps actually were.

Certain facts emerge, however, which seem beyond dispute. The first words in *This Is My Story* are "My mother was one of the most beautiful women I have ever seen." Later she was to revise her estimate to the flat statement that her mother was *the* most beautiful woman she had ever known, a remarkable recollection since Anna Hall Roosevelt died when her daughter was only eight years old. [8] It is indicative, however, of what was to become an unshakable belief in Eleanor Roosevelt as a little girl, that she herself was unwelcome because she was plain. In a vignette written in the late 1920's, ostensibly fictional but unquestionably autobiographical, she sees

> a green eyed rather ugly little girl standing in the door of a cozy library looking in at a very beautiful woman holding, oh so lovingly, in her lap a little fair-haired boy. Through Sally's heart passed the old sensations, the curious dread of the cold glance which would precede the kindly and indifferent "Come in Sally, and bring your book." [9]

Thus sensitive about her lack of beauty (she has recorded that her mother, when particularly vexed with her, called her "Granny"), she developed "an inordinate desire for affection and praise." "Attention and admiration," she said, "were the things all through my childhood that I wanted, because I was made to feel so conscious of the fact that nothing about me would attract attention or would bring me admiration!" And she tells a pathetic little story of how she lied to her convent mentors about swallowing a penny, for she had seen a girl who actually had done so and become the center of her schoolmates' attention.[10]

Anna Hall Roosevelt died of diphtheria in December, 1892, and "the little fair-haired boy" whom she had held "oh so lovingly" succumbed in the same epidemic a few months later. For the little girl, and for her baby brother Hall, it might be expected that their father would now assume charge of their upbringing. This possibility was the child's greatest hope. Elliott Roosevelt had spoken of her birth on October 11, 1884, as "a miracle from Heaven," and he continued to lavish a constant stream of affection upon his "Little Nell" until his death some ten years later.[11] Much of this endearment was, unfortunately, carried on in the form of letters; for drinking had become an acute problem for him, and he was forced to reside at Abingdon, Virginia, where relatives tried to assist in the vain effort to throw off his inclination toward the strong waters.

All the love that the little girl found frustrated by her mother she concentrated upon Elliott Roosevelt. She has touchingly, even movingly, described their brief moments together (that "somehow it was always he and I") and her utter desolation at the news of his death.[12] The memories she treasured of her father were enhanced by the kindly treatment she received from his relatives. She later testified that on her visits with them her shyness and timidity were considerably dispelled, that they were "a great joy" in contrast to the somber climate of her own residence.[13] She was to feel this way throughout the years of her youth, and when she was married it was her father's brother Theodore, then President of the United States, whom she asked to give her away.

The warmth involved in the relationship between Eleanor Roosevelt and the paternal side of her family perhaps helped to shape aspects of her own later social outlook. For in contrast to her mother's almost exclusive concern for the activities of New York's social elite, Mrs. Roosevelt recalled "being taken by my father to serve Thanksgiving dinner for the Newsboys' Club which my grandfather had established in New York City" and his explanation "that many of them had no homes and lived in little wooden shanties in empty lots." [14]

What could be more natural, in view of experiences like this one, than incorporating such activities of her beloved father into her own later rationale for helping youth? His interests, and those of her Uncle Theodore, were to be the ones toward which she would gravitate; the concerns of her mother and the Halls the type she would come to feel of little consequence. It would be overstating the case to say that her later interest in aiding young people was to be modeled on the memory of her father. At the same time, there can be little doubt that the proclivities of those she held most dear as a child reinforced her later belief in the importance of the causes to which she attached herself.

Soon after her mother's death, she and her brother were placed in the household of her maternal grandmother, Mrs. Valentine G. Hall. The atmosphere here, at least from certain of Mrs. Roosevelt's accounts, seems to have been something of an improvement over her previous existence:

> . . . there were long days in the summer when I lay under the trees and read or climbed into the cherry or the apple tree, according to the season, and filled my tummy as well as my mind and sometimes I even forgot to appear at meals but no one disturbed me. Rainy days the attic was my favorite spot and many later [sic] autumn afternoons and evenings do I remember before an open fire roasting chestnuts with a book on my lap.
>
> Life was leisurely. We lived without moving away, six months in one place. A child had time to read and dream and live.[15]

If this mellow nostalgia appears to have little in common with the manufactured legends of later biographers, there was yet an atmosphere in the home of her guardian which could hardly lead to a thoroughgoing sense of security or happiness for an already timid and uncertain girl. Her mother had been part of a large brood, and two of Eleanor's uncles still lived with their mother, either at Oak Terrace (the Hall summer place on the Hudson) or in New York City. Both drank excessively, and when Eleanor reached the age when acquaintances were permitted to call, the family lived in dread of some sort of scene the boys might create.

Nevertheless, as she grew older, she apparently enjoyed the companionship of certain of her maternal relatives and the friendship of an increasing circle of acquaintances. She later recalled that she had "adored" her young aunts Maude and "Pussie" (both of whom lived with Grandmother Hall), and that one of her primary misgivings when she returned, at the age of eighteen, from three years of finishing school in England was that "I had lost touch with most of my friends." [16]

This schooling, the only real formal educational training that Eleanor Roosevelt was ever to have, was at Allenswood, near London, and it remained one of the most powerful experiences of her life. Before 1899, her education had been (with the brief exception of a few months at a French convent as a child) in the hands of private tutors. It was sturdily traditional; she knew French well and was thoroughly versed in English and Continental literature.

Genuine intellectual stimulation, however, came only with Allenswood. This was almost wholly due to the influence of its owner, Mlle. Marie Souvestre. Mrs. Roosevelt recalled that she had the good fortune

> to be under a really great teacher for the years that I spent in Europe. It was not the actual subject which mattered, it was the inspiration of her personality and character, and the fact that she created in her pupils a curiosity and gave them the tools with which to satisfy it. [17]

Mlle. Souvestre had had as a student one of Eleanor Roosevelt's aunts (Mrs. Sheffield Cowles), and she appears to have given the niece an unusual amount of attention. She invited her to private suppers for visiting dignitaries and took her as a traveling companion to Europe. For the first time in her life the youthful student heard religion attacked and was subjected to long and earnest monologues on the righteous cause of the Boers. For the girl who, as a new arrival at Allenswood, had written that she could "never succeed in doing what I mean to do, never, never," the novel experience of a certain freedom of mind and action and a sense of responsibility led her to state later that when she returned to the United States for her debut, "I knew what I was expected to do and did it more or less successfully." [18]

Aside from increasing her poise and confidence, however, the finishing school years in England did not seem to stimulate in her the "vast intellectual curiosity" which she later claimed that they did.[19] Though she taught calisthenics and "fancy dancing" at settlement houses for a short time before her engagement, she rapidly adjusted her patterns of life and thought to those of the pre-Allenswood days.

> As I try to sum up my development in the autumn of 1903, I think I was a curious mixture of extreme innocence and unworldliness with a great deal of knowledge of some of the less attractive and less agreeable sides of life — which, however, did not seem to make me any more sophisticated or less innocent. . . . I had painfully high ideals and a tremendous sense of duty at that time, entirely unrelieved by any sense of humor or any appreciation of the weaknesses of human nature. Things were either right or wrong to me.[20]

Once again, as her girlhood drew to a close, there thus exists an apparent confusion in her testimony. She recalled that "I was lonely as a little girl"; she also stated, "I can never remember being lonely." She mentioned "the rigidity of my early bringing up" in a household where "no one disturbed me" if "I . . . forgot to appear at meals" and where "[I] had time to read and dream and live." She reminisced about books from the family library which mysteriously disappeared when she tried to read them, while on another occasion she praised the fact that "I was brought up in a home that did not believe in censorship" and where "there were no forbidden areas in the library bookshelves." She spoke of the dreary Sundays during which old-fashioned religious rules were enforced with gloomy exactness, yet she recalled the same residence in which "I don't think [religion] was spoken of a great deal. It was more or less taken for granted." She wrote "that in my own teen-age I had so much responsibility that I never knew what it was to be carefree"; she remembered elsewhere that her grandmother had sent her away to school because "she considered that at fifteen I was getting too much of the social side of life." [21]

This contradictory testimony extends to the Allenswood experience as well. If the influence of Mlle. Souvestre's school was all she later asserted it to be, that influence was to manifest itself only well after the fact. For intellectual curiosity was not to become a part of Eleanor Roosevelt's personality until many more years had passed.

What Mrs. Roosevelt seems to have done in her later appraisals of her youth was to reverse the old adage about never knowing when one was well off. With the profound changes of outlook that had accompanied her advancing years, she could see, in the 1930's particularly, almost nothing worthwhile in what her childhood represented. Society, as personified by her mother, was anathema to her. Wealth, when employed selfishly, was against every tenet she would come to hold as First Lady. Service, such as attending sewing circles for the poor or becoming active on charity boards, she would regard as a mere balm to the conscience. And, by compounding these objective dislikes with the genuine lack of affection and periods of unhappiness she had experienced in her early life, she could, in her own mind, find it possible to associate herself and her younger years with the agonizing insecurity and aspirations of American youth in the thirties.*

* In this connection, the conclusion of Mrs. Roosevelt's youthful friend, Joseph Lash, is interesting. Lash had been ready to take out a Communist Party card and join the staff of the *Daily Worker* just before the Soviet government signed its pact with Hitler. Completely disenchanted and in an emotional turmoil, he turned to Mrs. Roosevelt for help. The reasons for their ripening friendship, he suggests, were, in addition to a "moral affinity" and "a real sense of kinship and satisfaction," the fact that "I was in trouble and my miseries re-

The experiences of Mrs. Roosevelt's childhood and youth were therefore to become an important part of her later rationale for helping the young. To these experiences, however, were to be added others she would undergo in the years of her marriage. And, in this latter period, few events were to bulk larger in forming her views toward youth than those associated with being a mother to children of her own.

~

Once, as a much older woman, Mrs. Roosevelt was asked what she regarded as her most important mistake. "Too much belief in discipline when my children were young," was her response.[22] Despite endowing her answer with the infinite qualification ("though I am not sure") that was to become a virtual trademark, the very fact that, as an experienced public figure, Mrs. Roosevelt should cite misconceptions of rearing her children as possibly the most serious mistake of her life is indicative of the importance she attached to such matters. Possibly of even greater consequence, however, is the manner in which the recollections regarding her own maternal experiences were to affect her outlook as it pertained to the treatment of youth more generally.

Early references to Mrs. Roosevelt as a parent exist, but they are, frankly, of little except esoteric interest, being concerned principally with visitations of diseases, accidents, and other maladies that afflicted her children.* She was by all accounts a devoted mother; Professor Freidel even goes so far as to remark

---

minded her of her own when she was young. Insecurity, shyness, lack of social grace, she had to conquer them all and helping someone she cared about do the same filled a deep, unquenchable longing to feel needed and useful." See Joseph P. Lash, *Eleanor Roosevelt: A Friend's Memoir* (Garden City, New York, Doubleday and Co., Inc., 1964), p. 140.

* The children were Anna (1906), James (1907), Franklin, Jr. (1909, d. 1909), Elliott (1910), Franklin, Jr. (1914), and John (1916).

that she was intellectually "dormant" during the first decade or so of her marriage, dedicating her time almost exclusively to the tasks of housekeeping.[23] The first great challenge concerning her children occurred when, because of her husband's illness, he was restricted from giving them the companionship they were used to. In order to help fill this void, she successfully learned to swim and to take them on camping trips.

It was, however, only as her children began to reach college age that Mrs. Roosevelt started to articulate a philosophy of parenthood. One of her first efforts in this direction was an unpublished 1927 article entitled "Ethics of Parents." The burden of her discourse demonstrated a good deal of liberality, especially in an era when so many parents agonized over the waywardness of "flaming youth." "Why not try letting our children go for a change?" she asked. "Start in being something ourselves and not worrying so much about the younger generation getting away from us. Conceivably with some effort we might become more interesting to them as well as ourselves." She then summed up her code of parental ethics in seven points:

1. Furnish an example in living.
2. Stop preaching ethics and morals.
3. Have a knowledge of life's problems and an imagination.
4. Stop shielding your children and clipping their wings.
5. Allow your children to develop along their own lines.
6. Don't prevent self-reliance and initiative.
7. Have vision yourself and have bigness of soul.[24]

As often occurs, Mrs. Roosevelt sometimes found it difficult to live up to her ideals as they applied to her own offspring. One of her sons, James, recalls: "In almost everything I can remember her doing, Mother seemed torn between the desire to raise her own children with reasoned discipline, and, on the other hand, not to interfere in our lives." [25]

Mrs. Roosevelt's ambivalence, the result of the pull of new ideas she was absorbing because of a more active public life as opposed to her own early traditional environment, was complicated by two other factors. One of these was her husband. His disposition was one which shied from inflicting direct punishment, and, as a result, any necessary disciplinary action against the Roosevelt children usually had to be assumed by their mother. Moreover, especially after his illness and subsequent political career, FDR was unable to devote the time to his family he otherwise might have.[26] Mrs. Roosevelt herself recounts some of the difficulties of official versus more intimate concern: the fact that FDR once continued to read a state document while one of his sons was reciting a personal problem — to the latter's mortification; the time when both she and the President were anxiously awaiting a telephone call regarding a crucial family decision by one of the boys, which, when it turned out adversely, moved the President to say, "Well, we can not help it. Do you want to hear my first peace note to the nations?"[27]

The second difficulty obstructing Mrs. Roosevelt's familial efforts took the form of her husband's mother, Sara Delano Roosevelt. Sara Roosevelt retained control of many of the purse strings in the family and often used this financial leverage to override disciplinary action against her grandchildren. She made them the recipients of lavish gifts — trips to Europe, horses and cars — the latter sometimes coming after the originals had been wrecked. One of the boys told John Gunther that his grandmother was "the source of all the good things in life when we were little kids, if you knew how to handle her."[28]

Such intrusive forays, customarily accompanied by bland protestations of innocence, drove her daughter-in-law to distraction. "I am so angry at her . . . that it is all I can do to be decent," she wrote FDR following one instance of his mother's largesse. Similar episodes helped force her into an occasional priggish outburst over her husband's apparent unconcern. "Too bad James needs the money, you never can get away from your many gold diggers, can you?" she wrote him following James' request for an initiation fee to Harvard's Hasty Pudding Club. "I can't say 3 nights drunk fill me with anything but disgust!" [29]

Constant missives from his wife pursued FDR even into the White House period. "Something has to be done to make ——— realize it is dishonest not to pay his bills," she wrote at one juncture. "I suggest you ask him to list *all* he owes. Pay it yourself & then take it out of his allowance $100 a quarter. Tell him he *has* to live on his income . . ." And again, "Will you speak seriously and firmly to F., Jr. & John about drinking & fast driving. I really think it's important." [30]

In spite of these difficulties, Mrs. Roosevelt moved consistently toward a more broad-minded outlook regarding parenthood. For a Movietone short, made after her husband had become Governor of New York, she reiterated her belief that

> parents must try to make themselves the type of people that the younger generation can respect and trust and desire to come to when the need arises. They must not be hypocritical in deed or in thought, for youth is seeking truth and will not be put off by old shibboleths and shams. They will accept honest differences of opinion but not the repetition of outworn traditions and beliefs.[31]

To an increasing extent Mrs. Roosevelt appeared able to implement these beliefs in certain segments of her own family life. In this she was aided by her husband, who "had a very strong feeling that our sons should be allowed to make their own decisions and their own mistakes. . . . I think his attitude came very largely from the fact that his mother had wanted to direct his every thought and deed and that he had had to fight for independence." Conversation in the presidential family, for example, was freewheeling, even raucous. Mrs. Roosevelt, who in these family sessions frequently assumed a particular position on a subject more for the purpose of conversational sparring than because of genuine adherence, recorded in 1936 that "last night we ranged from the Townsend Plan . . . through the Social Security Act . . . workmen's compensation . . . to labor conditions"; and Harold Ickes recalled an occasion when

> Mrs. Roosevelt precipitated the discussion by raising some social question and her three sons at once began to wave their arms in the air and take violent issue with her. She expressed belief in a strict limitation of income, whether earned or not, and the boys insisted that every man ought to have a right to earn as much as he could. The President joined in at intervals, but he wasn't the President of the United States . . . he was merely the father of three sons who had opinions of their own . . . It was really most amusing.[32]

Some things there were, however, that were not so amusing, and Mrs. Roosevelt's wistful mention of her family's marital trials implies that they affected her more than she otherwise openly admitted.[33] Nonetheless, even as she might privately berate her children's errant conduct, she never failed to defend them publicly. When James' stomach ulcers reached a point where an operation was necessary, she indignantly replied to "a very kind note" which advised her that her son's troubles "would be all over if he would give up strong drink":

> Dear lady or gentleman, don't you know that for well over a year before this type of operation this particular patient has indulged only in milk and the type of food which a two-year-old baby is usually given?[34]

Each of her progeny, she told Joseph Lash, had come to face problems differently. Anna had "developed most in the way of understanding and compassion." John "was completely differ-

ent from the others . . . industrious, deliberate in all his actions." Franklin, Jr., was possessed of great charm but had perhaps known almost too few hardships, while Elliott's experience
was entirely the opposite; he had become embittered.[35] Possibly
because of the latter conviction, Mrs. Roosevelt was inclined to
be more lenient in matters concerning Elliott. In July, 1937,
wrote James Roosevelt,

> Mother wrote Father from Texas that Elliott was "dreadfully
> upset" because there had been no action by the Federal Com-
> munications Commission on the licensing of the stations which
> were being sought in the name of his second wife. He had be-
> come convinced — perhaps with good reason — that he was be-
> ing discriminated against because of his name, and Mother asked:
> "Couldn't you or James [at that time acting as his father's secre-
> tary] say a word which w^{ld} hurry them — You know Elliott's
> disposition, he is beginning to think you are both against him." [36]

Notwithstanding occasional misgivings, Mrs. Roosevelt thus
firmly supported her sons whenever she felt them to be targets of
unjustified public criticism. She argued, understandably, that
values were rendered more difficult to grasp because of dwelling
in the public spotlight. She continued to argue, somewhat less
convincingly, that if her family did not accept special privileges
"they are considered ungracious and unappreciative." [37] She assumed this attitude in spite of the fact that such conduct often
drew the fire of some of the administration's strongest supporters. Oswald Garrison Villard, for example, commented acidly:
"With all friendliness to Mrs. Roosevelt and the President, I am
sorry to have to record my sincere belief that the example set by
the Roosevelt children in their money-making is not one in
which I as an American can take any particular pride." [38]

From Mrs. Roosevelt's experiences as a mother, then, came
firsthand observations of young people who had undergone

strong contrary, and at times mutually exclusive, pressures. Her children had known an indulgent grandmother, a mother who had been emotionally split between procrustean notions of discipline and more novel beliefs in parental leniency, a father who through self-occupation or conviction sometimes seemed indifferent to their dilemmas, and the temptation of emoluments offered via the beguiling simplicity of use of their family name. The resultant disappointments which Anna and the boys experienced were to cement in Mrs. Roosevelt's mind the idea that her children, like herself, had been the victims of an absence of security. She became persuaded that they had lacked sympathetic guidance when it was most needed, and yet that they had not been allowed sufficient latitude, when younger, to acquire the self-discipline and clarity of vision which militates against later mistakes.

By the time her husband was to assume the presidency, she could well echo the sentiments she had first publicly uttered in 1924: "The young people are the ones who have the spirit of adventure and imagination which drives us forward. The older generation is the balance wheel that keeps the young from going too far." Her generation had "allowed things to happen which should not have taken place," she had asserted then. She had but a short emotional distance to travel to be able to write in 1933: "I believe very strongly that it is better to allow children too much freedom than too little." Young people need help, she concluded; they "do not need criticism or interference." [39] Her philosophy of youth was all but fully formulated.

~

One additional aspect of Mrs. Roosevelt's experience contributed to her close attention to the problems of youth. In 1927 she became assistant principal and teacher of literature, American history and current events at the Todhunter School in New York City. Todhunter was an institution that had been purchased and was run by Miss Marion Dickerman, a close friend of Mrs. Roosevelt whom the latter had met through New York political work in the 1920's. Its student body numbered roughly one hundred girls from kindergarten through high school age.[40]

As an active teacher, Mrs. Roosevelt was able to apply certain educational theories of which she had frequently spoken in a more general vein. Reflecting her own background, she considered the absorption of literary classics to be of the utmost importance. Scott, Dickens, Jane Austen, Latin and Greek classicists, Dante and the Italian poets "should be read before one is fifteen," for they "teach people to deal with ideas easily and familiarly." Almost defensively, she stated:

> I think if I had to choose between going to school and having an opportunity to read and have a love of reading, I would choose the latter. I feel that in the end, I would probably have as good an education as the child that went to school.[41]

These ideas rather obviously stemmed from her own formative experience. They mirrored her childhood habit of omnivorous reading and her lack of early formal educational training. Once again, however, against this stress upon the traditional, Mrs. Roosevelt simultaneously counterposed more unorthodox notions. The field of history, for example, she believed "must be taught with a greater emphasis on economic and social development and the connection between these questions and the actions of government must be sought." [42] With this in mind, Mrs. Roosevelt guided her young charges through such unlikely locations as the children's courts, city hall, Ellis Island, and the headquarters of the Democratic State Committee. On occasion she led some of her students into slum areas, experiences which she tried to make genuinely meaningful to them:

To these children of the rich, I had to explain what it meant to sleep in a room which had no window, what it meant to pant on fire escapes in hot July with people draped on fire escapes all around you, what it meant for a woman with her husband and eight children to live in three rooms in the basement. . . .[43]

Even the novel approach of tenement excursions, however, was not entirely out of accord with her own experience. "It has long been a pet theory of mine," she wrote, "that the basis of all real education is the contact of youth with a personality which will stimulate not only to work but to thought," for "no matter what young people study, the important thing is that the study should be vitalized for them by the personality of the teacher." [44] The expeditions with her students, which harmonized with her own growing interest in and knowledge of social conditions, were also perhaps as close as she could come to the equivalent of her own trips with Mlle. Souvestre so many years before. By all accounts these experiments were popular, and Mrs. Roosevelt was remembered with special pleasure by large numbers of her students.* Later on, when she became First Lady, she continued to be hostess to the Todhunter girls on their monthly visit to Washington as well as inviting them to Christmas festivities at Hyde Park. She maintained her association with the institution until it merged into the Dalton School in June 1939.[45]

Mrs. Roosevelt's educational activities had the vital effect of convincing her, as she was to recall later, that "most people could achieve what they wanted if they were given an opportunity for education." [46] Education thus came to represent the primary

---

* Mrs. Roosevelt was similarly conscientious in the classroom, preparing all her own lecture material with the exception of the portions which pertained to her "American Biography" series. Copies of the latter are on file at the Franklin D. Roosevelt Library; they bear a signature other than Mrs. Roosevelt's. Miss Marion Dickerman, to whom this writer is indebted for many informative comments on the Todhunter venture, confirms this. Interview with Marion Dickerman, May 25, 1965.

route through which progress for all people might become possible.* There was, for instance, "only one way to prevent recurrence of war and that is by better education." For the Negro, to use a second example, she could "urge first of all that you concentrate your effort on obtaining better opportunities for education." [47] As might be expected, she also believed that the teacher, rather than the teacher's physical plant, should receive more attention:

> I would like to see us spend more money on our preparation for teachers [and] on our salaries of teachers. I would like to have our schoolhouses equipped with the necessary equipment to make teaching easy, but I think sometimes we have spent too much money on the outside [sic] of schoolhouses and too little on the important thing, which is that the people who are teaching . . . may be constantly more useful. [48]

This laudable interest in education, as will become apparent later, was to carry her down some curious byways.

The Todhunter years, then, completed the background of Eleanor Roosevelt's interest in America's youth. Working directly with young people outside her own home appeared to intensify her belief that they, through education, understanding, and a broad tolerance, would mature into the kind of useful citizens she thought desirable. They could avoid the sense of insecurity that had plagued her in her own childhood, overcome the kind of problems that had faced her offspring, and determine better solutions for the social, economic, and international uncertainties that beclouded the present. As she set forth on her career as First Lady, she was ready, in this cause, to give of herself generously:

---

* Especially public education. Mrs. Roosevelt repeatedly stated that she had been blocked from sending her own children to public schools, principally by her mother-in-law. ER, "Ideal Education," *Woman's Journal*, XV (Oct., 1930), p. 9; ER, *It Seems to Me* (New York, W. W. Norton and Co., Inc., 1954), p. 65.

As we grow older it is more important that we be something which furnishes youth with stimulation and courage and, occasionally, when youth is a little too hot-headed, with a word of restraint.

And to this statement she was to add — characteristically — "although I do not favor much restraint." [49]

~

Exact figures are impossible to obtain, but the numerous surveys conducted by government agencies between 1933 and 1940 demonstrate beyond question that there were between three and four and one-half million Americans under the age of twenty-one who were unemployed during each of those years. In 1938, for example, the WPA found 14 percent of all youth, or 21 percent of youth in the labor market, out of jobs; and this estimate did not include large numbers of others occupied only by part-time work. [50] The gravity of youth's plight, concerning which the above figures gave only partial evidence, led Mrs. Roosevelt to utter a solemn admonition. "I have moments of real terror," she declared in 1934, "when I think we may be losing this generation. We have got to bring these young people into the active life of the community and make them feel that they are necessary." [51] To her basic solicitude for the young, the miasma of depression appeared to add a note of despair.

Her husband's administration had already embarked upon one program, the Civilian Conservation Corps, which involved employment and participation in "the active life of the community" for hundreds of thousands of young men. For the CCC's future she had expressed "great hopes" that it would

relieve not only the mere physical distress . . . but what is quite as bad, the mental distress of men who are out of work . . . these camps . . . are being organized to get men, unemployed

men, young men, as far as possible, out into the forest areas and
the park areas throughout the country where they can do work
which will be of value to the nation. . . .

While admitting that the plan contained imperfections, that some
of the men might be "quite unhappy, particularly if they are not
accustomed to . . . this kind of work," she nevertheless took
comfort in the thought that "at least they will have food and
shelter and work." [52]

A second objection, unstated but no doubt present in Mrs.
Roosevelt's mind, was the fact that by its very nature the concept of the CCC would help provide only for men. To meet this
imbalance, with the cooperation of Harry Hopkins and other
personnel of the Federal Emergency Relief Administration
(FERA), she became active in the establishment of camps for
young women. One of them, Camp Tera (at Bear Mountain
Park, New York), in which she was particularly interested, was
representative of similar camps which were set up in other parts
of the country. In order to be eligible for admission, it was necessary for a girl to show actual need; that is, she had to demonstrate that she was without physical resources either of money,
work, or family assistance. A physical examination to insure
against communicable disease was also required. The girls who
were admitted lived in tents or rustic cottages. They had the
services of a camp director, a dietician, a nurse and various coun-
selors. On occasion, adult instructors taught typing or handicrafts. The girls also enjoyed physical instruction, recreation
and entertainment. [53]

But these camps were not successful, and all of them were dis-
banded by the late 1930's.* No work could be found for which
women would be paid as were their male counterparts in the
CCC camps, and they had instead to be given a small allowance.

---

* Camp Tera, which was renamed Camp Jane Addams, was closed permanently in the summer of 1937.

Few of them stayed at the camps for any length of time, often because the rural environment held little appeal for them. Principally, however, the reason for the failure of these experiments lay in the fact that FERA personnel were too much immersed in the enormous problems of trying to assist older women, women who were in no position to leave their families, rather than being able to concentrate on the difficulties of young girls.

In truth, the CCC itself turned out to be something of a freak. Mrs. Roosevelt's statements to the contrary, it had not been designed out of any special consideration for the employment of young men. Indeed, it had hardly been conceived as a relief measure at all. Its actual purpose had been conservation, and it was only as a result of circumstances that it became primarily attractive to youth. Older men, like women, could not, except with the greatest difficulty, leave their homes; young, single men were able to do so — at least for comparatively short periods of time. Even then a surprisingly high rate of desertion or discharge occurred.[54] What seemed to be needed was a kind of enterprise which, unlike the Civilian Conservation Corps and its smattering of semi-analogous camps for women, aimed squarely at alleviating the predicament of youth *as youth*. Toward this goal Mrs. Roosevelt was by 1935 to devote much of her energy.

The chief official medium through which her efforts were to be directed was the National Youth Administration, created by executive order on June 26, 1935. Mrs. Roosevelt, with her customary disclaimer of responsibility for policy, later stated that Harry Hopkins and Aubrey Williams had come to her with the idea of a relief program for youth to be administered under the Works Progress Administration (the successor to FERA), but that they were reluctant to present it to the President in the fear that it might be construed as a fascist-like attempt to regiment youth. She was merely the agent, she contended, in agreeing to sound her husband out on the idea.[55] That her role possibly bulked larger than her own account would have it appear, however, is indicated by a letter to her from Charles Taussig, who was to become chairman of NYA's National Advisory Committee, soon after FDR's executive order. "My dear Mrs. Roosevelt," it began, "May I take this opportunity to congratulate you upon the creation of the National Youth Administration. The intensive and sympathetic work you have been doing for the youth of the country has, in a large measure, made this new venture possible." [56] Another close confidant of Mrs. Roosevelt reports a 1941 conversation in which

> Mrs. R. told us that the original suggestion for a National Youth Administration had been hers. She had urged it upon Harry Hopkins and Aubrey Williams. They were dubious, afraid it would be attacked. . . . Was the President aware of that possibility? they asked her. She would bring it to his attention, she said. There was that possibility, the President agreed, but should it be done anyway? When she said yes, he had given the go-ahead signal.[57]

Once the NYA was a fact, Mrs. Roosevelt propagandized continually in its behalf. Throughout the late 1930's her column abounded with favorable references to its projects; during her lecture tours (normally a period of three weeks to a month) scarcely a day passed without a paragraph extolling its virtues.[58] By early 1940 a national magazine could say:

> Mrs. Roosevelt's pet Government agency is the National Youth Administration, and on her trips she functions as a kind of inspector-general of NYA projects. . . . When she gets back to Washington, she makes a written report to the Youth Administrator, Aubrey Williams, which is most specific: "This swimming pool is too small. . . . That man could do a better job. . . ."[59]

Nor did her interest in this agency stop with mere reports. Frequently she asked that various people be given jobs with it. "I am interested in a man named Johnson of Rogers, Arkansas," she wrote Williams in 1936. "I have tried to help them through [his wife] but I think the real solution would be a permanent job for the husband. Is there anything in W.P.A. or N.Y.A. that he could be given?" Or,

> Mr. William Christy, who has been working with the N.Y.A. here in Washington for about a year is going to Los Angeles in the hopes of affiliating in the production end of the moving picture business.
>
> In the meantime, I wonder if you could not use him in the N.Y.A. work there until he gets located.[60]

Such requests on the part of the First Lady appear to have been given careful attention. Evidence of the importance attached to them may be seen, for example, in the replies to the two letters just cited. "Mr. Floyd Sharp, Works Progress Administrator for the State of Arkansas, happens to be in town today," wrote Aubrey Williams promptly, "and I am asking him to undertake to secure something in the way of a position for Mr. Johnson." And, as for the gentleman in need of interim employment until joining the movie industry: "I shall be very glad to take this matter up with our California office and see if something can be worked out for [Mr. Christy]." [61]

Furthermore, Mrs. Roosevelt was, as the wife of the President, in the unique position of bringing to his attention certain ideas to which she herself was sympathetic. Sometimes, as letters from Taussig point out, it was by merely providing the occasion ("What I do wish to emphasize is how effective the conference was after dinner, which you so kindly arranged with the President"); at other junctures she could be more direct (". . . probably your most valuable contribution to the meeting [with her husband] was calling attention at its close to the fact that we had hardly addressed ourselves to the problem of those millions of youth still at the bottom of the pyramid"). At still other times, as she herself indicated, she acted as liaison ("I talked with the President about your idea, and I think he has it in mind and you will be able to discuss details with him very rapidly. He is entirely favorable").[62] That her position, though entirely unofficial, was understood to be a powerful one can be inferred from the following letter sent by a St. Louis educator. Here the author, writing to Mrs. Roosevelt, enclosed a copy of a missive he had previously addressed to FDR "proposing that additional opportunities for expression be given young people and suggesting a plan which will furnish such opportunities." In his letter directed to the First Lady he urged her

> to give this proposal your careful consideration and inform me of your reaction. If you are favorably impressed I respectfully request that you assist by conveying your ideas to the proper authorities and to the public. . . .[63]

Correspondence of the above nature provides additional indication that Mrs. Roosevelt's role as regards NYA was considerable. Whether she was the inspiration for the agency's birth or whether she was but a willing midwife in its creation, her influence can be judged vital. For she had, and used, access to the President. Without that access, even according to her own version of events, Hopkins and Williams would not have introduced the idea to the Chief Executive, at least at that time. Secondly, she enjoyed a large public audience, and it is abundantly clear that she made every effort to impress that audience with the virtues and accomplishments of the National Youth Administration. Williams himself, who headed NYA, referred to her as the "first publicist of the nation." [64] Gratuitous propaganda of this nature must have been very welcome to an agency which constantly struggled for greater funds, if not for its very existence. Moreover, as her correspondence with high officials such as Williams and Taussig indicated, neither was she loath to make recommendations in matters both of policy and personnel nor was she reluctant to bring these ideas to the attention of her husband. It is difficult to imagine that Mrs. Roosevelt engaged in these activities without a reasonable certainty that they would be given serious heed. Evidence seems to indicate that her suggestions did indeed receive thoughtful consideration, though it is by no means sure that they were invariably carried out.

Finally, as it matured, the directions in which NYA policy moved were compatible with her own perspective. Mrs. Roosevelt was not much enamored with the concept of relief itself, expressing instead the opinion that such practices were merely "stopgaps" rather than fundamental solutions.[65] Better than orthodox relief was some form of vocational guidance; better still was education of a more general nature, her interest in which has already been commented upon. NYA reflected these preferences. From stressing unemployment relief in 1935–36, from conferring more attention upon recreational aspects and unskilled clerical training in 1937–38, the agency, by 1939, was concentrating upon "outdoor labor, metal and woodworking shops for boys, and sewing workshops for girls." Outright loans were also being made to students.[66] It therefore seems entirely possible that, given Mrs. Roosevelt's position within the orbit of NYA policy, these shifts of emphasis were more than coincidental.

~

While the First Lady attempted to discount the importance of her activities when they were concerned with official personnel and policies, she did not regard the same circumspection as necessary in dealing with unofficial bodies. Hence, her relationship with the American Youth Congress and her espousals of faith in its objectives and its leadership were subject to the merciless glare of constant, and often hostile, publicity. Some of this commentary was twisted and unfair, for Mrs. Roosevelt's kindly intentions were cynically misused by certain of her youthful beneficiaries; all too often, however, she displayed, in the defense of a cause she considered worthy, a stubbornness, a frenzied indignation and an astonishing gullibility which cast genuine doubts on her motives and sense of proportion.

The AYC was originally the brainchild of a young magazine authoress named Viola Ilma, a girl of considerable enthusiasm but no pronounced political views. Miss Ilma's notion was that the myriad youth groups, many of which had sprung up and become active with the onset of the depression, should have some sort of coordinate body to enable them to more effectively bring their ideas to the attention of nationally influential leaders. Among the youth groups which subscribed to this plan and sent delegates to the first convention in 1934 were such widely diverse organizations as the pro-Zionist Avukah, the War Resisters League, the Esperanto Association of North America and the National Council for Methodist Youth. None of these types of organization, however, had any concrete program relating to what the posture or goals of the AYC should be. The result was that the participating Communist-controlled student groups, such as the National Students League and the Young Communist League, which *did* have both their methodology and their ends well formulated, were able to assume leadership of the Youth Congress virtually even before it became an established entity.

The first victim of the leftist thrust was Miss Ilma herself; and the tactics by which she was ousted have since become mournfully familiar in other contexts. The Communist-led groups caucused before the convention, secretly decided on their slate of candidates for important posts, accused Miss Ilma (who had made a trip to Germany the previous year) of being in the pay of fascists and discriminating against liberal and radical youth groups, harassed and heckled her on the floor of the convention, railroaded through their own set of declarations and elected most of their own candidates.

The radicals then proceeded to consolidate their control of the AYC by the creation of "dummy" local organizations which sent delegates to subsequent conventions and were hence entitled to "representation" on the National Council. They also employed the device of electing sympathizers from innocuous-appearing groups like the Epworth League and the Student Division of the YMCA. The manifestos which they sponsored were purposely vague and diffuse rallying cries to liberals of good will; they meant nothing, but allowed the Communists great operational freedom. Moreover, by the middle thirties, Popular Front tactics meant that most Communists moved toward the political "right," thus enabling them and the liberals to cooperate without the public rifts which had been apparent in earlier years.[67]

It was some eighteen months after the founding of the American Youth Congress that Mrs. Roosevelt's name first appeared in conjunction with it. She addressed the organization in January, 1936, commenting afterward that because of certain social evils and violations of civil rights many of its members had had their faith in a democratic form of government shaken. The First Lady, however, had pointed out to them "that we had lived through a great variety of changes in the past, and our conception of social justice had evolved year by year, and that in all probability we would live through this situation and still remain a democracy." Despite the necessity of this gentle reproof, Mrs. Roosevelt was impressed with "the earnestness of these young people. They have a real desire to contribute to the solution of their own problems, and to try to think through the questions before them. They consider themselves as a part of a whole situation and not as a special group." [68]

Mrs. Roosevelt did not, however, come into intimate contact with the AYC until some time later, in 1938. In August of that year, the AYC was host to the World Youth Congress, whose conference was held at Vassar College near Mrs. Roosevelt's home at Hyde Park. Her comment upon meeting its leaders was to be a harbinger of her position in the next two years:

> I have just spent an interesting couple of hours with 14 members of the American Youth Congress. The head of the Congress, Mr. [William] Hinckley, had made a statement in this morning's press denying that the group is Communistic, which seems to me rather unnecessary, for it is quite obvious that a group with such varied organizations in it could hardly be called a branch of the Communist Party.[69]

Instead of what she regarded as irresponsible criticism, Mrs. Roosevelt felt that what youth needed was

> a confidence that they may try new things with the backing of their elders, that they may call upon the experience of their leaders, not to hold them back, but to help them. . . . We cannot expect in a changing world, to stand still and to find in the old conditions answers to new problems.

As for the AYC, the First Lady described it as a group which had "learned an extraordinary amount. . . . I don't think I know any group of people, young or old," she stated, "whom I consider today to have grown more over a period of years than that group of young people." [70]

This hospitable viewpoint was not without its response. Early in 1939 she was given a testimonial dinner in appreciation of her labors in behalf of youth, and soon afterward she was able to record that she was "much touched" by the fact that the American Youth Congress had named their annual fellowship after her.[71] Such, in fact, was her reputation for generosity and aid to youth by late autumn 1939, that when, in November of that year, the Dies Committee on Un-American Activities offered AYC leaders a chance to testify, the latter immediately turned to Eleanor Roosevelt for advice. Although up to this time she had made no secret of her association with the Youth Congress and certain of its constituent groups such as the American Student Union, it was actually the Dies Committee hearings which brought that association into widespread national prominence.

On November 30 youth leaders were waiting to be heard while the committee finished taking the routine testimony of one William Odell Nowell. "At this point," reads the official transcript,

Mrs. Franklin D. Roosevelt entered the hearing room.

Mr. Starnes [Joseph Starnes, Alabama Democrat, acting as Chairman in the absence of Martin Dies]: We will suspend for a moment. I notice the presence here of the First Lady of the Land. I would like to invite Mrs. Roosevelt to come around and sit with us at the committee table, if she will.

(Mrs. Roosevelt thanked Mr. Starnes for the invitation to sit with the committee and took a seat in the front row of the audience.)

Mr. Starnes: Proceed, Mr. Whitley [Rhea Whitley, committee counsel].[72]

Throughout the rest of that day, and the next, Mrs. Roosevelt did all she could to demonstrate her confidence in and friendship for the youth leaders. She had deliberated with them on the train from New York, and now she took them to lunch during recesses and opened the White House bedrooms to them at night.

The hearings themselves had their farcical side. Jack McMi-

chael, president of the AYC, asked for contributions. Other
youth leaders distributed handbills, and Joseph Lash of the
American Student Union recited:

> If you see an un-American
> Lurking far or near
> Just alkalize with Martin Dies
> And he will disappear.[73]

Mrs. Roosevelt, summarizing her impressions of the hearings
in her column, found the committee members to be "genuinely
courteous and helpful in their attitude." She felt that the only
exception to this "extremely heartening exhibition of government operating helpfully" was the committee's director of research, J. B. Matthews, whose approach was that of trying a
prisoner at the bar rather than seeking information. Indeed, while
that erratic gentleman (Matthews himself had been a close fellow
traveler in the early 1930's) had been questioning Lash, Mrs.
Roosevelt had moved up to the press table. The impression that
she was preparing to discuss his performance in her column apparently caused Dr. Matthews to soften his tactics.[74]

Mrs. Roosevelt's overt demonstration of friendship toward
youth groups was viewed with mixed emotions. Fulton Lewis,
Jr., in those remote days something of a liberal, presented her
with the "Statesman of the Week" award, and declared that,
without intending to pass on the merits of the controversy,

> . . . the judges do feel that the personal — and almost maternal
> — interest, which the First Lady of the Land has taken in these
> young Americans is an outstanding example of that invaluable
> kind of statesmanship, that gives friendly counsel and construc-
> tive guidance — rather than oratory and criticism.*

* Copy of press release, Dec. 15, 1939, "President's Personal File #2," Box 2,
FDRL. The other three judges were Robert Sherrod, Washington editor of
Time; Ernest K. Lindley, who held a similar position with *Newsweek;* and col-
umnist Ray Tucker.

On the other hand, to the New York *Sun* Mrs. Roosevelt's action appeared to be "a bold move to discredit the Dies Committee." There was some agreement, however, that the committee was not all it should have been in any event. Heywood Broun was of the opinion that, since the Nazi-Soviet Pact, Mrs. Roosevelt and her husband had been considered by the Communist Party its greatest enemies. He thereupon concluded that "when Dies toils to move public opinion against either Public Enemy No. 1 or No. 2 he may hear . . . a rumble of cordial approval from the left."

Others were not prepared to negotiate such a formidable broad jump of logic. The New York *World-Telegram*, although deploring the methods of the committee, nevertheless declared:

> There are many — and we are among them — who do not share Mrs. Roosevelt's conviction that the American Youth Congress is free from Communist control. We strongly suspect that Mrs. Roosevelt, a person of great frankness who likes to give others credit for equal candor, has been deceived by devious minded followers of the party line.

More outspoken still was the New York *Herald Tribune*. That she had invited AYC leaders to the White House, editorialized that newspaper, was "to confuse rather than to clarify the issue." The Communists, it continued, "have made it impossible to tell who is a Communist and where Communist influence begins and ends." For this reason,

> When any lie or evasion is justified in the party's service; when any "front" may be used for any ulterior purpose; when any sincere impulse toward domestic radicalism may be exploited for the private benefit of a foreign dictator, the public is compelled to draw inferences and has a right to demand that any suspect organization give some clearer account of the sources of its in-

spiration than mere proof that its heads do not hold Communist party cards. And any one of Mrs. Roosevelt's high position and influence has an obligation to use them in defense of such organizations with a caution that once would not have been necessary. The Dies Committee may have its faults. But for Mrs. Roosevelt to bring its hearings under this peculiarly direct sort of pressure is scarcely a public service.[75]

Notwithstanding this kind of criticism, the First Lady held to her course. She explained her position at length in her column of December 5, 1939:

When an organization stands up under this amount of investigation, I fail to see how there can be hidden either a Communist or Fascist program or a surreptitious control of any kind. It is true that there might be a number of members who might willingly work for the objectives of an organization and yet belong openly or secretely [sic] to subversive groups, but you cannot fight shadows and you must wait till you find the objectives of an organization are being changed or interfered with.[76]

The comparatively mild reaction which greeted her decisive gestures in behalf of the American Youth Congress in late 1939 developed into more outright criticism as a result of her participation in the AYC Citizenship Institute the following February. Two factors were instrumental in this hostility. The first concerned the great wave of public sympathy for Finland and concomitant outrage against the Soviet Union because of the latter's invasion of Finnish territory the previous December. The second was that instead of the Dies Committee as an antagonist, Mrs. Roosevelt appeared to oppose the stand of her husband. Furthermore, growing suspicion of Soviet motives generally and increasing impatience with youth groups' apologies for them combined to produce a much more unfriendly reception to youth's behavior than had been the case in the past.

The Citizenship Institute, held in Washington from February

9 through 12, 1940, marked the summit of the AYC's militancy and influence. Young people descended on the capital bearing banners with such slogans as "Jobs – Not Guns," "Keep America Out of War," and "The Yanks Are NOT Coming." To the current Hit Parade jingle, "Oh Johnny, Oh!" they substituted their own lyrics:

> No Major, no Major, we will not go.
> We'll wager, we'll wager, this ain't our show.
> Remember that we're not so green
> As the boys in 'seventeen.[77]

High-powered speakers had been induced to address them including, besides Mrs. Roosevelt, United Mine Workers leader John L. Lewis, Attorney General Robert Jackson and the President of the United States.

President Roosevelt's speech, on the evening of February 10, shocked the group. Instead of the customary petting and cajolery they were used to in high places, the young people heard FDR express himself in unusually outspoken terms. He told them that under a different form of government the kind of meeting they were holding could not take place; that their opportunities for employment were not more drastically limited than had been those of their counterparts in the past three decades; that they should not become deluded into expecting "Utopia overnight . . . some wonderful new law that will give to everybody who needs it a handout." He informed them that they had "no American right, by act or deed of any kind, to subvert the Government and the Constitution of this Nation." And he denounced their resolutions against loans to Finland as "unadulterated twaddle." [78] Treated for once without condescending flattery, youth responded with either offended silence or an occasional undisguised jeer.

The First Lady must have felt a keen sense of disappointment at this exhibition. Already, in both time and effort, her generosity in trying to make the Institute a success had been enormous. Besides regularly attending their meetings, she had arranged for two showings of the motion picture, *The Grapes of Wrath* (then premiering in New York), and for accommodations for one hundred and fifty male delegates free of charge in the riding ring at Fort Myer and for fifty girls free of charge in the Industrial Home. She had further seen to it that three hundred additional hotel rooms (including forty at the Shoreham) were provided at only one dollar a night and that Army trucks would take care of the transportation of the one hundred and fifty delegates at Fort Myer.[79]

Notwithstanding the President's brusque message and the rude reaction accorded it, Mrs. Roosevelt chose to face the young people in an hour's question-and-answer session the following night.* Hers was again the gentle, motherly approach. Although she did not give ground in her beliefs (she was highly sympathetic to the Finnish plight), the First Lady appeared, in contrast to the President, almost desperate to communicate a sense of understanding and good will. For the American Youth Bill, now scaled down to a demand for $500,000,000 to be channeled through NYA for the benefit of America's young people, she had only kind words.† In answer to a question concerning

* Between the President's speech and Mrs. Roosevelt's appearance the delegates had heard an address by John L. Lewis castigating FDR and inviting the AYC to associate itself politically with Labor's Non-Partisan League.

† The original American Youth Bill, which had been drafted in 1935 and which Mrs. Roosevelt had opposed because of anticipated excessive costs, provided for the following: (1) government sponsorship of vocational training and employment on public enterprises for all those between the ages of sixteen and twenty-five who needed it, wages in the latter case to be equal to prevailing local rates as established by recognized labor unions, but in any case not lower than $15.00 per week with $3.00 additional for each dependent; (2) government support of students, tuition plus living expenses and fees not to be lower than $15.00 per month for high school and vocational school students; (3) a program of work on college projects "of an academic nature" for college and graduate students who needed it at prevailing wages but not to be less than $25.00 per

why the administration had not been able to solve the unemployment problem, she declared: "It is a world question, a basic economic question. The administration doesn't know the answer."
In the area of foreign policy, Mrs. Roosevelt refused to indict
the AYC's failure to condemn the Russian push into Finland;
rather, she avoided judging its action by saying it should not
pass resolutions in which its members did not believe. She then
presented an earnest summary of her position:

> I don't see today the slightest reason why we should go to war
> and I hope there is not going to be any war and I think it prob-
> able that one answer is that up to now we have kept ourselves in
> armaments . . . a strong nation that nobody wishes to attack.
> . . . We don't want war. . . . Do you think the President
> wants war? But nobody knows what they may face when the
> world is going through a cataclysm. I could agree with you
> right this minute that I don't want war, but I don't know what
> you might say under different conditions six months from now.
> You are sure you will say the same thing . . . but I am not go-
> ing to be a prophet until I know what I am prophesying about.

In conclusion, Mrs. Roosevelt thanked her audience for its fairness in hearing her — for, she said, only through an exchange of
opinion was it possible to mature, learn and grow. She received a
standing ovation.[80]

Mrs. Roosevelt's decision not to forsake the American Youth

---

month; (4) all rates to be raised in accordance with the cost of living; (5) administration of the proposed bill to be composed of youth commissions: one-
third youth, one-third organized labor, one-third representation from local social service, educational, and consumers' organizations; (6) no projects to be of
a military nature or to subsidize private profit-making entities and no discrimination because of sex, color, nativity, religion, or political beliefs; (7) funds for
the bill to be provided by a tax "levied on inheritance, gifts, and individual and
corporation incomes of $5,000 a year or over." The revised (1939) bill was not
nearly so ambitious. *Congressional Record*, 74th Congress, 2nd Session, Jan. 14,
1936, H. R. 10189; see also George P. Rawick, "The New Deal and Youth: The
Civilian Conservation Corps, the National Youth Administration and the American Youth Congress" (unpublished Ph.D. dissertation, University of Wisconsin, 1957), pp. 325–27.

Congress, but to appeal to and help it, caused certain legislators to accelerate their criticism of her. In the House of Representatives the irascible Michigan Republican, Clare Hoffman, who had begun to attack her the previous autumn, was now seconded in such assaults by Republicans Karl Mundt of South Dakota and Frank B. Keefe of Wisconsin. This carping, however, because it was partisan and narrowly based, was of little consequence. Furthermore, the First Lady had defenders in Congress as well, among them Democratic Representatives Matthew A. Dunn and Leon Sacks of Pennsylvania and Lee Geyer of California, and American Labor Party Representative Vito Marcantonio of New York.*

More important was the disapproval evident in much of the press. While her husband's speech had been greeted by almost complete endorsement, Mrs. Roosevelt's position was a source of widespread misgivings. According to the Salt Lake City *Tribune*, for example, the President's "frank and timely" remarks "had a tendency to offset the solace communists have tried to extract from Mrs. Eleanor Roosevelt's misplaced confidence in this misled group of youngsters who needed exactly what the President gave them." Walter Lippmann lashed out strongly against the AYC, terming its members "shockingly ill-mannered, disrespectful, conceited, ungenerous and spoiled." There had been much discussion, he continued,

> about how many of them were Communists and how far they were under Communist control. They answered the question beyond any reasonable doubt . . . like a weather vane the opinions of the Youth Congress were . . . pointed infallibly by

---

* *Congressional Record:* for Hoffman, 76th Congress, 2nd Session, Oct. 9,. 1939, p. 219; Oct. 20, 1939, pp. 661–62; all others 76th Congress, 3rd Session: Mundt, April 9, 1940, pp. A1952–54; Keefe, Feb. 8, 1940, pp. 1237–38; Dunn and Sacks, Feb. 8, 1940, p. 1238; Geyer and Marcantonio, Feb. 9, 1940, p. 1346. Most of the Congressional outbursts against Mrs. Roosevelt were incidental to the main purpose of attacking the American Youth Congress.

the winds of doctrine which blow from Moscow . . . . It is not
necessary to know how many of them are active members of
Communist organizations. The fact is that they are hypnotized
by Moscow.

The Detroit *Free Press* agreed: "If the youngsters had set out to
justify criticisms which hitherto have been launched at them, and
suspicions about what they stand for, they could not have done a
better job." And it added:

> . . . regardless of what she may say out of the abundance of her
> charity, it is impossible to believe that even Mrs. Roosevelt can
> any longer be under much illusion about the extent to which the
> goodness of her heart has allowed her to be exploited and un-
> gratefully mistreated.

There were few indeed who, like Ernest Lindley, thought she
had "rendered a distinct service by giving those young people a
hearing, by making them feel that our democratic government
was interested in the problems of youth, and that they could and
should work through the forms of democracy." Even the usually sympathetic Lindley, however, was constrained to note:

> Whether Mrs. Roosevelt was wise in going further, by making
> herself the leading patroness of the American Youth Congress,
> was a question in my mind long before the gathering in Wash-
> ington last week. Without the presence that she lent to it, the
> organization probably would have faded out of existence.

In any case, it was Lindley's opinion that the American Youth
Congress "has washed itself up as an effective political force.
. . . It is doubtful," he concluded, "whether even Mrs. Roosevelt could obtain another hearing for this organization. . . ." [81]
   Despite notes of incredulity with respect to the First Lady's
further support of the AYC, Mrs. Roosevelt nevertheless persisted in her reluctance to part company with it. To Leslie

Gould's *American Youth Today*, a eulogistic account of the AYC's history written in the spring of 1940, she gave her imprimatur by writing a foreword. In it she declared that "people will be able to find out the real facts about the American Youth Congress. . . . The author . . . has, I think, given a picture which is historically correct. . . ." [82] In addition, she arranged a fund-raising ceremony in the group's behalf at the home of Edward J. Flynn in May and a conference between its leaders and her husband and Harry Hopkins in June.

As the Allied position in Europe grew increasingly critical, however, and as the AYC showed no disposition to modify its stand with regard to aid to the enemies of Hitler and Stalin, she allowed a sense of apprehension to seep into public print. Soon after the fall of France she expressed the hope

> that youth will always feel that war is a horrible thing, but we know that we have to meet circumstances as they exist and that when there is a war of opposing ideas and it becomes a war of force, there is nothing to do but accept force as a weapon, unless we wish to accept that which submission represents.

In July she was declaring that "The American Youth Congress . . . seem[s] to me to be discussing the world of a year ago, not the world as it is today." [83]

At the AYC's 1940 national convention at Lake Geneva, Wisconsin, Mrs. Roosevelt absented herself for the first time since she had originally shown interest in the group. It was probably fortunate that she did: at that conclave the organization voted 319–19 against the administration's armament measures; and a resolution which expressed opposition to being led by "a political dictator as are Germany, Italy, Russia, Japan or Spain" received but 10 votes out of the 533 delegates present. [84] Although she continued to see certain of its leaders, the Lake Geneva convention in fact signaled the termination of Mrs. Roosevelt's active sponsorship of the Congress. She began, instead, to transfer her allegiance to a far less controversial organization, the International Student Service.

In the summer of 1941, hard upon the German invasion of the Soviet Union, leaders of the AYC once more requested an audience with the First Lady. "I would feel," she said, "[that] any delegation organized under the American Youth Congress auspices was probably more interested in what was being done for Russia than in what was being done for young people in the U.S." [85] It was the end.

~

The significance of Mrs. Roosevelt's somewhat tardy disavowal of the AYC lies in the illumination it sheds upon certain facets of her perspective and character. She had reached a point, as a result of her own experiences, where a permissive attitude toward youth had assumed the proportions of being almost an absolute guide to her conduct. As she had stated in 1930, adults must allow young people to "meet their own difficulties, find their own solutions to knotty problems and gain experience for themselves." [86] Freedom to "think through" to their own answers in combination with education to supply them with a wide fund of alternatives would, by some mystical process, produce the suitably democratic citizen. Given this optimistic base, it was little wonder that she was "deeply persuaded of her ability to win the Youth Congress leaders to her way of thinking." [87]

The possible pitfalls of this faith, however, were penetratingly exposed by Walter Lippmann. In a column written soon after the February, 1940, Washington meeting of the AYC, he pointed out:

What is serious about this is not the nature of these [youthful] opinions but what has been revealed about how, as a result of recent theories of education, this new generation, or at least an articulate part of it, has learned to form its opinions. So-called progressive education is based on the notion that if you remove authority and discipline and tradition in the upbringing of young people, the unobstructed natural goodness of their hearts and minds will by spontaneous creation bring them to good ideas.

Our generation, the one to which Mrs. Roosevelt belongs, has made many mistakes. One of its very greatest mistakes has been to misunderstand and then break down the true relationship between youth and age. The true relationship is, so to speak, verti-cal — father and son, teacher and pupil, thinker and disciple, master and apprentice. In this relationship, experience is trans-mitted to the young and vitality is renewed in the mature. We have substituted a horizontal relationship in which we separate the young in youth movements . . . this segregation is most reactionary, in that it breaks the connection by which the new generation takes possession of experience and improves upon it. . . .

In the older, and truer, relationship between the generations, there is none of this sentimental foolery about youth as youth. . . . To be young was to prepare for the duties and responsi-bilities to come, and what was respected in youth was not their immaturity but the eternal fact that a boy is going to be a man and a girl is going to be a woman.[88]

To this kind of viewpoint Mrs. Roosevelt did not subscribe. On the contrary, she continued to maintain a rigid faith in the efficacy of latitudinarianism and good will. She was convinced that the baleful domestic and international situation characteris-tic of those years lent, if anything, additional force to her posi-tion. Growing up, in itself no easy process, had become further burdened by actual depression and the threat of war. Thus she could find, in the shifting posture of youth's collective security debates, its deeper hopes for full employment and lasting peace.[89]

Also to be taken into account was the First Lady's propensity for what one well-disposed observer was to call "the very human and lovable sign of gullibility." More simply, as Dorothy Thompson phrased it, "She never suspects anyone of ulterior purposes." [90] Careful reading of the record suggests, in fact, that these comments may have been understated; her professions of faith in youth groups, in contrast to what these groups were actually doing, were at times so uncompromising, so unqualifiedly positive, as to appear almost stupefying in their credulity. At the World Youth Congress at Vassar College in 1938, Joseph Cadden (AYC executive secretary) jammed through a "Peace Pact" which favored collective security but on which no floor discussion was permitted (with the excuse that time would not allow such discussion). Mrs. Roosevelt, commenting about the meeting, declared: "If there was central control over that group [Cadden was also organizational director of the meeting], I really am the fool people said I was because I found no evidence of it." Following the Youth Congress' 1939 annual convention, during which a resolution specifically denouncing communism and fascism was opposed by leading delegates in what were obviously prearranged remarks, the First Lady lauded "their adherence to democratic principles in open discussion" and expressed "a great confidence in the wisdom, the idealism and the honesty of the group as an entirety." At the conclusion of the 1939 Christmas week meeting in Madison, Wisconsin, of the American Student Union, which had declared itself against a condemnation of the Russian invasion of Finland by a vote of 322–49 and which was, by any reasonable standard, run by the Communists, she defended the ASU by stating that its resolution was "practically identical with the resolution passed by the National Student Federation which is a conservative student body." *

* The American Student Union had been formed by an amalgamation of the (communist) National Students League and the (socialist) Student League for

Subsequent to the February, 1940, Citizenship Institute in Washington, where a New Jersey Young Democrat, Stephen McArthur, was physically removed for shouting "What about Finland?" in the midst of a lachrymose recital by Abbott Simon about the victims of fascist aggression, Mrs. Roosevelt commented lamely that "the congress was not as well run as it might have been." And, at the termination of the AYC's 1940 annual convention at Lake Geneva, where the only group in the Congress supporting her husband's policies was barred because of technicalities, she was quoted as saying, "There still remains [sic] the same cordial relations between the American Youth Congress and myself as there always has [sic] been." [91]

Furthermore, it was difficult for Mrs. Roosevelt justifiably to plead, as she did later, that her misplaced confidence in youth groups was due solely to the fact that their leaders had lied to her.[92] Indeed, in addition to being physically present at every occasion just described except the two meetings in Wisconsin, she proclaimed that she was far better acquainted with the facts of youth organization activities than those who were suspicious of them. She herself elaborated upon this at some length. There was a difference, she said, in merely contributing a sum to an organization, the aims of which one might be in sympathy with, and being closely engaged in assisting a group:

> If . . . we give our names to appear on the letterhead of an organization and work with it actively, it seems to me that we have a more serious obligation. A conscientious person reads all the publications put out by the organization which they are joining, attends as many meetings as possible, knows as many people working in the organization as possible.
>
> It seems to me that something which was said many years ago applies in this instance: "By their works ye shall know them." [93]

Industrial Democracy at Columbus, Ohio, in December, 1935. Mrs. Roosevelt's characterization of the National Student Federation of America as a "conservative student body" was, at least in the 1930's, incorrect. See Rawick, "The New Deal and Youth," pp. 279–81.

She spelled out what she regarded as her knowledge of the AYC's activities even further in a letter written to a critic of that organization. The critic, a member of the Americanism Committee of the American Legion, had demanded "that she deny or substantiate a statement attributed to her that the AYC board members were not communists." Her reply was:

> I certainly did make that statement and I think that I have taken a good deal of trouble to get at the facts in this situation.
>
> How many of your representatives and those of other organizations you mention have met the Chairman of the American Youth Congress and the members of the board of directors, who are mapping out the program of work and raising the money — not only once, but many times?
>
> How many of you have spent hours at a time discussing various questions with them?
>
> How many of you have been over their finances and know how much money they have had and where it came from?
>
> How many of you have not only attended their general meetings but have spent some time attending special meetings at their national congress this year?
>
> How many of you have read the minutes and resolutions passed at all their meetings?
>
> How many of you have obtained the record of the Federal Bureau of Investigation and carefully studied it?
>
> I have done all these things.[94]

This self-righteous response, with its implication that her correspondent was ignorant about AYC activities whereas she was not, typified her own attitude as well as that of many liberals generally. Her claim, for example, that she had "carefully studied" FBI records pertaining to the leadership of the youth group took liberties with the truth. What she had in fact done, as she was to recall later, was to read the reports and find so many people who were obviously not Communists listed as contributors to "Communist fronts" that she decided all such reports

were worthless.[95] A closer and less prejudiced appraisal might
have led her to become less enthusiastic about some of her youthful friends. George P. Rawick, after an exhaustive study of various leaders of the Youth Congress, reached the following conclusions with respect to their communist inclinations:

> [William] Hinckley has been identified often as a member of the
> Communist Party; his wife was openly a member. [Jack] Mc-
> Michael has in all probability never been a member of either the
> Young Communist League or the Communist Party, but it is also
> true that he has been a leading fellow-traveler for almost twenty
> years [Rawick's study was made in 1956–57]. Of [Joseph]
> Cadden, [Miriam] Bogorad, [Abbott] Simon and [Frances]
> Williams it can be clearly stated that whether they were mem-
> bers of the YCL or the CP in the days of their activity with the
> Youth Congress is immaterial. They followed every twist and
> turn of the Communist line from 1935–36 through 1942.

Elizabeth Scott, Rawick believes, was only a "dupe"; Rose Ter-
lin and Rose Troiano, though following the Party line, probably
did so innocently. Edward Strong, on the other hand, was ad-
mittedly a Communist, Waldo McNutt was one in all but name,
and Joseph Lash changed his pro-Soviet orientation only with
the Russo-German pact of 1939. James Wechsler, at that time a
member of the Young Communist League, has stated that the
Communists "ran the show" almost from the first, and he has
received corroboration from Murray Kempton and Joseph
Lash.[96]

It was in fact more than credulity and a predisposition toward
youth that led Mrs. Roosevelt to her stubborn defense of the
American Youth Congress leaders. Like many liberals of her
time, Mrs. Roosevelt despised the imputation of Communism as
applied to what she believed were progressive, democratic ideals.
She herself, in certain of her other activities, had been accused of
harboring Communist sympathies. Such charges were absurd.

She had, indeed, frequently indicated her opposition to Communism. Speaking before a youth group in 1938, for example, she had made the unqualified declaration: "I don't hold any brief for young people who are Communists." Later, when a youth group, apparently laboring under the misguided notion that the First Lady was "one of us," had named a branch of the Young Communist League after her, she had angrily written: ". . . this is perhaps too serious a matter for joking. They cannot use names without permission and, in addition, I am now and always will be opposed to the Communist form of government." [97] To the suggestions about her own Communist sympathies she could further cite the inaccuracy of similar charges directed against other aspects of youth's activities. She recognized, for instance, that much of the depression generation had an honest and non-ideological commitment to peace, and would have agreed with the estimate of the *Christian Science Monitor* when it observed:

> No generation in the history of America has been so continuously and persistently bombarded with anti-war propaganda as the young people of today. . . . The deep impression peace propaganda has made on them is having its effect.

She also had correctly diagnosed the American Youth Bill (before its revision in 1939) as being unwise because it would result in exorbitant costs rather than because it was allegedly communistic and "not the American way." [98]

For these reasons, Mrs. Roosevelt had a tendency to "overreact" whenever the issue of communism was associated with her friends or activities. Her position was sound when she declared:

> I am ashamed of the fear we have alowed [sic] to be put over us, so that when somebody says that a particular group is Communist, we don't even take the trouble to find out how many are Communists. We are afraid to have anything to do with them. It is too foolish.[99]

But her grounds were less tenable when, in the face of over-whelming evidence that it was Communist-oriented, she continued to lend aid and comfort to a group she *had* had something to do with. For, by 1940, it was no longer merely partisan Congressmen, headline-hunting investigating committees or professional patriots who were warning her against the AYC. Her mail was flooded with protests, many of them by no means stemming from persons basically antagonistic. One such individual, for example, who signed herself "A gal who likes you for yourself," wrote "the kindest and best hearted woman in the world" to "please be the dignifyed lady you know you can be" and "don't have a rabble of youngsters . . . crumming up the place." Mrs. Roosevelt herself mentioned in her column the amount of critical reaction she was receiving due to her championing of youth groups. Moreover, people in whom she personally trusted were rapidly becoming disillusioned. James C. Patton, President of the National Farmers Union, and Dexter Keezer, President of Reed College, were sent by Taussig to the February, 1940, gathering, and both came back very much soured. David Dubinsky, President of the International Ladies Garment Workers Union, and Malvina Thompson, Mrs. Roosevelt's personal secretary and a close friend, both warned her against the Congress.[100]

A part of Mrs. Roosevelt's persistence in defending the youth groups might perhaps have been due to a reluctance to face squarely the results of the Russian "experiment." She had been able, for instance, to casually use a phrase like "some of my Communist friends" without irony or without self-consciousness, and she had thought that the Soviet Union "should be sympathetically watched and regarded." She had felt, in other words, the same semi-hopefulness about Russia, sometimes apparently justified but so often frustrated, which prevailed in most liberal-progressive circles in the decade of the 1930's. Like those circles, she had feared atrophy of domestic reform when the administration had turned its attention to military defense; like them, also, she had felt totalitarianism of the right to be a greater danger than tyranny of the left.[101]

Important, too, was the rhetoric of the Popular Front years, so hazy and yet so comforting, in which the youthful debates and resolutions were couched. One of Mrs. Roosevelt's more grievous minor shortcomings was that she seemed unconcerned with the context in which words were used, the emotion conveyed by them being itself sufficient. Hence, such terms as "jobs," "security," "democracy" and "peace" usually found in her a ready response. She did not appear to comprehend fully the fact that they could also be employed, with a glib cynicism, by such uncongenial agents as the *Daily Worker* (as were the words just cited, in a resolution of 1938) or by Gil Green of the Young Communist League (who called the U.S.S.R. "the truest representative of democracy in the modern world").[102]

The difference in this respect between the First Lady's instincts and those of one of her prominent contemporaries is instructive. Perhaps the only woman to rival Eleanor Roosevelt during the latter 1930's, both in influence and popularity, was the journalist Dorothy Thompson. Outspokenly anti-Nazi, Miss Thompson was at the same time in no way deceived by the Popular Front rhetoric of Communism. Her reaction to the AYC's antics was therefore devoid of either the frills of rationalization or the evasions of strained apologetics. Instead, following the occasion of the 1940 Citizenship Institute, she addressed to the group's leadership

a very simple question. How come that you take in Communists?

I'm not arguing whether people have the right to be Communists. That's not the issue. But you people are pledged to a creed. You come before the public and say, "This is what we believe." And then you say, "We've got Communists, too."

Now the result is that an adult like myself begins to think:
"Either these kids are phonies or they're idiots."
Because no Communist believes this creed.*

There remained, lastly, one further element of Mrs. Roosevelt's philosophy that contributed to her stubborn championship
of the American Youth Congress. She believed in complete and
untrammeled freedom of thought. Even as late as the summer of
1940, when evidence indicates that she was experiencing unset-
tling notions about the motives of the Youth Congress, she could
still write the AYC that she saw "no reason now and I never
have, why you should put the young communist league
out." [103] This should in no wise be construed as indicating sympathy, on the First Lady's part, for the Young Communist
League. It demonstrated, rather, the lengths to which she was
prepared to go in order to uphold the *sine qua non* of her entire
attitude toward youth.

No limits, she had repeatedly stated, should be placed upon
young people in seeking their own solutions to their own problems. Adults should be a part of this process only by virtue of
their capacity to help; "old shibboleths" and "outworn traditions" existed only to be thrown off. With the shackles of restraint removed, youth would remake the world into a better
place, would not be guilty of the mistakes of their elders. *How*,
then, in view of this set of assumptions, could any barriers be
imposed around what doctrines the young might choose to believe? Limitations of this nature would negate their freedom to
find solutions. *By what right* could elders place restrictions upon

---

* Dorothy Thompson, "On the Record." New York *Herald Tribune*, Feb.
16, 1940. Although Miss Thompson and Eleanor Roosevelt were to work
closely in behalf of a more militant pro-Allied policy in 1940 and 1941, there
could be little genuine sense of empathy between the shrewd, tough-minded
reporter and the emotive, trustful First Lady. As Miss Thompson's friend Vincent Sheean has indicated, the two women "did not fervently admire each
other." Vincent Sheean, *Dorothy and Red* (Boston, Houghton Mifflin Co.,
1963), fn., p. 264.

youth? The former were incompetent as judges; their own mistakes belied their claims to any restrictions. And *why* should youth be circumscribed in any case? Given freedom to think for themselves, they could not but improve upon the situation they had inherited.

Nothing so clearly summarizes the discordant series of influences which operated upon Mrs. Roosevelt throughout her first fifty-odd years. The times of her youth, her childhood and her young motherhood were, with the single exception of the Allenswood years, spent in absorbing the ideas and practices of an older generation. With these ideas and practices she could never quite, subconsciously, break. Her experiences in social work, education and public life thereafter, on the other hand, opened her mind to new sets of goals and new methods. These, she had determined consciously, were somehow "better" than the old. Caught in this dilemma, she was left to try to twist the old and the new together.

That she managed it, however crudely, is indicated by her attitude as it pertained to youth and freedom. For, in adopting the attitude she did, she turned a belief in freedom into a dogmatic assertion of the rectitude of laissez faire, and she molded nineteenth-century optimism into a blind faith for the accomplishment of twentieth-century goals.

II

FRIEND TO
A NEGLECTED PROMISE

FRIEND TO A NEGLECTED PROMISE

For the first time Negro men and women have reason to
believe that their government really does care. . . .

> From a message delivered to Mrs. Roosevelt
> by a Negro delegation. Summer, 1939.

THE IMMENSE STRIDES made by the Negro American toward
greater equality of opportunity and treatment in the decade
of the 1960's has tended to dim the light of his earlier advances.
This is understandable, for there seems little room for dispute
that former gains, both qualitatively and quantitatively, did not
rival this later progress. Nevertheless, small as his earlier tri-
umphs may appear when viewed on a comparative scale, they
were no mean achievement. This is especially true because the
impetus for advance had to be created almost *in vacuo;* one of
the most difficult aspects of any long-term movement is simply
getting it started.

What Professor W. W. Rostow might call the "take-off
stage" on the route to fuller citizenship for the Negro occurred
in the 1930's.[1] Certain "pre-conditions" for this development
already existed: The massive colored migration to the North
during and after the First World War, for example, gave many
Negroes their first taste of urban life, higher incomes and a less
permeating inflexibility of race prejudice on the part of the white
community than had been the case in the rural South. A few
Negroes acquired unusually fine educations, and these individ-

uals began to articulate the sentiments of protest and aspiration of great masses of their brethren. W. E. B. Du Bois, Carter Woodson and E. Franklin Frazier can be counted in this group. Others found success in the arts. Countee Cullen in letters and Marian Anderson in music were building high reputations by the onset of the 1930's. Jazz, accepted widely in Europe, had also made many white converts in the United States. In athletics, Jack Johnson had already been heavyweight boxing champion, and Paul Robeson had received national attention because of his football exploits at Rutgers. In isolated pockets of society, therefore, the efforts of individual Negroes had won for their race a certain admiration, no matter how reluctant or how comparatively small.

Ironically enough, national depression was, in a manner, to assist them further. Always extra vulnerable to the caprices of the economy, Negroes felt the effects of widespread economic stagnation earlier and more deeply than any other group in American society. At the bottom of the economic scale, they were customarily the first to be fired, the last to be hired. Depression thus brought them incalculable hardship.

Negroes were not, of course, the sole American group which suffered. The breadth of the crisis meant that virtually every citizen was affected. The Roosevelt Administration, confronted with such unprecedented distress, believed that only a correspondingly massive counterattack led by the national government could bring about recovery. And the very scope of the government's plans, since they aimed at alleviating misery wherever it existed, necessarily included the Negro as a beneficiary. The New Deal, with its heretofore unheard of relief methods, its *inclusive* attack upon unemployment, came inherently to improve the plight of great numbers of colored Americans. Programs like the CCC, AAA and FERA filtered their gratifying results to the black man, if for no other reason than that he was so often in the economically stricken class these programs were designed to help.

Incidental benefits of such a nature could not, however, make for genuine advance. As important as they were in the immediate sense and as grateful as the Negro may have been for them, they could not in the long run fundamentally further his quest for greater political, legal, economic and social rights. The generative force which sparked these aims was in a narrower area of the government. It embraced individuals who wished not only recovery and jobs for those who had suffered most the blows of economic calamity; it was deeply concerned also with the Negro per se. The people who composed this group wanted, in brief, not only recovery in the economic sphere but reform in the racial one as well.

The kind of approach which concerned the Negro *as a Negro* was *specific* rather than incidental, *exclusive* rather than inclusive. Although there were many officials of relatively minor influence within the group which held such sentiments, certain major figures were prominent in it as well. Henry Wallace and Frances Perkins were well disposed; Harold Ickes had headed the Chicago chapter of the NAACP. W. Frank Persons and Aubrey Williams were part of this *locus;* later, Negroes themselves — Will Alexander, Robert Weaver and Mary McLeod Bethune — were brought in to augment it.

These individuals, sometimes in the face of considerable odds, accomplished much. Vital to what they were able to do, however, was the forceful leadership given their efforts by Eleanor Roosevelt. This is not to say that Negro advancement would not have occurred without her presence. It is, on the other hand, very doubtful that it would have taken place on the scale it in fact did without her active intervention and encouragement. She brought to bear upon the entire question, besides the prestige of her name and the advantages peculiar to it, a lack of rigidity, a sense of caution, a political finesse and, withal, a spirit of dedication that resulted in what may well have been her most substantial achievement during her first eight years in the White House.

~

Mrs. Roosevelt did not carry with her interest in the American Negro the same dogmatic tenets which governed her approach to youth. Unquestionably, her entire social outlook rendered her hospitable to the aspirations of minorities; contrarily, she had had but limited experience with such problems before she became First Lady. Her first acquaintance with Negroes, she recalled, occurred this way:

> On Saturdays we visited my great aunt Mrs. James King Gracie, who had been born and brought up on a Georgia plantation. She would read to us from the Brer Rabbit books and tell us about life on the plantation. This was my very first introduction to Negroes in any way.
>
> It was rather a happy way to meet the people with whom I was later to make many friends because all the stories our aunt told us were about delightful people. Our aunt had conducted a school for little Negro children and taught many of them when no other facilities for education were available to them.
>
> But it was not until I was more than 15 and in Europe that I actually met a Negro. It was even after I had worked in a Rivington Street settlement in New York that I met and knew Negroes. That was after I returned from Europe . . . .
>
> While in Paris I very likely met Negroes but they made no special impression, very likely because they were English-speaking Americans just as I was. I never dreamed that they had a special problem of any kind.
>
> I think I really began to understand their problem when I went to Washington, D.C., for the first time [in 1913]. Millie and Francis came to work for us and I learned a great deal about them. I think Millie and Francis were the first Negroes I ever shook hands with.[2]

From her own testimony, it therefore seems clear that as a young woman Mrs. Roosevelt had only the most casual contacts with Negroes. The first intimation that she was aware that any racial tension existed appeared in a letter written from Europe to her mother-in-law in 1905 in which she indifferently mentioned overhearing some American tourists discuss the "negro question." [3] During the Wilson years in Washington and the early 1920's, when she was becoming politically active in New York, no word pertaining to colored Americans occurred either in her writings or her speeches. In 1928, during the course of a lengthy article in which she elaborated upon the issues of the forthcoming presidential election, statements concerning the Negro were notable only by their absence.[4]

Notwithstanding her apparent indifference, Mrs. Roosevelt seems to have known that, in certain areas at least, colored Americans were subjects of discrimination. Among her early writings at Hyde Park is an interesting fragment, dated 1928, containing the words "I have never attacked the South for its attitude toward the Negro." It continues to the effect that if Southerners were going to enforce the Prohibition Amendment, then for consistency's sake if nothing else they ought to enforce the Fourteenth and Fifteenth Amendments as well.

> . . . I quite realize that the south is leagally [sic] within its rights in debarring the negro from voting and after the reconstruction period, I do not think anyone could blame the southerners for their feeling not [sic] for what was done but it seems to me that the need is gradually passing away and that though they are legally entirely right they often do not live quite up to the spirit of these amendments. However, I have never said this in any public statement.[5]

In spite of the caution which marked this passage, the sentiments behind the statement itself seemed clear enough. They suggested that Mrs. Roosevelt was both aware that Negroes were not enjoying their full rights in the South and that she was hesitant to take a public stand on the issue.

Forces were at work which, by however circuitous a route, may have helped nudge her toward a more forthright position. In the Smith-Hoover presidential campaign of 1928, a contest in which she labored diligently in the New York Governor's behalf, she witnessed an unparalleled amount of intolerance directed toward her candidate. This illiberality, much of which stemmed from Southern sources, was an outgrowth of an older America's and a more tradition-minded Democratic Party's battle against allegedly hostile forces which were changing the nature and power structure of American society. Al Smith seemed to be representative of many of these forces: he was the product of an urban environment, closely associated with Tammany Hall, "wet" on the liquor question and a Catholic.

On certain of these issues Mrs. Roosevelt's position was one with that of the New York Governor. Her surprisingly strong attachment to the virtues of a rural life did not mean for her a concomitant suspicion of the city.* She was, after all, like Smith a native of New York City. Nor was she opposed to the political organizations the metropolis so frequently spawned. The "boss," she stated plainly, was often "an enlightened, high minded leader"; Tammany Hall had inaugurated many things in which all citizens could take pride.[6]

The prohibition question was more perplexing. She was, at that time, a very convinced "dry" and delivered the optimistic forecast that "we'll have a drier country than ever before. . . . Congress, if I am right, will continue to grow drier. . . ." Nevertheless, she recognized that there were pockets of highly vocal pro-repeal sentiment; to accommodate them was proper,

---

* Mrs. Roosevelt's philosophy regarding rural environment is examined in Chapter IV of the present work.

she felt, for it would insure better enforcement of the law as a whole. Her position, as a matter of fact, was characteristic of the pro-Smith "drys": namely, that Smith "supported absolute prohibition if a State wanted it, and favored modification only to improve the workability of and respect for the law." [7]

The issue of Smith's Catholicism also found Mrs. Roosevelt in the Governor's corner, albeit with a certain lack of militancy. She was "willing to grant that the Popes, past and present, have written in a way which would lead us to fear a growth of temporal power and a control by the church of the civil government," but she regarded this as no longer a danger. Most Catholics now looked to the pontiff as merely "their spiritual father and leader." *

What must be borne in mind concerning Mrs. Roosevelt's views on these questions and her support of Smith was the apparent effect upon her made by the attacks on Smith's position. The Governor's more outspoken opponents almost invariably adopted the strategy of assailing Smith on several fronts at once; they believed that his vulnerable points were closely interwoven.[8] What could one expect from a candidate whose origins

---

* ER, untitled MS (1928), "ER, Speeches and Articles," Box 1, FDRL. Mrs. Roosevelt's attitude toward Catholicism has been the subject of some debate. Joseph Lash records that he was "struck by her hostility to the Catholic Church," and Bess Furman Armstrong confirms the fact that she spoke critically of it from time to time.

It is to be remembered, however, that it was the Church outside the spiritual sphere, not in it, of which Mrs. Roosevelt was wary. James A. Farley, himself a devout Catholic, told this writer that he could recall no instance of antagonism in Mrs. Roosevelt's dealings with him or any one else of his faith at any time, and many Catholics came to her defense when Cardinal Spellman intimated in 1949 that she was anti-Catholic. Even Lash concluded his recollections by stating that whatever antipathy she might have held was not directed toward the Church's faith or doctrine, but only its political activities. Joseph P. Lash, *Eleanor Roosevelt: A Friend's Memoir* (Garden City, New York, Doubleday and Co., Inc., 1964), p. 242; interview with Bess Furman Armstrong, June 11, 1965; interview with James A. Farley, May 14, 1965; Seymour P. Lachman, "The Cardinal, the Congressmen, and the First Lady," *A Journal of Church and State*, VII (Winter, 1965), pp. 48–49.

were in that Sodom of civilization called New York City?
Wasn't it only logical that he favored corrupt machine rule,
championed immoral liquor swilling? And wasn't it also natural,
continued his detractors, that he was a representative of Rome,
intriguing to saddle the country with the popery which had laid
such a heavy hand on the homeland of his Irish ancestors? The
mark of the alien was truly upon him.

One element only remained to complete this horrendous picture for the South, that, of course, being the ancient standby of
the race issue. Although prominent Negro spokesmen such as
W. E. B. Du Bois were quick to point out that the New York
Governor "has sedulously avoided recognizing Negroes in any
way" and that "a vote for Al Smith is a vote for the Bourbon
south," [9] anti-Smith leaders, after some vacillation, began to link
him with threats to white supremacy. The fact that Southern
white nuns "were teaching colored children, and that the Catholic Church everywhere accorded 'such equality in church relations as is not extended to [Negroes] by other religious organizations'" was widely circulated. Senator Furnifold M. Simmons
of North Carolina was convinced that Democratic National
Chairman John J. Raskob was lining up Negro support "with
the lure of liquor," and the Ku Klux Klan seconded this view
and "was active particularly in the rural areas" against the New
York Governor.[10]

The bigotry — and the frequent scurrility — which accompanied this barrage of anti-Smith propaganda seems to have impressed Mrs. Roosevelt deeply. Soon after penning the fragment
in which she pointed out that she had "never . . . in any public
statement" spoken out on the Negro question, she became em-
broiled in an acrimonious dispute with Mrs. Jesse W. Nicholson
whose National Woman's Democratic Law Enforcement
League was "opposed to Governor Smith because he represents

Tammany and . . . would, if elected, use his power . . . to re-
peal or amend the Eighteenth Amendment." Mrs. Nicholson
also feared that the Governor's friends "are counting on the
negro support because he [Smith] does believe in equality between blacks and whites." Although Mrs. Roosevelt denied that
this was in fact Smith's position, she was nonetheless sufficiently
aroused to overcome her earlier scruples about refusing to express herself publicly on the racial issue. Unless, she wrote Mrs.
Nicholson, the latter's organization began to concentrate its
efforts on upholding the Fourteenth and Fifteenth Amendments
as well as the Eighteenth, it should consider changing its name to
the "National Woman's Dry Enforcement League." By 1930,
she was openly of the opinion that Southerners had "brought to
a free country a subject race which has cost us much and created
for us a problem which is far from satisfactorily solved even today," and two decades later she could still recall being "outraged
at the campaign of . . . bigotry waged against [Smith]" and
appeared particularly incensed over the ignorance of "Southern
farmers" and "Georgians." [11]

The road to open advocacy in behalf of the colored American's aspirations was also considerably eased by Mrs. Roosevelt's
religious outlook. Possibly because of the cheerless Sabbaths of
her youth and because of her exposure to the freethinking doctrines of Mlle. Souvestre, she seems to have dispensed with the
more formal trappings of religious dogma at a comparatively
early date. When her children were very young, she remembered that she asked her husband

> how much religion he felt we must teach them, or whether it
> was our duty to leave them free minds until they decided for
> themselves as they grew older. He . . . said that he thought
> they had better go to church and learn what he had learned. It
> could do them no harm. Heatedly, I replied: "But are you sure

that you believe in everything you learned?" He answered: "I really never thought about it. I think it is just as well not to think about things like that too much."

Frances Perkins says that on a later occasion, upon hearing the opinion that FDR was "really a very simple Christian," Mrs. Roosevelt raised her eyebrows and replied, "Yes, a *very simple* Christian." [12]

Although her religious views were perhaps dissimilar to those of her husband, Mrs. Roosevelt shared his indifference to theological niceties. A belief in God appears to have been the sole underpinning of her religious metaphysics.* Instead, religion represented to her a social and ethical guide. It consisted, as she expressed it in 1932, of "the striving of the human soul to achieve spiritually the best that it is capable of and to care unselfishly, not only for personal good but for the good of all those who toil with them upon the earth." Mrs. Roosevelt believed, in other words, in unselfishness. To this belief she attached religious terms, in this case "soul" and "spirit." That she was little concerned with defining these terms with any precision became evident the following year when she attempted to explain "spirit." "I haven't any idea whether the scientists have ever discovered it," she said, but "this really matters very little. I recognize it in other people." After giving several instances of selfless service despite bitter hardship, she declared that such examples were "proof conclusive that there is something in us which we must call spirit because there is no other word which describes it!" [13] Her emphasis was once again placed upon the ethical key, "unselfishness," when she wrote in 1940 that the "best and most unselfish life we have known in history" was that of Christ. We "may not all believe in Christ's divinity," she concluded, but

---

* She also harbored an element, however slight, of mysticism, occasionally commenting that she sensed "a presence" in her room at the White House. *The Wisdom of Eleanor Roosevelt* (a compilation of her columns done for *McCall's Magazine*, New York, n.d.), pp. 18, 110.

"His life is important chiefly because it becomes a shining beacon of what success means." [14] Organized religion thus appears to have concerned Mrs. Roosevelt but slightly. Rather, her interest was in the example of Christ, which symbolized unselfishness and the overcoming of adversity.

To an individual of this persuasion it would be virtually impossible to overlook the situation confronting the black man, or for that matter, racial or ethnic minorities more generally. Although her name was to become most specifically identified with attempts to help the American Negro, her sympathies lay with other minority groups as well. Her references to the plight of the American Indian, while not extensive, were warmly understanding. He was, she felt, "little understood, and often maligned," and she frequently praised his art and other handicraft achievements.[15] Similarly, the First Lady regarded American Jews with high esteem. If, on occasion, Mrs. Roosevelt allowed her respect for them to take the form of overly lavish praise (as when she informed a Philadelphia Jewish women's group that "the women of your race and their husbands are the best citizens this country has"), she, much more typically, minimized their uniqueness and addressed them merely as American citizens rather than as a special group.[16]

It was, in fact, the latter approach — treatment of minorities as Americans rather than as singular human enclaves of society — which was one of Mrs. Roosevelt's most distinguishing characteristics. That her auditors understood and appreciated this is indicated by the words of a Jewish commentator who, in remarking on an address by the First Lady to a New York Zionist group, expressed gratification that "although she stood under the Zionist flag she avoided making any statement on specifically Jewish questions. Personally," this observer continued, "we regard it . . . as an additional instance of her tact that at the beginning of her address she emphasized that she was speaking not as a non-Jewess to Jewish women but as an American to fellow-Americans." [17]

The First Lady carried this attitude into her relations with Negroes as well. She would often preface her remarks to them with phrases like "Much that I am going to say tonight would apply with equal force to any of us living in this country," or would address herself "to you as citizens of the United States on things which are not only of interest to you but which are of interest to every citizen of this country" or "to you not as a special group, but as American citizens." The dignity which she thus gave to her listeners earned the plaudits of the Negro press, the Chicago *Defender*, for example, pointing out during one of her major speeches:

> Not once . . . did she find it necessary to refer to the racial identity of the members of the audience . . . . Her utterances bespoke a genuine interest in the major problems which confront, and have confronted American Democracy.

And the remarks of Dr. Carrie Weaver Smith were probably representative of much of the Negro community when she declared that the First Lady's gestures of helpfulness and friendship to colored girls were made with "courage and enthusiasm and, what is far more important, without . . . the insufferable patronizing manner which so many persons in like position would manifest." [18]

Exchanges of this kind between Mrs. Roosevelt and her admirers from ethnic and racial groups were not to transpire until after she had been First Lady for some little time. They were, however, presaged by her statement, made shortly after her husband's election to the presidency, in which she declared that

> the fundamental, vital thing which must be alive in each human consciousness is the religious teaching that we cannot live for

ourselves alone and that as long as we are here on this earth we are all of us brothers, regardless of race, creed, or color.[19]

Even in view of such assertions, her evolution to a solid commitment on behalf of Negro aspirations was comparatively slow. In 1933 she was, according to her later recollection, still naïvely dismayed at a proximate manifestation of racial prejudice. She remembered clearly an engagement with Mary McLeod Bethune that year

> because of something shocking that happened before the lunch. The lunch was with a white lady who was deeply interested in Bethune-Cookman College. Mrs. Bethune told me there had been considerable question as to whether she could lunch with us in Florida. It was quite a shock to me because it seemed so perfectly dreadful that there should be any question about it.[20]

It is not difficult, in view of examples like this one, to understand why, when Mrs. Roosevelt took up residence in the White House, she did not at once embark upon a flurry of activity in behalf of the Negro. She was simply not yet wholly cognizant of the critical nature of his position. She seemed to be aware that discrimination existed without fully realizing its extent.

Despite these factors, she participated in enterprises which increased her interest in the colored race. Her trip to Puerto Rico and the Virgin Islands, taken in March, 1934, for the dual purpose of demonstrating the President's personal interest in the islanders and to publicize the wretchedness of native conditions, could hardly have helped but enlarge her sympathy for the black man. Her friendship with Negro educator Mary McLeod Bethune, whom she had met in 1927, was deepening. And, in the course of her other activities, she was receiving letters like the one from a Negro mother which reported that her children were "so nere necket they cant get out on the street" and pleading for intervention with the local relief office.[21]

That she was increasingly aware of the need for taking up the cudgels on behalf of the Negro became obvious when on May 11, 1934, she made an NBC radio address to the National Conference on Fundamentals in the Education of Negroes. The First Lady minced no words, proclaiming: "We can have no group beaten down, underprivileged without reaction on the rest." *Opportunity*, the journal of the National Urban League, quoted with approval these "brave and sincere words spoken with deep conviction," and continued emotionally:

> And then this for those who would rise on the backs of their fellow citizens: "We must learn to work together, all of us regardless of race, creed or color. We must wipe out the feeling of intolerance wherever we find it, of belief that any one group can go ahead alone." [22]

The speech was sufficiently precedent shattering to attract comment in Congress. Representative Joseph A. Gavagan, a New York Democrat whose district included the greater part of Harlem, stated that socially as well as economically there was "no color line at the White House." He singled out Mrs. Roosevelt for special praise:

> The little 6-year-old colored boy during the Easter-egg rolling fete who was "shot" in the picture with three other youngsters got a great thrill out of holding the hand of the First Lady of the land while she beamed the Roosevelt smile before the battery of cameramen for the edification of all and sundry everywhere, at home and abroad. It recalled a like picture taken on her visit to the Virgin Islands. Mrs. Roosevelt's deeds have been no less significant than her speeches, especially the admonition to the educational leaders of the Nation assembled in Washington when she stoutly condemned double standards in teachers' salaries, buildings, equipment, and educational opportunities practiced to the detriment and [sic] social welfare of the whole country, and the colored citizen more specifically . . . .

We congratulate Mrs. Roosevelt on her courageous stand . . . .[23]

In addition to giving public voice to her sentiments of concern for the Negro, Mrs. Roosevelt began to exercise her influence in other ways as well. Clarence Pickett of the American Friends Service Committee remembered her having invited a prominent colored gathering to the White House as early as January, 1934, to discuss the admission of Negroes to the government homestead projects. On another occasion Walter White recalled that, desperate after presidential secretary Marvin McIntyre kept intercepting his requests to see the Chief Executive about the Wagner-Costigan Anti-Lynching Bill in 1935, he turned to the First Lady, who promptly secured him an appointment. On the date of the meeting FDR was late, and Mrs. Roosevelt and White went over the bill together. After appearing and, in their subsequent conversation, listening to White rebut all of his prepared objections, the President "turned sharply and declared, 'Somebody's been priming you. Was it my wife?' " [24]

Mrs. Roosevelt was also a determining force in certain appointments. "Why Mary McLeod Bethune became head of the Division of Negro Affairs [of the NYA] presents little mystery," states Allen F. Kifer. "Besides being the obvious choice among Negro women in public life, her personality and qualifications were known to and appreciated by the President's wife." Kifer concludes that their earlier friendship "probably led directly to Mrs. Bethune's appointment." [25]

Expanding activities of this nature, besides gaining the admiration of the Negro community,* drew the attention of white supremacists as well. "The emotionalism of the professional Southerner was perhaps stirred more by the democratic speeches and

---

* Mrs. Roosevelt was, for example, asked to deliver the principal address at the Urban League's Twenty-Fifth Anniversary dinner in 1935.

attitude of Mrs. Roosevelt than by the acts of the New Deal Administration," commented Louis Martin, a colored Detroit publisher. "To him she became a sinister figure because she dared to express some positive beliefs in racial equality." Wrath against the First Lady below the Mason-Dixon line began to manifest itself at a grass roots meeting of Southern Democrats at Macon, Georgia, in early 1936. Delegates to the convention found on every seat a copy of the *Georgia Woman's World*, in which was featured a large photograph of the First Lady being escorted by two Negro ROTC officers during one of her visits to Howard University. Vance Muse, a moving spirit of the Macon conclave, described the picture as being "of Mrs. Roosevelt going to some nigger meeting, with two escorts, niggers, on each arm." To it was soon added a crude drawing which depicted the First Lady dancing with a Negro and which bore the legend, "Nigger Lover — Eleanor." [26] Picture and drawing were distributed over certain parts of the South by the Texas Election Managers Association, a self-styled super-patriotic group closely identified with a similar Houston organization, the Committee to Uphold the Constitution.*

In May, 1936, Mrs. Roosevelt further outraged Southern sensibilities by holding a garden party on the White House lawn for sixty girls, all except eight of them colored, from the National Industrial Training school in Washington, D.C. Whereas this gesture caused the institution's Negro superintendent, Dr. Carrie Weaver Smith, to assert that "Mrs. Roosevelt knows what the word 'lady' means," so great was the ire in parts of the South that at the South Carolina Democratic Convention a few weeks later Northern party speakers were cautioned to "make no lau-

---

* The Macon affair had received financial backing from the extreme rightest American Liberty League; Vance Muse later admitted, however, that the anti-Negro aspects of it were introduced without the contributors' knowledge. George Wolfskill, *The Revolt of the Conservatives: A History of the American Liberty League* (Boston, Houghton Mifflin Co., 1962), p. 242.

datory references to the President's wife; she had just entertained
a bunch of 'nigger whores' at the White House." *

Such blatant prejudice in one quarter could only heighten the
luster of Mrs. Roosevelt's reputation in another. Her growing
role in the racial sphere, however, began to have far greater implications than those which merely touched upon her personal
image. Paul Ward of *The Nation* seemed to sense this when, in
reporting the antics of the Macon meeting and the venom characteristic of the South Carolina Democratic Convention, he suggested that similar instances could become powerful vote-makers
for the administration. Highly placed officials in the Democratic
Party were quick to agree; if Mrs. Roosevelt's evident friendship
for the Negro could cause such outrage amongst certain white
Southerners, it might also corral vast support elsewhere. In areas
where it felt that the controversial photograph would be sympathetically received, the Democratic National Committee therefore "took pains to distribute more than a million [copies]" of
the picture of the First Lady at Howard University.[27]

These efforts made it plain that the influence exercised by Mrs.
Roosevelt's words and actions had undergone a substantial enlargement. No longer did her activities concerning racial matters
result merely in attracting gratitude toward her as an individual.
By 1936 they transcended a purely private relationship between
any single person and group. Instead, her position had assumed
the dimensions of a full-blown political issue. And it was as such,

---

* *New York Times*, May 17, 1936; Paul W. Ward, "Wooing the Negro
Vote," *The Nation*, CXLIII (Aug. 1, 1636), p. 120. It was not only among
Southerners that anti-Negro, anti-Roosevelt biases teamed together. In an in-
credibly tasteless effort to embarrass the President and his wife, FDR's neighbor
Howland Spencer sold his Hudson River property to the gaudily eccentric Negro cultist Father Divine. Both the Roosevelts accepted the situation with grace
and good humor, the First Lady commenting deftly that "I always feel sorry
for anyone who has to sell a country place they have lived in and enjoyed for
many years . . . . It must, however, be pleasant to feel that in the future this
place will be 'heaven' to some people, even if it cannot be to its former owner."
"My Day," Aug. 1, 1938; *New York Times*, Aug. 10, 1938.

in addition to whatever intrinsic help she could render the black man, that her increasing zeal in behalf of the Negro was to attain its greatest significance.

~

Although colored voters had defected from their traditional Republican allegiance in large numbers in the midterm elections of 1936, their course in 1936 was regarded as unpredictable. One favorable ballot doth not a party man make, and Democratic leaders viewed with some concern the opinions of various Negro journals. Franklin D. Roosevelt, declared the official organ of the NAACP,

> is no improvement on Wilson and Lincoln. He, too, is in the class of almost, nearly, well-nigh, not-quite, and all-but. He, too, is just short of doing what he knows to be right and just. After all, we haven't made a great deal of progress in the White House in seventy years.[28]

This position had, in fact, some justification, for FDR had shown a certain ambivalence toward Negro aspirations throughout his public career. In personal relations he appeared benign; as Assistant Secretary of the Navy in 1917 he had written "a strong letter to . . . the Surgeon General on behalf of a Negro doctor who wished to enter the Army Medical Reserve Corps." [29] Furthermore, as President, he shone the warmth of his personality on one Sylvester Harris, a colored Mississippi farmer who, when he placed a personal telephone call to the White House in an effort to stave off a mortgage foreclosure, was put straight through to the Chief Executive and had his property saved by a loan from the AAA.*

Taken as a whole, however, Roosevelt's record was far from satisfactory according to the Negro standpoint. In 1932 Walter

---

* Harris' "testimony" was given credit for being instrumental in the defeat of Congressman Oscar De Priest, a Republican, by Democrat Arthur Mitchell in Chicago in 1934. Both victor and vanquished were Negroes.

White complained that FDR "had made overtures to the Southern Bourbons" and that Negroes had reason to be suspicious of
his earlier boast "that he wrote the Constitution of Haiti when
without real justification that black republic was invaded and
seized and governed by American marines serving American
financial powers." A Negro historian, Henry Lee Moon, was
more explicit:

> Nothing in the public career of Franklin D. Roosevelt prior to
> his election to the presidency had given any convincing indica-
> tion of a sympathetic understanding of the problems of the Ne-
> gro in America. As governor of New York he had paid but
> slight attention to the colored population of the state. What
> casual contacts he had were chiefly through James A. Farley
> who, as Democratic leader, overlooked no potential voter. He
> made no outstanding appointments of Negro Democrats. He
> initiated no legislation which was of immediate concern to this
> minority. Indeed, the Negroes of New York received little rec-
> ognition from Governor Roosevelt either by way of appoint-
> ment or legislative program.[30]

As President, Roosevelt continued to equivocate. While denouncing lynching as "a vile form of collective murder," he refused to push for anti-lynching and anti-poll tax measures on the
ground that such a course would endanger other legislation
which was more immediately pressing. His public statements as
they pertained to the colored man — typified by his 1935 Emancipation Proclamation Anniversary message wherein he affirmed
that Negro progress had been "remarkable" and that he hoped to
see colored Americans "go forward to even greater things in the
years to come" — were flat and uninspired. In view of such am-
biguity, it was little wonder that a Negro journal could say in
disillusion:

> The hopeless thing about us is our brain storms of love and hate.
> We rush to kick a Harding to Hell and a Roosevelt to Heaven

with a mass unanimity all out of proportion to facts or proba-
bilities. It is a pitiable proof of lack of reason and judgment.[31]

Negro spokesmen did not confine their charges of inconsist-
ency to the occupant of the White House. They appeared to
regard much of the entire New Deal as surfeited with racial prejudice. Though the Act which made the CCC a reality contained
the clause that "in employing citizens for the purpose of this Act,
no discrimination shall be made on account of race, color, or
creed," and although W. Frank Persons, with Secretary Perkins'
support, worked to eliminate discrimination in enrollee selection,
the Corps "continued to run afoul of local laws and customs"
with which it did not generally quarrel. In 1935 FDR was receiving letters similar in tenor to the one which wondered:
". . . if war was declared, would they pick all the white boys
first and leave the negro boys as the last called for service? This
is what they do in the CCC." [32]

Analogous complaints were leveled at other agencies. In the
summer of 1933 it was reported that although "the NRA banner
literally clutters the scenery" in the South, an "unfortunate
phase of government-regulated wages is the injustice it has
worked upon the Negro. It is certain that already Negroes are
being displaced by white persons in a number of lines of work."
Editor Virginius Dabney thought it "doubtful if the NRA has
helped the Negro at all," and in the United States Senate Royal
Copeland, Democrat of New York, read into the *Congressional
Record* these remarks of New York City Collector of Internal
Revenue James J. Hoey:

> I have learned that wherever there is a condition of unemploy-
> ment the Negro is the first to be fired, and as conditions improve
> he is the last to be rehired. I find that this condition is Nation-
> wide; that Negroes as a group are the greatest sufferers in the
> depression and do not receive the benefits of employment under

the N.R.A. In fact, the minimum-wage provision of the N.R.A. operates to the distinct disadvantage of the Negro.

For example, where an employer had a Negro elevator operator at $10 a week, finding himself forced by law to pay a minimum wage of $15 weekly, he fires the colored man and hires a white man to take his place.

Nor was General Johnson's Blue Eagle the only prey for potshots. The NAACP condemned the "widespread deprivation of crop reduction bonuses under the AAA due to Negro tenants and sharecroppers but appropriated by white landlords," and TVA administrators were accused of showing bias in their hiring policies.[33]

In view of this less than inspiring record, the heavy endorsement given the Democrats by Negroes in 1936 can justifiably be considered a matter for some astonishment. Upon closer examination, however, that result is not so surprising as may at first appear. Despite the variety of complaints which concerned discriminatory policies in a number of New Deal agencies, there existed at the same time the undeniable fact that many Negroes *were* being hired, *were* being taken off the relief roles and receiving succor from administration programs. The Pittsburgh *Courier*, for example, carried a lead announcing "Over 26,000 Negroes Receiving Benefits Under NYA." Robert C. Weaver asserted that "the New Deal, insofar as it represents an extension of governmental activity into the economic sphere, is a departure which can do much to reach Negro citizens." This notion that the colored American could not help but share in any anticipated benefits aimed toward alleviating economic distress as a whole was well summarized by a highly placed government official brought into the administration specifically to protect Negro interests. Stated Dr. Clark Foreman:

The whole question of the future of the Negro population is intimately involved in the administration's attempt to plan and regulate industry. Although undoubtedly there will be displacement and misfortune in the transitional period, the Negroes along with all minority groups seem certain to benefit by a greater centralized control.[34]

Thus, the fact that countless Negroes were taken from the relief roles, were given a job, and often received enough for at least a subsistence income must have been reason enough to predispose them favorably toward the New Deal philosophy. They could join with many of their equally deprived white brethren in reciprocating with their ballots the advantages they had received from various administration measures.

Expressions auguring more general equality of citizenship for the Negro also began to manifest themselves. Despite the President's hesitation with respect to certain civil rights legislation, what one historian has called his "consummate ability to personalize his understanding of human exploitations and underprivilege" communicated itself, as in the case of Sylvester Harris, to the Negro. For the first time, moreover, genuinely important posts in the government were going to colored men and women. To the names of Robert Weaver, Will Alexander and Mrs. Bethune would soon be added those of William Hastie to the federal bench and Lester Walton as Minister to Haiti. Finally, certain highly placed administration figures were hiring without discrimination. Hallie Flanagan of the WPA Federal Theatre Project employed her personnel on the basis of their ability rather than their color, and NYA administrators strove to eliminate racial factors in their recruitment policy. Mary McLeod Bethune, in order to make certain that Negroes were aware of such happy occurrences, traveled frequently to inform the black man of "a great humanitarian spirit that men call Franklin D. Roosevelt." [35]

Most gilt-edged of all, however, appeared the image of Mrs. Roosevelt. Whereas Negroes might complain about FDR's intransigence, whereas they might be chagrined at discrimination permitted in certain agencies of his administration, no such hesitations occurred in their estimate of his wife. In December, 1935, her picture appeared on the cover of *Opportunity*, and the magazine's pages subsequently hailed her Urban League Anniversary address of that month as "unparalleled in the history of America. . . . never before has a First Lady made a plea in behalf of fair play and equal opportunity for Negro citizens." [36]

Nor did she hesitate to carry this refulgence directly into the political arena. To James A. Farley she suggested in 1936 that "it would be well to start some negro speakers . . . to speak at church meetings and that type of negro organization," and she herself was active in forming the Good Neighbor League, a group of Negro ex-Republicans whose announced object was "to stop voting for Lincoln and vote for Roosevelt instead." [37]

This Good Neighbor League motto is worth noting. For the abject ineptitude of the Republican Party in offering a political alternative to colored Americans was to provide yet another impetus in molding them into what Louis Harris was later to call "the most solidly Democratic voting group in the United States." [38] Indeed, signs of Negro dissatisfaction with the GOP had appeared as early as 1932 because of the Hoover Administration's alleged attempts to build up a lily-white "Republicrat" appendage in the South. Colored leaders had also been disenchanted about the nomination of North Carolina's John J. Parker, who was supposedly unfriendly to Negroes, to the Supreme Court. Furthermore, there had been ugly rumors to the effect that the wife of Representative Oscar De Priest of Illinois had been snubbed at a Hoover White House tea.[39]

As important as any resentment the Negro might have felt about matters of patronage or social acceptability was his economic distress. In spite of the Negro's obvious share in the general hard times, the Republicans persisted in their failure to treat him as an integral part of a suffering nation. Rather, they continued to believe that the black man would respond to appeals from the past. The Hooverian approach — that the Republican Party would not "abandon or depart from its traditional duty toward the American Negro" — suggests the ineptitude and irrelevance of GOP appeals to that minority. In analyzing Negro defections to the Democrats in 1932, Arthur Krock wrote:

> . . . it simply means that the shallow, materialistic old arguments went down with the spiritual ones about the Emancipation Proclamation when the lean stomach and the hapless heart uttered a stronger call for a "new deal" . . . [Negroes] have few bank accounts, wealthy friends or parents, or even diminished dividends to save them. . . . The Negro, in brief, voted as a citizen on Hoover and Roosevelt, forgetting Lincoln and Jefferson Davis, who were not running in 1932.[40]

Like Krock, however, many observers felt that the Negro would in time return to his traditional Republican home. Defections in 1932, as Arthur M. Schlesinger, Jr., was later to put it, came "essentially from the top . . . the opinion-makers had abandoned the Republicans. . . ." Although this was serious enough (for, as one analyst said, these opinion-makers "are influential factors" in the Negro's life), it yet appeared that by a reassertion and modernization of its appeal, the Republican party might halt or even reverse the colored drift into Democratic ranks.[41]

By 1934, however, the GOP was so shattered and demoralized that there seemed very little it could offer; and indeed, it did not offer much. Commenting about Republican tactics following the 1934 debacle, *The New Republic* remarked, "Generalizations about liberty and regimentation mean little to those who are still chiefly concerned with the liberty to have bread and butter."[42] The Republicans in 1936 accordingly were confronted with the problem of cultivating the Negro by a different sort of approach. They were at a disadvantage in being unable to claim sponsorship of the inclusive types of benefits the Negro had enjoyed under the New Deal; but they might have capitalized, by taking advantage of the inherent antipathy of Southern Democrats toward the black man, upon the exclusive, or more humanitarian, side of the Negro question.

In their endeavors to appear as the party which might lead the Negro toward a fuller participation in American life the Republicans failed abysmally. Even before either national party convention assembled, political observers were noting that

> up until now there has been no special effort of Republican leaders to return this vote to their fold. On the other hand, the Negroes have been attracted by the bids of support from the Democratic organization generally, and especially by local machines in the Northern and border states. They claim, furthermore, to have fared better in party patronage. . . .[43]

Negro suspicions were further aroused when, at the Republican National Convention, the credentials committee seated lily-white delegations from the South. Nor was the GOP cause enhanced in Negro eyes when Republican Senator William E. Borah of Idaho, for a time a presidential aspirant, came out with a slashing attack on proposed anti-lynching legislation. Even though the eventual Republican presidential nominee, Alfred M. Landon, endorsed such legislation, he for the most part played upon familiar and threadbare themes throughout the campaign.

The American Negro thus became a major instrumentality in helping deliver the incredible Democratic victory in November. In that election every Negro ward in Cleveland, for example, voted Democratic; in Cincinnati's Ward Sixteen heavy colored voting gave FDR 65 percent of the ballots. Chicago more than doubled its 1932 preference for the President, and Roosevelt carried Pittsburgh's Negro Third Ward by an almost ten-to-one margin.[44]

The explanation for such Negro voting patterns can be found in several factors. Of immediate concern to the Negro was simply getting a living; for this opportunity he, in common with millions of other economically distressed citizens, was grateful to the New Deal. Secondly, the Negro had virtually no voting alternative among the major parties; the Republicans spoke a language — the theory of the elite, the sanctity of property rights, the idea of limited government, the existence of irrefutable natural laws — that was, if not incomprehensible, at least of negligible interest to him.[45] And — of extreme political significance — one should note that the Negro, by and large, would not in future years return to his erstwhile Republican home. Other groups and other interests might, for one reason or another, wend their way back to the GOP sanctuary, but the black man was to seek his bed and board elsewhere. Nor was his exile due only to Democratic succor for his "lean stomach"; of increasing importance was its response to his "hapless heart" as well. And perhaps, in reality, it was the latter which was most instrumental, over the long run, in sealing the Negro-Democratic allegiance.*

~

Following the election of 1936, *The Crisis* printed an unusually perceptive editorial. It asserted that although many colored citizens cast Democratic ballots because they expected a continuation of relief, "we believe that underneath their concern for

---

* By autumn, 1939, it was the opinion of the New York *Age* (Oct. 21, 1939) that the Republican Party "utterly disregarded" the Negro and "made no effort to enfranchise Negroes in the South and went 'lily-white' at every opportunity." Most Negroes appeared to agree in the election a year later. Large northern cities, wherein dwelt vast congeries of colored citizens, registered heavily in favor of a third term. An investigator who later polled 581 Negro residents of Harlem found that 82 percent of them had cast their ballots Democratic. Negroes in the border states also endorsed the New Deal. Kentucky Negroes, for example, were estimated to have gone Democratic by a margin of more than two to one. Paul N. Lazarsfeld, "The Negro Vote," *The Nation*, CLXIX (Sept. 30, 1944), p. 379; *The New Republic*, CXI (Aug. 28, 1944), p. 243.

immediate relief, either in jobs or direct assistance, they had a feeling that Mr. Roosevelt represented a kind of philosophy in government which will mean much to their race." [46] The magazine did not spell out this philosophy, but its implication seemed to be that Negroes were in accord with the sentiments of Mary McLeod Bethune, who was reported as "joyously [admitting] that 'never in American history has the Negroes' future seemed so secure.'" The *Literary Digest*, continuing its account of Mrs. Bethune's optimism, declared:

> She ought to know, for frequent have been her conferences at the White House with the President and his wife. Under her auspices, Negro officials recently met to draw up an agenda to present to the President and Congress, with an eye to having it incorporated into the general plan for the Second New Deal.[47]

The high expectations entertained by Negro spokesmen were not primarily based upon further economic benefits. Rather, they were grounded on the fact that Negroes *were* being considered in administration circles, that they *could* get a hearing in White House meetings and that their voice *did* count for something. Colored Americans came to believe, in other words, that perhaps for the first time in American history there was an occupant of the Executive Mansion who intended to give the black man a special place on his agenda.

And yet this belief, as it pertained to the President himself, rested upon rather flimsy accomplishments. Throughout FDR's first two terms of office, there was simply no legislation or executive move of any kind which was in fact *directly* ameliorative of Negro disadvantages. Eleanor Roosevelt recalled

> wanting to get all-out support for the anti-lynching bill and the removal of the poll tax, but though Franklin was in favor of both measures, they never became "must" legislation. When I would protest, he would simply say: "First things come first,

and I can't alienate certain votes I need for measures that are more important at the moment by pushing any measure that would entail a fight." [48]

The President's record and attitude of political caution would therefore hardly appear to justify the immense regard in which he came to be held by many colored Americans. His actions would scarcely seem to warrant the impassioned outburst of Negro Congressman Arthur Mitchell, who in 1939 called him "the greatest humanitarian this Nation or any other Nation has seen. He is second only to the Christ." [49]

One of the possible reasons for the emotion which the President seemed to inspire in the Negro community was expressed by Representative Mitchell again in 1940. In a somewhat more sober judgment than his peroration of the previous year, he declared: "The President, his splendid wife, and the outstanding members of his Cabinet have all shown unusual interest in the welfare of the Negro." [50] Evidence of the attention to Negro causes by the Chief Executive's "splendid wife" were reflected by headlines such as "Mrs. Roosevelt Among the 200 Guests Who Attend Opening of Harlem Art Center," "Mrs. Eleanor Roosevelt Heads List of Prominent Persons . . . Who Will Raise $20,000 to Erect Memorial to James Weldon Johnson," "Mrs. Franklin D. Roosevelt Among Those Attending Showing of New Portraits of Negroes," and "Mrs. Roosevelt Dedicates New Negro Community Center in Ithaca." [51]

The context of Congressman Mitchell's remark demonstrated once again to what extent the many activities of the First Lady had become conjoined in the Negro's mind with the image of the President himself. If FDR was unable to risk an outspoken position on discrimination in New Deal agencies, his wife could nonetheless assure colored audiences that it was "not the intention of those at the top" that Negroes should be subject to such discrimination. If the President might not push strongly for anti-lynching and anti-poll tax legislation, she was able to place the Roosevelt name publicly in support of such legislation "as soon as possible." Where the Chief Executive did not dare risk the ire of powerful Dixie Congressmen by associating himself unqualifiedly with Negro aspirations, his wife could do so and subject herself to all manner of Southern vilification. Southern aspersions against the First Lady in fact raised the stock of the Roosevelts another notch in the eyes of the Negro. Thus, by 1940, one Negro journal could claim that the best proof of New Deal friendship for the colored American lay "in the smearing, race-hating propaganda" employed against the President and his wife. Negro historian Henry Lee Moon was later to say that the Roosevelts became "greatly admired by the masses of Negroes, who loved them for the enemies they made — the most infamous of Southern reactionaries — as much as from positive benefits derived from [FDR's] administration." [52]

That she was aware of the political advantages in appearing as the President's "second self" when he himself found it inexpedient to take a firm position on behalf of civil rights legislation is attested to by one of her closest friends. Writes Lorena Hickok:

> When she publicly took her stand on the race question she did not do it simply because she felt sorry for Negroes, although she was horrified by lynchings and race riots, and her sense of fair play was outraged by the poll tax and the educational and economic inequities forced upon them. Her attitude was based on some clear, hardheaded thinking, plenty of American common sense and political instinct of a high order. It undoubtedly swung millions of votes to the Democratic party. . . .[53]

Franklin Roosevelt appeared also to be aware of the political advantages inherent in his wife's being able to place the Roosevelt name on the side of an issue which, as President, he could not flatly endorse. As Mrs. Roosevelt remembered later:

I knew that many of my racial beliefs and activities in the field of social work caused Steve Early and Marvin McIntyre grave concern. They were afraid that I would hurt my husband politically and socially, and I imagine they thought I was doing many things without Franklin's knowledge and agreement. On occasion they blew up to him and to other people.[54]

The implication in this statement that she did in fact *have* her husband's consent for her stand on racial matters is borne out by his comment to her to the effect that he could always inform Southern critics that "I can't do a thing with you." [55] In truth, it is impossible to believe that FDR, with his magnificent sense of political realities, was not fully aware of the tremendous advantages which occurred from the First Lady's public posture. For it allowed him, in effect, to assume two different attitudes at one and the same time. This "dual identity" helped him to gain the approval of over 80 percent of Negroes polled by *Fortune Magazine* in 1938.*

Mrs. Roosevelt further contributed to welding the entire administration's reputation to her own outlook by praising various inclusive agencies as though they were, at least in part, directed exclusively toward Negroes. Many of her activities were devoted to Negro creative projects under the auspices of the NYA and WPA, and she often emphasized the relationship between these agencies and the realization of Negro artistic aspirations. After praising Negro talent in a speech before the National Urban League, for example, she suggested:

* William E. Leuchtenburg, *Franklin D. Roosevelt and the New Deal, 1932–1940* (New York, Harper & Row, 1963), p. 187. While the overwhelming devotion of so many blacks does not seem warranted by FDR's record, it is not fair to draw the conclusion that he was cynical about Negro aspirations. That his wife was the workhorse in the family in this respect is true enough, but as Louis Harris reports, the President, in his personal contacts with colored leaders, repeatedly "made it known . . . that he was sympathetic to Negro problems." Louis Harris, *Is There A Republican Majority?* (New York, Harper & Brothers, 1954), p. 155.

. . . perhaps the NYA is beginning to take advantage of their opportunity and is showing to the country as a whole what a contribution can be made to the culture and the art of this nation. And I am sure that the WPA and its art program has given many of us an opportunity to know Negro artists that we would never have known otherwise. We may be sorry that we have the WPA and NYA. I happen to think some day we are going to be glad, for perhaps we will have discovered in our country many things that otherwise might have been left undiscovered.[56]

Such apparently casual linking of benefits to the Negro with administration policies as a whole tended, in the Negro's mind, to infuse the entire New Deal program with the humanitarian, pro-Negro attitude exhibited by the President's wife.

It should not be inferred, however, that political considerations were paramount in Mrs. Roosevelt's concern for greater justice for the Negro. Gestures, small in themselves, demonstrate that she possessed a deep belief that the evils of discrimination must be eradicated. Though she frequently encountered situations in which expediency seemed to dictate compliance with local customs and prejudice, she chose instead to give practical application of the viewpoint she expounded. Of one instance of this kind which occurred in Birmingham, Alabama, Mrs. Roosevelt wrote:

The meetings of the Southern Conference on Human Welfare . . . were attended by both colored and white people, although they were segregated in the meeting place. Aubrey [Williams] and I were late at one session and dashed into the church where the meeting was being held and sat down on the colored side. At once the police appeared to remind us of the rules and regulations on segregation. I was told that I could not sit on the colored side. Rather than give in I asked that chairs be placed for us with the speakers facing the whole group. At a later meeting word came to us that all the audience was to be arrested and taken to jail for breaking one of Birmingham's strongest laws against mixed audiences. However, nothing happened. . . .[57]

Determination to stand upon principle in comparatively minor matters led to an incident in regard to Negro rights which was one of the most widely publicized of Mrs. Roosevelt's entire career. Early in 1939 the Daughters of the American Revolution made it known that they had refused the facilities of their headquarters, Constitution Hall in Washington, D.C., for a concert by the outstanding Negro contralto, Marian Anderson. The reason for this action, according to DAR president-general Mrs. Henry N. Robert, was the organization's desire to maintain conformity to "existing and still prevailing 'conditions and customs' in the capital which the community itself must work out." *

Protests against the DAR policy were immediate, and they arose from persons of widely different social and political viewpoints. Chief Justice and Mrs. Charles Evans Hughes, Associate Justice and Mrs. Hugo Black, New York Mayor Fiorello La Guardia, Senator Charles McNary, Republican of Oregon, and Senator Bennett Champ Clark, Democrat of Missouri, were among those lending their names to petitions of objection. The *New York Times*, after paying tribute to Miss Anderson's artistry, declared:

> If [her] inability to find a suitable hall in the national capital for her April concert is due to social or racial snobbery, all that can be said is that such an attitude is inconsistent with the best American traditions, including those which were born in the fires of the American Revolution. It is hard to believe that any patriotic American organization in this country would approve of discrimination against so gifted an artist and so fine a person as Miss Anderson. In fact, no organization could do so and still merit the adjective patriotic.[58]

* *New York Times*, April 19, 1939. Constitution Hall was virtually the only auditorium in Washington, D.C., suitable for concert purposes.

A group of New York clergymen signed a petition which called the DAR's policy "pagan." In Washington Democratic Senator Robert Wagner of New York spoke at a protest meeting where resolutions condemning the DAR position were drawn up. At Howard University Senator Robert A. Taft, Republican of Ohio, promised a colored audience that they would "have the support of the great majority of white people, and all of the intelligent white leaders" in their "fight against certain narrow prejudices, such as that which seems to have excluded Marian Anderson from a proper auditorium in the city of Washington." [59]

Mrs. Roosevelt, however, did not confine her indignation to verbal protest. She had become, on April 20, 1933, life member number 281,200 of the Daughters of the American Revolution. Soon after the DAR released the news of its policy concerning the Anderson concert, the First Lady wrote in her column:

> I have been debating in my mind for some time, a question which I have had to debate with myself once or twice before in my life. Usually I have decided differently from the way in which I am deciding now. The question is, if you belong to an organization and disapprove of an action which is typical of a policy, should you resign or is it better to work for a changed point of view within the organization? In the past, when I was able to work actively in any organization to which I belonged, I have usually stayed in until I had at least made a fight and been defeated.
>
> Even then, I have, as a rule, accepted my defeat and decided I was wrong or, perhaps, a little too far ahead of the thinking of the majority at that time. I have often found that the thing in which I was interested was done some years later. But, in this case, I belong to an organization in which I can do no active work. They have taken an action which has been widely talked of in the press. To remain as a member implies approval of that action, and therefore I am resigning.*

---

* "My Day," Feb. 27, 1939. Besides its immediate consequences, Mrs. Roosevelt's resignation set a standard by which Negroes measured subsequent First

The First Lady's action received widespread approval. Only in the South was she criticized to a substantial degree, and there disagreement was expressed primarily in terms of the impropriety of the President's wife "making a fuss about" the incident rather than the correctness of excluding Miss Anderson. In the country as a whole, even including the South, Mrs. Roosevelt's decision was estimated to be favored by at least a two-thirds majority of those questioned about it.[60]

The colored community was, of course, pronouncedly enthusiastic. *Opportunity* felt that the First Lady's withdrawal was but the expected result of her well-known opinions:

> The resignation of Mrs. Eleanor R. Roosevelt from this organization under the circumstances is easily understood. Herself a gentlewoman inherently courteous to people no matter what their station or race or nationality, a true daughter of the American Revolution, she was repelled by an exhibition which is as crude as it is un-American.[61]

Further comment, in addition to confirming the high esteem in which Mrs. Roosevelt was held by Negroes, indicated how successfully she had thrown her own pro-Negro mantle over the shoulders of her husband's administration. That her actions had come to be viewed in a much larger frame of reference than merely that of a private citizen was evident from the assertion of the Minneapolis *Spokesman*, a Negro journal:

> Those who marvel at the Negro's steadfast adherence to the New Deal after years of traditional subservience to Republican-

---

Ladies. In 1945 the DAR closed Constitution Hall to another celebrated Negro artist, jazz pianist Hazel Scott. President Truman compared the ban to the policies of the Nazis. However, Mrs. Truman, when asked whether she would continue to attend DAR functions, responded, "Why not?" Harking back to Mrs. Roosevelt's stand in 1939, Walter White commented that Mrs. Truman's reply "is most disappointing, particularly in contrast with the action of her distinguished predecessor as First Lady." *The Crisis*, LII (Nov., 1945), pp. 313, 362.

ism have presented before their eyes this week, if they will see, one of the chief reasons. When Eleanor Roosevelt, first lady of the land, resigned from the Daughters of the American Revolution, because another great American woman, Marian Anderson, was not permitted to use Constitution Hall, she broke another shackle in the chain which binds so much of our country in racial intolerance and bigotry.

The *Spokesman* went on to suggest the cumulative effect of Mrs. Roosevelt's conduct in the Anderson affair as well as a host of lesser ones that had been faithfully reported in the Negro press. "It is the little things that the Roosevelts do . . . which makes them great and increases in the mind of the thinking Negro respect for the New Deal and most of what is represents," editorialized the Minneapolis newspaper.[62]

Miss Anderson's failure to procure a hall in Washington resolved itself triumphantly when, with the assistance of the Interior Department, she was given use of the space adjoining the Lincoln Memorial where she presented her concert before an audience of 75,000 people on Easter Sunday, April 9, 1939. The following July the great contralto was given the Joel E. Spingarn Medal, an award to the Negro who "shall have made the highest achievement during the preceding year or years in any honorable field of human endeavor." Chosen to present the medal was Mrs. Eleanor Roosevelt, whose name, besides that of Miss Anderson herself, had been most associated with the whole imbroglio. The First Lady did not, in the course of her address on that occasion, touch upon her own prominent place in the incident of a few months before. In her acceptance speech, however, Miss Anderson made special reference to Mrs. Roosevelt's stature among Negroes by saying, "I feel it a signal honor to have received the medal from the hands of our First Lady who is not a first lady in name only but in her every deed." "It was a great occasion," declared the Chicago *Defender,* "surpassed only by the greatness of Mrs. Roosevelt." [63]

Thus, by the latter part of her husband's second term, Mrs. Roosevelt could well look upon her labors in behalf of the American colored minority as having resulted in gains of a very substantial nature. This progress was perhaps not all that she had wished it might be; but one of the reasons it had occurred at all was that she had exercised a caution which, in other fields, she sometimes did not display. She had come comparatively slowly to a full realization of the Negro's plight, and she reached her position without the encumbrance of excessive preconceptions. This induced in her a growing steadiness of purpose which nonetheless did not try to overreach practical, workable goals. She consistently sought to assure the Negro of the fact that although he had "been through and will continue to go through many periods of disappointment" — a disappointment shared by his friends of all races — she had, withal, "come to realize that what seemed to be slow and halting advances, in the aggregate make quite a rapid march forward." She urged, *"above everything else,* [that] *no action . . . be taken which can cause so much bitterness that the whole liberalizing effort may be set back over a period of years"* [this writer's emphasis]. Mrs. Roosevelt herself, in harmony with this moderate spirit, avoided temptations to "bait," but instead took pains to make cordial reference to areas and personalities that might have been expected to take exception to her beliefs. Her columns were replete with remarks such as "I do not think I have ever been in a city which gave me a greater sense of being among friendly people than Shreveport, Louisiana," or "there is certainly a friendly, cooperative spirit in Natchez, Mississippi." After having read Jonathan Daniels' *A Southerner Looks at the South,* she commented: "I have chuckled even when the mistakes we 'Yankees' made were pointed out. I think, perhaps, I have enough of my Southern grandmother in me to understand a real Southerner's feelings about certain things." [64]

These complimentary allusions helped reduce antipathy to her views in the South. Even in a locale where her stand on the racial question might have been expected to make for sizable opposition, she was accorded a generous welcome. A Montgomery, Alabama, newspaper, for example, could feel its city "fortunate indeed" to have the opportunity to hear "one of the inspiring messages she brings her countrymen," and a correspondent from the same state could write the President: "This afternoon the people of Alabama gave Mrs. Roosevelt the largest and most appreciative audience ever to be assembled in the City of Birmingham." [65]

She was not visionary about what could be accomplished in the immediate future. What she spoke for was in the classic American tradition — equality of opportunity. Education was basic to winning this. Speaking to a group of Negro educators, she confessed that she

> could not help but think how stupid we are in some ways, for of course in any democracy the one important thing is to see as far as possible that every child receives at least the best education that that child is able to assimilate . . . [but] we have been slow, many of us who are of the white race, in realizing how important [it is] to our race, that you should have the best educational opportunities.[66]

In addition to educational opportunity, the First Lady advocated equality of opportunity to employ the skills education would presumably provide. "Equal opportunity for training," Mrs. Roosevelt once said, "and equal opportunity to hold jobs for which you are trained. These are basic things to a democracy of any country." Even, however, as both education and equality in jobs were reached, "you cannot expect people to change overnight." ". . . we know quite well," she repeated on another occasion, "that we cannot expect anyone who has had limited opportunities to do as well in one generation or two generations as do people who have had for many generations every opportunity." [67]

Simultaneously, Mrs. Roosevelt in no way slackened her efforts in behalf of the Negro's advance. Prudence, in her case, was not synonymous with apathy. She summarized her philosophy on this point by declaring:

> . . . we must not just accept things that are wrong and placidly sit back and say, "Well, people have stood that for a long while, they'll probably live through it some time longer," and be content with things as they are. You've got to want to change the things that are not satisfactory. You have got to want to do it so much that you will take some trouble about it.[68]

It was her underlying conception — that "intrinsically every human being has the same value before his Maker" — that drove Mrs. Roosevelt to "take some trouble" about the racial inequities she saw all about her.[69] If, in so doing, she reaped political dividends for her husband's administration, that was a gratifying side result. But it was a side result only. Her prime objective remained to help wipe out racial injustice in the interests, not of the Democracy, but of democracy. It is for this reason that the reaction to the Marian Anderson episode surely must have pleased her. For it was a reaction that crossed all party, social and racial lines. And that was the goal, after all, which she had really hoped and struggled to achieve.

III

PARTNER IN A CHAMPION
POLITICAL COMBINATION

PARTNER IN A CHAMPION
POLITICAL COMBINATION

. . . every major gesture of a President's wife
has a political effect, whether intended or not.
New York Times, March 19, 1939.

ANDREW SINCLAIR has said of Warren G. Harding that he
liked to play the part of the "political innocent." By that
Sinclair meant that the twenty-ninth President — publicly — was
not averse to having it believed that his political prominence
stemmed from sources mainly apart from those of his own making. Harding wished to create a legend, in other words, that he
was not involved in whatever manipulation and bargaining might
have occurred in the process of bringing him to high office. Instead, he preferred to have people think that the fact that he
became an important public figure was due to extraneous pressures or to other facets of his personality.[1]

In something of an analogous way, Eleanor Roosevelt elected
to assume the same role. The difference in her case was that, in
addition to denying that her motives were in any way induced
by political considerations, she also disclaimed that her actions
themselves were of any political importance. Thus, when in the
summer of 1940 she was desperately summoned by Frances Perkins and James A. Farley to calm a Democratic National Convention hostile over what it felt was the "dictation" of Henry
Wallace as vice-presidential candidate, she asserted that it was
incredible that she was "called upon to do things like going to

Chicago" for she "was not important or influential." So also, she was later to recall that "I never tried to exert any political influence on my husband or anyone else in the government," and that the "political influence that was attributed to me was nil where my husband was concerned. . . ." [2]

Nothing in the nature of the broad claims that Mrs. Roosevelt ever made about herself is more contradicted by the evidence. Not only were political calculations present in almost everything she said and did, but she possessed what Democratic National Chairman James A. Farley called a genuine "sense of politics." [3] She exercised this talent as a logical complement to her belief in the progress of racial minorities. She utilized it to an even greater extent in her advocacy of an enlarged political role for women. She employed it in the course of campaigns for candidates of her choice and in the Democratic Party generally. She used it in attempting to press her beliefs on government officials, especially her husband. And it was always present, often subtly but sometimes obviously, in her efforts to convey to the public the virtues of the personalities and programs which she favored. No understanding of Mrs. Roosevelt's unique position both within and without the government can be complete without a grasp of this aspect of her activities. This "sense of politics" was as instrumental as her humanitarian zeal in shaping the growth of her prestige and influence.

~

Although her Uncle Theodore had made politics his career and although she visited him a number of times after his accession to the White House, Eleanor Roosevelt was, both as a girl and a young woman, profoundly ignorant of governmental and political matters. Such topics were simply not discussed in her home.[4] She was later to recall with acute embarrassment an occasion on her honeymoon when she was utterly unable to cope with a question by a British friend, Lady Helen Ferguson, regarding the federal system in the United States; and so disinterested did she continue to be in the complexities of politics that, in 1912, she departed from the scene of the Democratic Party's convention in Baltimore well before the national ticket had even been decided upon.[5]

Her lack of concern over governmental issues and processes was accompanied by a similar naïveté about basic political methodology. At the time FDR held the position of Assistant Secretary of the Navy during the First World War she committed, during the course of a newspaper interview, the unhappy *faux pas* of blithely implying that hers was a household of prodigal wealth. "My bills are no larger," she stated in answer to the query of how she met the rising food shortage and consequent inflation. "Making the ten servants help me do my saving has not only been possible but highly profitable." Of this impolitic performance her husband was moved to write:

> All I can say is that your latest newspaper campaign is a corker and I am proud to be the husband of the Originator, Discoverer and Inventor of the New Household Economy for Millionaires! Please have a photo taken showing the family, the ten cooperating servants, [and] the scraps saved from the table. . . . I will have it published in the Sunday Times.[6]

Mrs. Roosevelt was properly abashed. "I do think it was horrid . . . to use my name in that way," she wrote, "and I feel dreadfully about it because so much is not true and yet some of it I did say. I never will be caught again that's sure and I'd like to crawl away for shame." The young matron did not in fact appear comfortable in the political maelstrom as a whole. "I hate politics!" she complained during FDR's 1920 campaign for the vice-presidency. ". . . I really don't see that I'm of the least use on this trip!" She was thought of by a Washington correspondent at that time as being "essentially a home woman" who "seems particularly to dislike the official spotlight" and who was quoted as saying: "Personally I had wanted Franklin out of government service for a few years at least. So in spite of the honor I really feel rather unselfish when I wish for his success." [7]

Despite her apparent innocence and a disinclination to mix in the turmoils of political life, Mrs. Roosevelt seems nonetheless to have been building up a knowledge of politics that was deeper and more far-reaching than she realized. By 1921 she had, after all, been the wife of a public official for eleven years. From the beery and smoke-filled sessions at the Roosevelt residence in Albany — when FDR had served in the New York State Senate — to the campaign swing of 1920, she had witnessed a great many of the countless variations of a public man's existence. Informal maneuver, grim reprisal, wild ballot scramble, endless protocol, and high statesmanship — all these she had seen and begun to appraise. Hence, by the late stages of her husband's hopeless quest of 1920, she discovered in her conversations with his chief political adviser, Louis Howe, that these experiences had given her grounds for a surprising number of political opinions of her own. [8]

Franklin Roosevelt's sudden illness in 1921 precipitated her into a field of activity in which she could draw upon and apply the political lessons she had subconsciously learned. She and Howe, as opposed to Sara Delano Roosevelt, who hoped that her son would now return to Hyde Park and become a country squire, wished to restore the patient to as active a life as could then be visualized for him. To this end, Howe encouraged the patient's wife to take part in political life in order that her activities and contacts might restimulate her husband's interest. The result seems to have been successful not only insofar as FDR was concerned; it also ushered Mrs. Roosevelt herself into politics as a full-time participant.

Many of her early ventures in the political realm embraced principally nonpartisan enterprises. She helped gather data for

the League of Women Voters, became active in the Woman's
City Club, was chairman of the Non-Partisan Legislative Com-
mittee, juror for the Bok Peace Award, and a member of the
Consumers League, the Foreign Policy Association and the City
Housing Corporation.[9] More ideological was her work with the
Women's Trade Union League, her growing interest in which
led her to "drop . . . out of what is known as society entirely."
"I gradually found myself more and more interested in work-
ers," she recalled, and "less and less interested in my old associ-
ates." [10]

She began to engage in outright party activity as well. Democratic fortunes in New York State in the early 1920's were at a
low ebb; in some localities outside New York City the party possessed no organization at all. Nancy Cook of the Women's Division of the Democratic State Committee, in need of a Democratic
woman with a "name" to assist in fund-raising, turned to Mrs.
Roosevelt and prevailed on her to speak in an effort to help re-
fuel the party treasury. The latter's debut in this kind of activity
impressed Miss Cook sufficiently for her to introduce Mrs. Roosevelt to Marion Dickerman and Caroline O'Day, both of whom
were laboring in the Democratic vineyard. Together they began
to tour the fifty-two counties of the state, endeavoring to place a
vice-chairman in every county and to form the nuclei of clubs
and study groups. A party organ, the *Women's Democratic
News*, was established, and Mrs. Roosevelt herself assumed the
editorship. She also became the finance chairman of the
Women's Division of the State Committee and commenced a
speechmaking career that would ultimately add up to literally
millions of words. By the summer of 1922, the *New York
Times* was already beginning to take note of her political remarks, describing her at the same time as being "actively engaged
in the work of organizing the Democratic women of the
State." [11]

Mrs. Roosevelt's early political remarks and electioneering tactics often reflected the techniques of Louis Howe; they inclined toward irony and cynicism. Concerning the Republican gubernatorial candidacy of her cousin, Theodore Roosevelt, Jr., in 1924, for example, she professed to be delighted. His nomination, she said, meant a sure victory for incumbent Alfred E. Smith, for how could Smith fail to win "when the Republican Convention yesterday did all it could to help him?" She and Howe then concocted the idea of mounting a steaming teapot (the Teapot Dome oil scandals were by that time in full force as a political issue) on top of an automobile, which followed young Roosevelt all over the state.*

Sarcastic barbs also punctuated certain of her speeches and articles. Her immediate reaction, when asked by a reporter to give her views with respect to Republican high tariff policies in the 1920's, took the form of an angrily satirical parody to the effect that "A little girl's doll will cost more, but it is important that we can get diamonds free — they matters [sic?] so much to most poor people." "Regarding the much discussed prosperity," she observed on another occasion, "I should like to ask whether the devastated Northwest is still part of the United States." She referred to New York's Republican Senator James Wadsworth as possessing "a Marie Antoinette type of mind." And, in an unpublished article written in 1928, she implied that her low opinion of male politicians in particular might be extended to include the entire male population in general:

News comes that the ladies of Thibet find it necessary to have at least three husbands each in order to make up between them the

* *New York Times,* Sept. 27, 1924; ER, *This I Remember* (New York, Harper & Brothers, 1949), p. 31. T.R., Jr's., connection with the scandals appears to have been extremely tenuous. He had been Assistant Secretary of the Navy when the Teapot Dome properties were transferred from the authority of his unwitting boss, Edwin Denby, to that of the Interior Department and Albert B. Fall.

necessary qualifications for a model spouse. . . . There is, perhaps, food for thought on the part of our sex in the Thibetan
idea of accumulating a number of husbands so as to get all of
the qualifications we consider should be possessed by our better
halves.[12]

This caustic streak, however, gradually ceased its intrusion upon
her public utterances. Only rarely after she became First Lady
does one come across such outbursts. Much more characteristic
were the methods she employed, for instance, in her attempts to
persuade women to take a greater interest in the nation's political
process. Although her later reputation and appeal would know
no boundaries as to sex, her energies for a great many years were
directed primarily toward the feminine side of the electorate;
and in this area she customarily abandoned narrowly partisan
carping and instead offered a case in the form of positive and
constructive proposals.

Most American women, when Mrs. Roosevelt began her political activities, had possessed the franchise for only a few years,
and their political efforts were still regarded lightly, or even re-
sentfully, by the more tradition-minded male. At the time Mrs.
Roosevelt carried the women's carefully formulated planks on
social welfare to the Democratic National Convention in 1924,
the National Committee gave her only the most cursory attention. And Marion Dickerman recalls an occasion in the early
twenties when a local party leader who had pretended to be elsewhere consented to see Mrs. Roosevelt and her co-workers only
after they had waited on his front porch for almost three hours.*

Such cavalier treatment was anathema to Mrs. Roosevelt. In
attempting to combat it, however, she did not adopt a classically
feminist line. Men and women *were* different, she contended:

* Interview with Marion Dickerman, May 25, 1965. Ironically, the gentleman
(John Fitzgibbons) to whom lady political visitors were such a nuisance was
himself later defeated in the Democratic primary by Caroline O'Day.

They are equals in many ways, but they cannot refuse to acknowledge their differences. Not to acknowledge them weakens
the case [for women]. Their physical functions in life are different and perhaps . . . certain questions are waiting to be solved
until women can bring their views to bear upon these questions.[13]

By taking this position, Mrs. Roosevelt mixed a distinctly old-
fashioned element (the notion that men and women *"are* different") with the more novel hope that such "differences" might be
useful in solving "certain questions," presumably of a political or
quasi-political nature.

The procedure by which this might be accomplished was obvious. Mrs. Roosevelt perhaps overstated it, but her meaning
was unmistakable when she asked: "Have women gained actual
political equality with men? No," was her answer, "and they will
not until they accept and back women political bosses." The
word "boss," she continued,

> may shock sensitive ears for it means to many all that is un-
> healthy and bad in our political machinery, but as things are to-
> day the boss is the leader, often an enlightened, high minded
> leader, retaining little of the old qualities attached to this ob-
> noxious owrd [sic], but still holding his authority over his dis-
> trict.[14]

What Mrs. Roosevelt sought, in other words, was for women
to become active in the day-to-day aspects of political life and to
acquire positions of power. Fundamentally, she believed, there
existed a "corelation of interests" and an interdependence in society which it was to women's advantage to understand. House-
wives must grasp the fact that farm income, farm prices, wages,
and commodity prices had a bearing on one another and upon
them. The homemaker, furthermore, should realize that she was
affected by events in every part of the globe, for international
policies ultimately determined whether there was to be war or
peace. ". . . when people say a woman's place is in the home, I

say, with enthusiasm, it certainly is, but if she really cares about her home, that caring will take her far and wide." [15]

Preferably, however, within the Democratic Party. Although from time to time she made a gratuitous curtsey in the direction of "the reasonable element of our citizenry, which votes according to its convictions and not on party lines," her record was that of a devoted adherent to the party of her choice. In 1928, for instance, although in principle she favored State Amendment #6 for a four-year gubernatorial term in New York, she presented an involved argument of opposition centering around the fact that the amendment called for the governor to be elected at the same time as the President. "I do not think that . . . we are going to improve the number of people who regularly attend elections or the quality of their intelligence by making it possible for them to vote on as many thinks [sic] as possible in the same year," was the reason Mrs. Roosevelt publicly gave for her stand.[16] It is likely, however, that a more fundamental reason for her position was her knowledge that the party out of power in Washington stood a better chance of success in midterm elections than it did when forced to run its state candidates in a presidential contest. The national political trend throughout the 1920's was, of course, Republican.

Her sense of party loyalty also led Mrs. Roosevelt to support candidates whose qualifications would otherwise probably not have strongly commended themselves to her. As an instance of this, she praised a letter by the notoriously easygoing James Walker which pledged that he would conduct his New York City mayoralty according to the ideals of his parents, who had taught him to "love the good and the pure." Moreover, she disagreed with a Republican women's group which had claimed that Tammany underworld connections would back Walker. "If these ladies would revert to the early history of New York," she declared, "they would find that the Tammany Society had

sponsored and started many things which they are proud of."
Leaving the Democratic Party, she told a close friend some
years later, would "break her heart." [17]

That party, she repeatedly affirmed, needed the help of
women. It was, she said in 1927, "wretchedly organized," for
the men in it were unable "to comprehend the value of sustained
organization. . . . Men think they can organize the vote six
weeks before election," she asserted, "but women generally believe in all-year-round active political work." Her own schedule
was certainly an earnest confirmation of this view. By the mid-
1920's she was writing her husband to the effect:

> Mrs. O'Day and I saw the Governor, our assemblymen and oth-
> ers and then Mrs. Greene and I went over to Saratoga, where we
> had a fine democratic tea. We dined at Skidmore College and I
> spoke afterwards to the girls. . . . Caught the midnight in Al-
> bany and had a busy day Thursday with a lunch for Miss Smith,
> dean of the Bryn Mawr Summer School, International coopera-
> tion meeting. . . . I read at the Women's Trade Union League
> in the evening. . . . This morning went to see Elizabeth Read
> as I'm to be treasurer for City, State and Nation, don't laugh!
> . . . I've written or am writing to every Democrat in the state.[18]

Dedicated political effort of this sort began to gain Mrs. Roosevelt considerable reputation. By 1928 she was being referred
to as "one of our most authoritative and trustworthy spokesmen
for the Democratic Party today." She was by no means unde-
serving of such accolades, for evidence indicates that she was becoming a crisply efficient political technician. One of her unedited memos written during the Smith-Hoover struggle of 1928
well demonstrates her grasp of campaign procedure:

> Send letters to all promi[n]ent Democratic women, asking them,
> what their contacts are, and inviting their suggestions as to the
> best method of managing their own locality.
>   Ask them about conditions?

What their locality produces?

Is their product prosperous?

If not, why not?

Then prepare special propaganda suited to their needs and de-sires, a propaganda suited to the special needs of each locality. We could not use the same propaganda in an agricultural district that we could in a mining town or in an educaijonal [sic] centre. Each must have seperate [sic] treatment arranged to suit.

Ask what is the most discussed subject, what the people are most interested in, ask the women what they personally can con-trabute [sic] toward the democrat party, time, cars, influence to obtain voluntsry [sic] workers.

Open a Smith Headquarters where ever possible, make it a comfortable rest room for the use of all workers, men and women, and well supplied with Smith literature, cards and etc.

Impress upon them that *time is short and to answere* [sic] *at once.*

Then get special literature out as soon as possible, and at work. And any thing of inportance [sic] that you may discover sent [sic] at once to the Democratic National Committe[e]. . . .[19]

Mrs. Roosevelt continued, and even expanded, her efforts in behalf of women and the Democratic Party after her husband was elected President. Her daily columns contained constant references to the methods by which women might go about en-tering a career in politics, the fact that they need not shed their femininity because of this vocation, and the many successes at-tained by women who had elected to go into public life.[20]

Certain individual cases, moreover, took the First Lady far be-yond mere general exhortation. In 1934, for example, when her close friend Caroline Goodwin O'Day was running for Repre-sentative-at-large in New York, Mrs. Roosevelt actively entered the campaign. Employing the device that she came "not as the wife of the President . . . [but] as a citizen of the State of New York," she conducted a two-day whirlwind speaking tour in the Rochester-Syracuse area. Republicans, as might have been expected, were somewhat indignant, and accused Mrs. O'Day of being "too dumb" to speak for herself. ". . . I shall gladly remain 'dumb,' " replied the latter, "since I have such a good friend to speak for me." Dorothy Frooks Peekskill, the Law Preservation Party's candidate in the same election, was also unhappy, wiring the President: "AFTER MRS ROOSEVELT WROTE ME SHE WOULD KEEP OUT OF LOCAL DEMOCRATIC POLICIES [sic] DID SHE NOT GIVE SPECIAL PRIVILEGE TO MY OPPONENT IN USING THE WHITE HOUSE PRESTIGE?" Notwithstanding these protests, Mrs. Roosevelt's active intervention seemed generally well received. *Newsweek* reported that "the well-fed diners" of the Erie County League of Women Voters "applauded enthusiastically" her spirited remarks concerning the virtues of the New Deal and Mrs. O'Day; and the latter received a commanding margin of the ballots in the subsequent election.[21]

The First Lady also maintained her energetic political pace in less obvious ways. Her correspondence with Mary (Molly) Dewson, director of the Women's Division of the Democratic National Committee, was voluminous, though the subjects to which it pertained — appointments, meetings, matters of procedure, and patronage — are, for a later generation, of purely antiquarian value.[22] By 1936, the regard in which her political judgment was held was indicated when, after having been asked by FDR to investigate the conditions of the party machinery, she drafted a three-page, single-spaced memorandum concerning Democratic strategy for the upcoming election. The questions which she raised compelled party chairman Farley to write a reply of twenty pages.*

* Memo from ER to FDR, James A. Farley, *et al.*, July 16, 1936, "Papers of Mary W. Dewson," Group 37, Box 3, FDRL. This memorandum appears in full in Elliott Roosevelt (ed.) and Joseph P. Lash (asst.), *F.D.R. His Personal Letters 1928–1945,* 2 vols. (New York, Duell, Sloan and Pearce, 1950), I, pp. 598–601, and is therefore not quoted here.

In addition to speeches, articles, *sub rosa* consultations and other behind-the-scenes efforts, the First Lady did not scruple to employ what were ostensibly nonpolitical devices for partisan objectives. Such, for example, was occasionally the case with her press conferences. She began these conferences at the suggestion of a newswoman friend, Lorena Hickok, shortly after she entered the White House; and thereafter they were held almost every week in the Monroe Room or in the west sitting room. Male journalists were not allowed, for Mrs. Roosevelt was of the belief that the lady reporters would be better able to hold on to their respective jobs if they alone were admitted. This viewpoint, which became well known amongst women members of the press corps, did nothing to damage the generous manner in which the First Lady's activities were written up by female reporters.[23]

Mrs. Roosevelt stated the purpose of her meetings with the press in March, 1933. The women journalists' goal, she asserted, should be

> to try to tell the women throughout the country what you think they ought to know and what you think they should know . . . a woman's job is to make her impressions go to leading the women in the country to form a general attitude of mind and thought. Your job is an important one . . . you are the interpreters to the women of the nation. . . .*

In order to dispel any impression that her news conferences would become a political vehicle for the administration, Mrs.

---

* ER, copy of a statement made during her first press conference, undated but March, 1933, "ER, Speeches and Articles," Box 5, FDRL. None of the other notes of these sessions are at this time available. Only two persons ever took complete notes of them; one, Martha Strayer, still possesses copies. The other set, taken by Mrs. Roosevelt's secretary, Malvina Thompson, was either destroyed or is in the unopened portions of Mrs. Roosevelt's papers at Hyde Park. Interview with Bess Furman Armstrong, June 11, 1965.

Roosevelt prohibited questions which concerned pending legislation. She did not, however, always narrowly pursue the spirit of this ban. As a national magazine pointed out in 1937:

> It was probably no accident that she asked Katherine Lenroot to be guest speaker during the first days of the row over the Supreme Court reorganization. Chief of the Children's Bureau, Miss Lenroot pointed out that it had taken thirteen years to get 26 child-labor amendments through 26 States. It was a handy example for the President to use to demonstrate how much time a Supreme Court reorganization amendment might eat up.[24]

Moreover, Mrs. Roosevelt's interest in women and Democratic politics sometimes led her to permit the conferences to serve as a clearing house for straightforward party propaganda. Soon after the New Deal came to power, Molly Dewson hit upon a contrivance she called the "Reporter Plan," which foresaw the appointment of twenty-two "reporters" in each community by the Democratic county women's organizations, each reporter to study intensively one aspect of administration policy. Roundtable discussions were to be held. The anticipated results of this scheme, according to Miss Dewson's flier of January, 1934, were to be

> All the reporters become informed on all the agencies.
> They speak before other groups.
> They tell their neighbors what they have learned.
> REPORTERS HELP ELECT DEMOCRATIC CANDIDATES [orig. emph.].
> They become a real force in helping shape the trend of government.

Miss Dewson later recalled that both the President and Mrs. Roosevelt were too busy to confer with her about the idea. Nevertheless, she continued,

. . . when I telephoned Eleanor I would like to tell the women newspaper reporters about my plan for developing the work of the Women's Division at her press conference at the White House . . . she agreed, sight unseen, or rather, hearing unheard. She did not even remind me that politics were "out" at her press conference[s].[25]

Emma Bugbee of the New York *Herald Tribune* related of this session that the plan, in addition to aiming at better organization of Democratic women, proved to be an attempt to "reach into Republican ranks also." For, as Miss Dewson had stated, " 'If the Administration policies are really understood by Republican women, they will discover that at heart they have been Democrats all along.' " Throughout Miss Dewson's presentation, the *Herald Tribune* reporter concluded, "Mrs. Roosevelt smiled but contributed not a word." [26] Molly Dewson was thus able, by the sufferance of the First Lady, to get an abundance of free publicity for a proposal which otherwise might have required the Democratic Women's Division countless hours (and dollars) to promulgate.

~

The foregoing activities did not, however, account for the totality of Mrs. Roosevelt's political effectiveness. Of great additional importance in this wise were her humanitarian concerns, many of which came to include activities of a quasi-political nature. The First Lady had long possessed a sense of sympathy for the "underdog," and she was appalled at the increased burdens depression brought him. Her sense of justice was deeply offended at the spectacle of so many Americans being denied the *opportunity* to get a decent living, and her efforts to alleviate this unhappy condition were heavily freighted with humanitarian motives. One is compelled to point out, however, that Mrs.

Roosevelt's aid to deprived groups of American citizens to an extent presupposed eventual advantage to the New Deal Administration as well as balm to her own altruistic conscience. Political self-interest fortuitously blended with genuine idealism in shaping the direction of the First Lady's activities.[27] Close observation of her career confirms the fact that Mrs. Roosevelt's charitable instincts continually served to build and solidify the political loyalty of countless thousands of people to the Democratic Party in general and to her husband and herself in particular.

In a political speech she delivered in 1928 Mrs. Roosevelt had included the prescient observation that Republican presidential candidate Herbert Hoover possessed few gifts in the way of being able to "bring government closer to the people." Her own belief was that a great nation "must develop the human side of government," should make each citizen aware, in other words, that his government was directly concerned with him as an individual.[28] As her own contribution toward furthering this objective, she began, during her husband's tenure as Governor of New York, to personally oversee the relief of certain cases of adversity. Grace Tully, one of FDR's secretaries, records that "during the early Albany days . . . she handed me a pathetic letter from a destitute young mother asking for help — not by any means an unusual type of appeal," and that Mrs. Roosevelt not only made out a personal check to cover immediate necessities for the distraught woman but brought her to Hyde Park, saw that she received instruction as a seamstress, and later secured her a job in the needle trade.[29]

Although after becoming mistress of the White House Mrs. Roosevelt could naturally not afford the time for such *intensive* personal supervision, the *extent* of her interest in cases of hardship and destitution all over the country increased enormously. In the year 1933 alone her mail was estimated as amounting to over 300,000 pieces, the vast majority of these being appeals for aid of one sort or another.[30]

Mrs. Roosevelt herself was for the most part responsible for this immense epistolary outpouring. She closed her series of broadcasts for Pond's on March 3, 1933, with a restatement of her belief in the necessity for an intimate contact between government and citizen:

> . . . I shall always hope in one way or another to keep in touch with you, the American people, for I feel that you are very close to me. Your interests are my interests. . . . The one great danger for a man in public life or for a woman who is that man's wife, is that they may be set apart from the stream of life affecting the rest of the country. . . .[31]

In accordance with this philosophy, she introduced her series of columns ("Mrs. Roosevelt's Page") for the *Woman's Home Companion* in August, 1933, with the open solicitation, "I Want You to Write to Me." After stating that for years she had been receiving letters from every sort of person all over the country, she continued:

> Always I have wished that I could reach these correspondents and many more with messages which perhaps might help them, their families, their neighbors and friends to solve the problems which are forever rising in our personal, family and community lives, not only with my ideas but with the ideas of others.[32]

Almost immediately a deluge of mail began to inundate the offices of the *Woman's Home Companion*. "Your invitation to write you will, doubtless, be met by an avalanche of letters," correctly predicted one correspondent before proceeding with her problem. "In one of your magazine articles you wrote asking mothers to write you in regard to their problems during the depression," began a second; it was "only because of your re-

peated and sincere invitations to 'write to me' and my own des-
peration that I am laying aside some pride and attempting to put
my troubles before you," confessed a third.[33] Such prefatory
remarks, representative of countless others of like sentiment,
demonstrated beyond question that the First Lady had come
upon an unusually effective method of bringing government
"closer to the people."

It is impossible to spend day upon day scrutinizing these missives without being deeply moved by the pathetic accounts they
contain. Loneliness ("death visited . . . and taken my only
son"); despondency ("but this we have agreed — that death by
any means is preferable [to the present circumstances]. . . .");
illness ("my sister . . . sick for two years . . . now I can not
get work nowheres"); poverty ("I am trying to hold my farm
and get food for my children but it is hard this year. Money is
scarce and hard to get. . . .") — all were present in wretched
profusion.[34]

Certainly such heartrending misfortune did not fail to stir an
individual of Mrs. Roosevelt's generous impulses. And this would
have been especially true in light of the almost childlike faith in
the First Lady reflected by so much of the correspondence.
People seemed to regard her as a kind of court of last resort
which, when appealed to in the extremities of distress, was
uniquely capable of devising some means of solving their problems. "Please, Mrs. Roosevelt will you not work out some
plan?" or "*Please* dear lady can't you help me . . . some way?"
are typical concluding passages.[35]

To the best of her ability, the First Lady did what she could
on a purely personal basis. In what she judged especially acute
situations she would send a small check or perhaps clothing, but
the extent of such aid was naturally curtailed by the limitations
of her own purse. "I wish very much that I could send you the
money for which you ask," she was forced to inform one peti-

tioner, "but unfortunately I have so many requests of this type that I have had to make it a rule to grant none of them." A few years later, still faced with similar entreaties, she noted in her column: "I did a little mental arithmetic this morning and found that if I said 'yes' to the requests that came to me just in this morning's mail, I would need $2000 before night to send out to various people." [36]

What the First Lady required in order to adequately meet the pleas for help which reached her was some mechanism which was designed to supply aid on a widespread scale. Furthermore, genuine alleviation would necessitate a medium which could furnish work; for, contrary to the comparatively few requests for direct handouts which reached her, the vast majority of appeals to Mrs. Roosevelt were for jobs. Most Americans wanted the opportunity to support themselves, not a dole.

As her mail piled up in the autumn of 1933, Mrs. Roosevelt turned to one of the New Deal's first massive relief vehicles, the Federal Emergency Relief Administration (FERA). The procedure by which that agency came to handle the problems posed by the correspondence to the First Lady involved, with minor variations, two steps: first, via one of her secretaries, she forwarded the letters to Ellen S. Woodward, Director of FERA's Women's Work Division;* and, second, Miss Woodward in turn customarily informed the appropriate local agency office, which then investigated the case. The most interesting aspect of this system is that it necessarily dovetailed the activities of an *unofficial* person, Eleanor Roosevelt, with those of an *official* government agency. What was ostensibly a personal correspondence stemming from the invitation of a private citizen became in fact a major route through which an administrative agency, identified with the New Deal and the Democratic Party, was put into contact with potential beneficiaries. Mrs. Roosevelt's private sympa-

---

* Mrs. Roosevelt's mail came, overwhelmingly, from women.

thies, in other words, became inextricably woven with public function.* This meant that the entire operation came to have political overtones, whether the First Lady meant it to do so or not.

The indications are that regardless of original intent, she did come to realize that political capital could be accumulated from this type of correspondence. First of all, she did not, as she might have done, write in her magazine or newspaper columns that she was swamped with such a quantity of mail that she could not possibly give most of it her personal attention.† She did not advise that women seeking a job for themselves or for members of their families should write to Miss Woodward at FERA. Rather, she apparently considered it advisable to keep the name "Roosevelt" in the picture. This would accord with her pronouncements in favor of "humanizing" the government; it would also forge a strong link in a chain which associated the name "Roosevelt" with securing a job.

Thorough examination of the records in the FERA files renders virtually inescapable the conclusion that the First Lady was aware of the essential duality — humanitarian and political — her correspondence entailed. A very large portion of the letters to her contain sentiments of the most flattering kind. Such forms

* This commingling of the "personal" and the "official" was noticed — and in some cases objected to — by various observers. During hearings held in December, 1933, on an appropriations bill for the Department of Labor, Republican Representative Robert L. Bacon of New York sharply questioned Mary Anderson, Director of the Labor Department's Women's Bureau, concerning the rumor that Mrs. Roosevelt was using Department personnel and the frank to answer mail received as a result of the *Woman's Home Companion* invitation. Miss Anderson readily admitted that much of Mrs. Roosevelt's mail reached her desk, but could not ascertain how much of it was traceable to the First Lady's magazine articles. See memo from R. Barrows to Marvin McIntyre, undated but Dec., 1933, "President's Personal File #2," Box 1, FDRL.

† Merely to handle and answer the immense amount of correspondence directed to Mrs. Roosevelt required, by the late 1930's, a staff of fourteen clerks and stenographers. Of the approximately one hundred fifty thousand letters she was receiving annually at that time, the First Lady personally answered about five hundred, and signed about twenty thousand more. *Life*, VIII (Feb. 15, 1940), p. 72.

of salutation as "Our dear First Lady of America," "Esteemed One," or "First Mother of the Land" presaged complimentary phrases of the same tenor in the *corpora* of the letters. Nor did these laudatory allusions have only Mrs. Roosevelt as their subject. "I believe in Franklin Roosevelt and his ideals," stated a New Jersey woman. "He is working as Christ worked for the good of the world." A Georgia correspondent expressed the opinion that "your good husband certainly is leading the country back from despair to hope and happiness," and another admirer from the same state wrote that the President "could not be the great man he is if he did not have the wonderful wife he has." "I was a born republican, voted republican but am a staunch supporter of the present regime," explained a lady from Oregon, while another, writing from New York, told of her business failing "for no other reason than that I believed 'Prosperity was just around the corner,'" and added, "I was a speaker for the N.R.A." [37]

These expressions of praise and support perhaps can hardly be considered surprising since they stemmed from individuals in search of a job. The frequency of such effusions, however, and the fact that they were meant for the First Lady's eyes, indicates that their authors were becoming increasingly aware of *her* power. Approached properly, it was felt, *she* could do something to remedy their plight. Missives replete with statements like "Having read that it is possible to get in touch with certain agencies thru your kindly offices. . . ."; "Recently I noted . . . that you have interested yourself in a movement . . . to find positions for white-collar women . . ."; and "Appreciating your able and active participation in Federal Recovery [sic] activities . . ." show very clearly the growing notion abroad that Mrs. Roosevelt was becoming a figure to reckon with.[38]

Her expanding role as it related to FERA was noted within government circles as well. As early as November, 1933, the

First Lady, an unofficial personage, was asked to preside over
that agency's Conference on Emergency Needs for Women.
During the course of the meeting, besides introducing FERA
Administrator Harry Hopkins and participating actively in the
discussion of problems with which the agency was confronted,
Mrs. Roosevelt was lauded by Democratic Congresswoman
Mary T. Norton of New Jersey for "the splendid interest you
have shown in this movement, so human and so fine. . . ." [39]

Succeeding months witnessed a further increase in the First
Lady's concern. Accompanying the dispatch of her correspondence to Miss Woodward were scores of notes from either her
personal secretary, Mrs. Malvina Thompson Scheider, or from
Mrs. Roosevelt herself to the effect: "Mrs. Roosevelt has asked
me to send you the enclosed letter in the hope you may know of
some place this girl could be used"; "Can you think of any place
for this girl? She needs a job very badly and Mrs. Roosevelt is
personally interested"; or, "This woman sounds educated and intelligent. Is there anything in Alabama she could be given to
do?" In what appeared to be critical cases, greater haste than use
of the regular mails was urged. "I think you had better wire,"
advised the First Lady concerning the plight of a Colorado family. Occasionally, one even comes across transcripts of long-
distance telephone conversations wherein can be found phrases
like "Mrs. Roosevelt has expressed the hope that we will immediately get in touch with you all and make a satisfactory investigation," and "I promised Mrs. Roosevelt I would telephone you
the first thing. . . . This is an emergency case." So frequent
became the communication between the First Lady and FERA
personnel that the latter, by the autumn of 1934, had to make
new arrangements to better expedite "the special White House
cases." [40]

The interest Mrs. Roosevelt displayed in relief activities and
the importance attached to "the special White House cases"

meant that she became involved, almost as a matter of course, in the intricacies of personnel and administration within FERA. Chicago employees of that agency evidenced their respect for her influence by wiring her their suggestions for appointments in a possible new midwestern branch. Moreover, the First Lady's unique position with regard to her husband was also appreciated. A Connecticut FERA worker telegraphed: "PLEASE ASK THE PRESIDENT TO HOLD UP REMOVAL OF OUR VERY FINE NEWTON BRAINARD . . . UNTIL HE [FDR] KNOWS ALL." Although the results of such deferential communiqués are frequently unavailable, existing evidence tends to show that Mrs. Roosevelt was not reluctant to make her views known. "THINK MRS. [CHARLES] SABIN ABLE WOMAN," wired Mrs. Scheider in answer to a request for the First Lady's ratification of a proposed appointment by New York's Governor Herbert Lehman. And, on another occasion, Harry Hopkins followed a phone conversation with the President's wife by noting to Miss Woodward: "Mrs. Roosevelt said that Massachusetts has fallen down on the whole [relief] program and thinks . . . a definite order must be given that a certain percentage of the jobs must go to women." "I will follow up the Massachusetts matter each day until we are [sure] the women's program is functioning effectively," Miss Woodward hastened to assure the First Lady.[41]

Mrs. Roosevelt's influence with respect to governmental boards and personnel, while perhaps exceptionally strong in the case of the Federal Emergency Relief Administration, was by no means directed to that agency alone. Although the evidence is fragmentary, that which is available indicates that she attempted to diffuse her viewpoint throughout much of the New Deal political and administrative hierarchy. She made, for example, unabashed use of the patronage. "Dear Louis," ran a representative letter to Howe, "I am anxious to see that Jo Coffin gets a job [in the Government Printing Office]. Will you tell me what can be

done." Party Chairman Farley estimated the President's wife to
have been responsible for the appointments of over four thousand women in fourth-class post offices. Harold Ickes, too, was
subject to the First Lady's suggestions. "I concur in your evident opinion regarding the retention of a woman as Assistant
Commissioner of Education," the Secretary of the Interior wrote
her in December, 1933, further promising to "see what can be
done about allotting half the positions to women under the plan
for giving work to unemployed teachers." Bespeaking the gratitude which such action aroused was a note from the friend of
one of the appointees who had written her request "in a sort of
religious fervor . . . mailed it, and then gulped. Can't you imagine how I feel," this correspondent enthused, "how grateful I
am? Believe me!" [42]

At times Mrs. Roosevelt was criticized for what was regarded
in some circles as unwarranted interference in party or national
affairs. In 1939, she strongly urged the appointment of Mary
Winslow as United States member of the Inter-American Commission of Women. The Commission, whose purpose was to col-
lect and sift certain juridical information and to work for "civil
and political equality for women," had had as its U.S. member
since 1928 Miss Doris Stevens, fluent in Spanish and the only
American woman who belonged to the American Institute of
Law. There was no question of a vacancy on the Commission,
but the First Lady wished Miss Winslow to have the place. The
latter, although untrained in law and unfamiliar with the Spanish
language, was a social worker and had worked with Mrs. Roosevelt in the Women's Trade Union League. The President's wife
was also criticized for her advocacy of the appointment of Congressman Thomas R. Amlie, a Wisconsin Progressive, to the In-
terstate Commerce Commission, and because of her reported
pressure to get Morris Sheppard to withdraw in favor of Lyndon
B. Johnson in the 1941 Texas senatorial primary. Her alleged

interference with State Department routine reportedly caused United States Ambassador to England Joseph P. Kennedy to remark, with characteristic tact and gentleness: "She bothered us more on our jobs . . . to take care of the poor little nobodies than all the rest of the people put together. She's always sending me a note to have some little Suzie Glotz to tea at the Embassy." *

Mrs. Roosevelt's desire to impress her ideas upon the various public agencies seems, ultimately, to have stemmed from her compassion for the unfortunate and a desire to do something to mitigate their ills. This part of her philosophy was basically personal; it could be implemented by unofficial engagement in the kinds of good works traditional to the wives of Presidents. One aspect of the First Lady's break with such comparatively limited activity came because she did not hesitate to use official personnel and media as means to further her own charitable objectives. This remarkable expansion of her role was doubtless due in part to the unprecedented misery which confronted so many Americans because of the Depression. The desperate plight of countless citizens, she must have felt, called for similarly unconventional measures of counteraction, even insofar as that might mean personal exertion of pressure wherever and whenever she deemed such a course necessary. Furthermore, she had for some years been impatient with certain forms of orthodoxy anyhow,

---

* *New York Times*, Feb. 17, 19, 28, 1939; Alfred Steinberg, *Mrs. R* (New York, G. P. Putnam's Sons, 1958), pp. 243–44; Victor Lasky, *J.F.K., The Man and the Myth* (New York, The Macmillan Co., 1963), p. 58. Miss Winslow got the position with the Inter-American Commission of Women, but Amlie's supposed left-wing views evoked such a hostile reaction in Congress that he withdrew his name from consideration for membership on the ICC. Johnson was thrashed in the Texas primary by the veteran demagogue W. Lee ("Pass the Biscuits, Pappy") O'Daniel. Kennedy's remarks, although taken from a book not otherwise noted for its accuracy, are in this case not the words as Lasky interpreted them but as were heard by Louis Lyons of the Boston *Globe* in an interview which Kennedy apparently thought was off the record. They seem to have reached the ears of the President where they did nothing to help salvage the already souring relationship between the two men.

having once commented in this connection: "I am popularly supposed not to be very fond of traditions. In fact, the older members of my family feel that I am rather prone to make too many changes rather than stick to old customs. . . ."[43]

To these considerations, however, should be added the motive of partisan calculation. This is true even as it concerned a less obviously political relationship such as that which she had with FERA. For, to the thousands in the ranks of the unemployed who, almost as a final gesture of futility, had written the First Lady and then — miracle of miracles, been offered a job — to them she must have possessed the attributes of an awesomely beneficent angel. Frequently, also, there would be a letter from Mrs. Roosevelt, from "Tommy" (Mrs. Scheider), or from the First Lady's daughter Anna.* It was the recipients of these letters and these jobs who would help form the constituency which would revere the Roosevelts all their lives. Mrs. Roosevelt, assuming the role of intermediary, surely had not been unaware that her good offices would stimulate this kind of reaction.

~

In taking account of Eleanor Roosevelt's active participation in the functions of an agency like FERA, one is impressed by the fact that her growing influence, in spite of the fact that it was subject to criticism in certain quarters, was nonetheless warmly welcomed by considerable numbers of persons in government service. This hospitable climate may be ascribed partially to her sincerity; partially, also, it may have been due to the fact that, in an agency like the Federal Emergency Relief Administration, she could claim a host of friends, particularly Administrator Hopkins. Another possible factor was that many women were connected with FERA; these women were presumably proud that

* There are several letters in the FERA files which are in substance "thank you" notes for missives emanating from Mrs. Roosevelt or one of her assistants. Unfortunately, the latter are not available.

one of their sex was willing and able to exercise such responsibility. Above all these considerations, however, was the fundamental reality of her position — she was the wife of the President of the United States. It was primarily as a result of this, more than anything else, that her letters received special attention in agencies like FERA; for, as one commentator remarked, "Any federal worker knows . . . that a request from her is treated by the Departments with a degree of authority second only to one from the President himself." [44] The very fact of her interest in any given enterprise was, furthermore, advantageous; she provided the clearest and most direct channel of communication to the ear of the Chief Executive. Paul U. Kellogg of Survey Associates, Inc. (a social work-oriented organization in which Mrs. Roosevelt took considerable interest), was accustomed to sending her articles which embodied his views, confident that such material would "reach . . . you — and, if you will . . . the President." Harry Hopkins worked through her constantly in the early days of the New Deal in order to gain access to the "inner circle." Molly Dewson commented that when she needed help on some definite point, "Mrs. Roosevelt gave me the opportunity to sit by the President at dinner and the matter was settled before we finished our soup; or Mrs. Roosevelt spoke to him herself and relayed the answer." Charles Taussig utilized the First Lady's good offices to reach FDR with proposals concerning youth; Walter White did the same thing with respect to Negro problems.[45]

In fine, there appears persuasive evidence that Eleanor Roosevelt was both willing and able to bring to her husband's attention a multitude of possible programs which might not otherwise have been subject to his consideration. Because of the sensitivity of her position she could expedite the flow of ideas in which she believed; she was able to free them from becoming bogged down, emasculated or lost in the lower echelons of government.

This in itself gave her great power, for any project which aroused her interest stood an excellent chance of being transmitted to the very highest levels of the entire decision-making structure.

One wonders, however, whether her influence as it concerned the President stopped at this point. Was the First Lady, in other words, willing merely to assume the role of conveyer of the projects of others, or did she act more positively by trying to impress upon her husband the virtues of such projects? Further, did she perhaps also introduce and advocate notions of her own? And, whatever the dimensions of her activities in this respect, how much consideration did President Roosevelt give to the proposals which reached him by way of his wife?

In grappling with a problem of this nature a note of caution should be struck at the outset. Exact calculations as regards it are in fact impossible; that is, the amount of influence that one person has upon another does not allow of precise measurement. This is generally true in any relationship; it is emphatically so when the subjects are as complex as Franklin and Eleanor Roosevelt. Further, because they were man and wife, much of the interaction between the two of them can never be known. The tone and content of their private conversations were, in the nature of things, not only often unofficial, but confidential. Hence, in trying to deal specifically with this problem the historian finds himself in an area that is considerably circumscribed. At best, what he may try to accomplish is to indicate, on the basis of whatever evidence is available, whether in fact a positive influence did exist, and, if so, the ways in which such influence manifested itself.

To begin with, Mrs. Roosevelt, from early on, entertained certain theories regarding the role of the wife of a prominent public figure, although these notions underwent a good many changes in the years before her husband became President. As has been pointed out, she was thought of, during FDR's vice-presidential campaign of 1920, as "essentially a home woman."[46] Despite the fact that she embarked upon a considerable amount of political activity not long thereafter, she indicated in 1927 that her set of priorities remained essentially the same as they were earlier. There was room "for countless other concerns," she admitted in a magazine interview of that year, but "home comes first." As a wife, then, she continued to stress the importance of matters domestic and private.[47]

In 1928 Franklin Roosevelt, after a seven-year struggle with infantile paralysis, again officially entered public life, as the Governor of New York State. His status as an officeholder, as opposed to that of a politically interested private citizen, appeared to bring about a change in the thinking of his wife as regards her emphasis of concern. For, in 1930, she had this observation to make:

> I think we must all agree that in the wife's job there are three fundamentals — being a partner, being a mother, and being a housekeeper and homemaker. Formerly, if we had been arranging the phases of the job in the order of their importance, I think we would have put being a mother first and next being a housekeeper and homemaker, and then being a partner. But today we understand that everything else depends upon the success of the wife and husband in their personal partnership relation. So from the modern point of view that comes first.[48]

Personal involvement in political activities, in addition to the return of her husband to official position, caused Mrs. Roosevelt to change her concept of what areas of concern were most valuable for the wife of a public servant. Such a reversal of preferences was, however, but the first step in outlining her philosophy of political partnership; there remained a plethora of methods by which this philosophy could be implemented. In an article written shortly before her husband's first election to the Presidency, she attempted to outline her views of what the best methods for aiding this partnership would be. The keynote of her beliefs was sounded in the lead sentence: "Wives of Great Men . . . May Have Their Own Convictions, but Must Keep Them to Themselves Says Mrs. Franklin D. Roosevelt." Sentiments in the same vein marked the remainder of the article: "It is imperative that a wife should not interfere with her husband while he is in office. . . . Decidedly she should not attempt to meddle with her husband's plans, his procedure, or his principles. . . . The wife's opinions must be subordinated. . . . She must never agree to try to convince him on any point . . . upon which he has not yet passed judgment." [49]

For awhile Mrs. Roosevelt attempted faithfully to carry out these modest admonitions. Sentiments such as "Franklin has asked me to get busy on this organization work and I have written the enclosed letter which is to go to all women whose names are sent in to us from different states," reflected her desire to restrict her role to that of a political helpmeet who loyally carried out instructions. During her early years as mistress of the White House she did not, for the most part, assert positively her political views, but instead followed the lead of her husband. "The President's instructions on [Upton] Sinclair's candidacy in California are (1) Say nothing and (2) Do nothing," Steve Early wrote in answer to her request concerning what conduct she should adopt with respect to that campaign; and, accordingly, she obeyed his advice.*

A striking example of Eleanor Roosevelt's determination to aid her husband during the early days of his Presidency can be seen

---

* ER to Molly Dewson, July 18, 1931, "Dewson Papers," Group 37, Box 1, FDRL; Steve Early to ER, n.d. but 1934, quoted in Arthur M. Schlesinger, Jr., *The Politics of Upheaval* (Boston, Houghton Mifflin Co., 1960), p. 120. Upton Sinclair, who shared certain of Roosevelt's views, ran for the California governorship in 1934 on an "End Poverty in California" (EPIC) ticket. He was defeated by a combination of Republicans and conservative Democrats.

in the role she assumed with regard to the so-called "Second Bonus March" in the spring of 1933. At the risk of some digression, it should be pointed out that there has been a certain amount of misunderstanding about the two bonus marches insofar as they involved the policies of the Hoover and Roosevelt administrations. In fact, there was no fundamental difference of policy between them. The contrast between the Hoover treatment of the first Bonus Expeditionary Force in July, 1932, and that of FDR as it concerned the second BEF in May, 1933, was solely one of method. During Hoover's incumbency some 25,000 destitute veterans made their way to Washington in the hope that their presence there would spur Congress to grant them immediate full payment of their Adjustment Compensation Certificates, which were otherwise not due until 1945. The Senate overwhelmingly rejected this proposal, embodied in the Patman Bill, by a vote of sixty-eight to eighteen. Still, many of the veterans, some of whom were occupying Treasury Department property, refused to leave. The situation was difficult; the threat of epidemic grew, construction work on the Treasury Department land was halted due to the encampment, and tempers on the part of both the ex-servicemen and local police and municipal officials wore thin. In late July rioting broke out, during the course of which two veterans were killed, and Hoover called for government troops to restore order. In the ensuing struggle the bonus marchers were routed from the property, driven to the mud flats at Anacostia where there was another BEF encampment, whereupon the veterans there were also driven out with tear gas.

The spectacle of masked troops with drawn bayonets pursuing the ragged and unarmed ex-servicemen was a sobering one for many Americans. Especially in retrospect, the man who seemed most blameworthy was Herbert Hoover. The *B. E. F. News* cartoonist sketched a wicked-looking portrait of the President wherein he was made to resemble Kaiser Wilhelm II, the personification of brutality in the eyes of many contemporaries. Wrote Arthur M. Schlesinger, Jr., later:

> When the grey mists rose from the [Anacostia] river in the morning, blue-white smoke was drifting over the ruins . . . Little . . . Bernard Myers . . . eleven weeks old, was dying in the hospital. The *B. E. F. News* suggested the epitaph: "Here lies Bernard Myers, aged three months, gassed to death by order of President Hoover." [50]

Franklin D. Roosevelt's methods of dealing with the second Bonus Expeditionary Force the following May made Hoover's course, by comparison, look even worse. At FDR's behest, the veterans were given coffee and a large tent for their meetings. Furthermore, he sent Mrs. Roosevelt out to the encampment where she acted as a good-will ambassador ("be sure to tell them that Franklin sent you," Louis Howe had advised) and led the men in a songfest. This excellent public relations gesture reportedly caused one of the veterans to remark: "Hoover sent the Army — Roosevelt sent his wife." Subsequently, most of the marchers signed up with the Civilian Conservation Corps.[51]

It was Mrs. Roosevelt's recollection that Herbert Hoover had played a truly villainous role with respect to the BEF imbroglio. She added to the legend of Hoover's alleged inhumanity when in 1949 she wrote: "I shall never forget my feeling of horror in 1932 when I realized that the Army had actually been ordered to fire on the veterans." But here her interpretation of events was faulty. For no such "orders" were ever given — by anyone. As for the President himself, one close student of the affair has concluded that Hoover had nothing to do with the Army's pursuit of the ex-servicemen to Anacostia; that he asked only for the eviction of those rioters who occupied Treasury Department buildings; and that, for this purpose, "in fairness to Hoover, it should be noted that he was led to believe that [Police Superintendent Pelham D.] Glassford and all District officials thought troops necessary." The idea of cleaning out Anacostia seems to have originated with the commander of the troops, General Douglas MacArthur.[52]

Moreover, if press comment was any guide, reaction was widely favorable to the Army's course. The *New York Times* published the results of an Associated Press survey concerning the events of July 28, and commented:

> Editorial opinion was practically unanimous in expressing the belief that President Hoover was justified in his course. The disorder was generally attributed to radical elements . . . while some editors held politicians seeking votes as being partly responsible for the gathering of the "army" at the capital.[53]

Dissent from this line of thought stemmed principally from the bitterly anti-Hoover Hearst press; indeed, it was the Hearst-owned Washington *Herald* that gave the Bernard Myers story such widespread coverage. When a doctor from Gallinger Hospital later said that the infant's death bore no connection to tear gas but that he had succumbed to congenital enteritis, the story was buried on the newspaper's back pages.[54]

The Democrats did not use the bonus army issue as campaign ammunition in the 1932 election, for Roosevelt's position on it was essentially the same as Hoover's. Stated FDR unequivocally at Pittsburgh: "I do not see how . . . a government running behind two billion dollars annually can consider the anticipation of the bonus payment until it has a balanced budget, not only on paper but with a surplus of cash in the treasury." [55] Roosevelt's method for sending the veterans home was also identical to that of Hoover. Those who did not join the CCC were given transportation funds which were deducted from their service certificates.[56]

The basic difference, and it was an important one, in the outcome of the two bonus expeditions resulted from a contrast of
mood. Beyond any doubt, states Maurice P. Sneller,

> . . . the bonus march of 1932 was instructive. It taught the
> Roosevelt Administration how to avoid the errors of its pre-
> decessor. . . . Roosevelt deliberately went out of his way to be
> friendly. He received a committee representing the veterans in
> the White House; told the men that he was opposed to their
> bonus and would veto any measure that Congress might pass; but
> at the same time he won their friendship. . . .[57]

The handling of the second BEF displayed the new administration's superior grasp of tact and political astuteness. It showed
that the President, especially, recognized the importance of grass
roots sentiment on the part of his constituency. Mrs. Roosevelt,
preceding her appearance with the veterans, had been instructed
to "get their gripes." [58] Such direct liaison work on the part of
the President's wife — so very important in the case of the bonus
marchers — was to become an increasingly effective ingredient
in the formula of political success enjoyed by her husband.

~

Eleanor Roosevelt had assumed a reportorial and liaison role of
this sort well before she became First Lady. Her husband, because of the effects of his illness, was prevented from being able
to engage in the activities of broad firsthand observation customarily essential to a politician. The function of moving among
various groups and ascertaining both the actualities involved and
the sentiments regarding those actualities therefore fell in considerable part to Mrs. Roosevelt. She became a virtual extension of
her husband — his eyes, ears and legs. Through verbal reports
and through a judicious selection of her own mail which she felt
her husband should see, she was able, both before he became

President and afterward, to materially assist him in maintaining a current grasp of the basic conditions, hopes and frustrations of large groups of the electorate.[59]

According to Frances Perkins, FDR placed unqualified faith in his wife's reports:

> In cabinet meetings he would say "You know my Missus gets around a lot," or "my Missus says that they have typhoid fever in that district," or "my Missus says the people are leaving the dust bowl in droves because they haven't any chances there. . . ."

Presidential secretary Grace Tully recalled that it was not unusual to hear the Chief Executive "predicate an entire line of questioning upon a statement that 'My Missus told me so and so.'" Although the First Lady's reporting to the President opened up possibilities of influencing him, because, as Rexford G. Tugwell observed, her conclusions were "prejudiced," the same thing could have been said of anyone bringing information to him.[60] In "getting the gripes" of the BEF ex-servicemen, Mrs. Roosevelt was still adhering to the principles she had set forth for the wife of a public man in 1932.

These principles had emphasized the importance of acting in behalf of her husband, which included going places and observing conditions that he, by force of circumstances, was either too involved to visit or unable to reach in the first place. It was essentially a passive function which involved little more than reportage. While Mrs. Roosevelt did not abandon this role during the time her husband was in the White House, she did, as time passed, expand and enlarge upon it to a considerable degree. Basically, she became not only a mere proxy for President Roosevelt, but a complement to him as well. She began, as one observer expressed it, to operate as "the extension of the generous side of the President's outlook."[61] She, as it were, broadened his image; without essentially distorting it, she came to accentuate a part of his philosophy — that concerned with various social justice movements — which otherwise might have remained in comparative shadow. The First Lady, in brief, gradually emerged as an active spokesman for her own beliefs, beliefs which, while not in direct contradiction to those of the Chief Executive, nonetheless seemed to be of considerably more importance in her hierarchy of values than they did in that of her husband's. Nowhere can this enlargement of her own role be better exemplified than in the changing tone and subject matter of her daily newspaper column; nowhere, also, did she render such yeoman service to her own ideas and to the image of Franklin Roosevelt.

The notion that the First Lady might become a daily columnist apparently occurred as early as 1933 and stemmed originally from Gretta Palmer, who edited the woman's page of the New York *World-Telegram*. Because of a multitude of other commitments, Mrs. Roosevelt was not initially very receptive to the plan, and this despite the fact that there evidently was keen bidding for her services. At length, in 1935 when McNaught Syndicate signed her sharp-tongued, anti-New Deal cousin Alice for a column of her own, she gave in; "My Day" appeared on December 30 of that year under the auspices of Monte Bourjaily and United Features. Distributed originally in some twenty newspapers, by early 1939 it was carried by sixty-eight of them, giving her column a total circulation of over four and one-half million readers. The column's format was originally that of a somewhat innocuous diary: it continued to retain vestiges of this blandness; but Mrs. Roosevelt, over the years, devoted an ever increasing amount of her space to public issues.[62]

"My Day" also became, often covertly but sometimes openly, a significant channel of partisan propaganda. The First Lady had the choice of several methods by which she could promulgate her political beliefs, and she seems to have employed virtually all of them. The first was to simply and openly praise administration measures; because this frequently involved her own social and economic views on a broader scale, discussion of it occurs for the most part elsewhere in this work.* Another way was to mention unobtrusively her own political activities; this she did continually. "My Day" brimmed with phrases like ". . . the Democratic Women's Division Dinner . . . last night was very successful"; ". . . it is encouraging to find so many young Democrats growing up to strengthen the party"; or, ". . . there have been many Democratic national and state campaigns in which I attended to the details of the organization. . . ." — passages which periodically reminded her readers of her party affiliation and loyalty.[63]

Of more direct concern, however, was the objective of helping her husband. Here again, she often employed the technique in which she had expressed so profound a belief — that of bringing "closer to the people" important and otherwise distant officials in the government. Thus, anecdotes about FDR's "human" qualities dotted her narrative — how he loved to "lose" his secret service guards when driving his car; his proclivity for never throwing anything away; the fact that he was invariably "calm as a May morning" before his important radio speeches; his easy capacity to forget the cares of high office and relax and enjoy himself.[64]

So, too, with the remainder of the family. The First Lady's readers were continually edified by accounts of her pretending to be a growling lion for the purpose of amusing her grandson Bill; the antics of her horse "Dot"; Franklin, Jr.'s sinus operation; her daughter Anna's book, *Scamper, The Bunny Who Went to the White House;* her grandchildren's table manners; Curtis learning how to play dominoes; Chandler cutting her thumb on a piece of paper; and similar momentous topics.[65] Inanities of this

* See Chapter IV.

nature caused certain of her followers much anguish; some, like Oswald Garrison Villard, were willing to excuse "the banality and intellectual poverty of her diary" because of her "sympathy for so many good causes"; others, however, protested. To a reader in the latter category, who begged her not to "waste your valuable time and the space in the paper with something so worthless . . . when you could so easily write something which might have marvelous results," the First Lady replied that we must not "always deal with the solemn sides of life." She was subsequently cheered by several letters in the following weeks which indicated that many of her readers enjoyed hearing about the family.[66]

It was at the time of the 1936 election campaign that Mrs. Roosevelt's column most overtly wielded the political cudgel. Its author did this principally by means of illustrative little stories, a device she had adopted in the 1920's. In 1924, for example, one finds that she employed the following tale concerning a poverty-stricken farm woman, who allegedly told her:

"Oh, I ain't got much time for politics but Mr. Williams, the R.F.D. man says I must vote for Coolidge because he ain't had a chance yet and I've always been a Republican anyways. . . . No," she went on, "he ain't done much as I can see for farmers, leastways I never had a worse time." [67]

Even to the most unsophisticated, narratives like this had an obvious moral; and Mrs. Roosevelt later dredged up a number of them for campaign purposes. One concerned a taxicab driver who, upon learning the identity of his passenger, uttered ecstatically, "I am honored. . . . Will you tell your husband he has my vote in November and I guess he has the vote of every plain man who has any sense!" Then there was the salesman who informed her: "Business is so good this year . . . there isn't going to be any change anywhere, either . . . business will continue being good." As election day drew closer, a note of pathos was introduced. "One of the most touching election stories that has come to me" was a letter about an ailing, ninety-year-old Bronx resident "who has been told that death is very near." Though he didn't fear the end, "he is hanging on to life with grim determination." So grim, apparently, that the old gentleman wouldn't even take to his bed — in fact he wouldn't go to sleep anywhere. "Instead he sits in a chair night and day fighting to stay awake. . . . He insists on doing this. Why? Because he is detirmined [sic] to vote for Mr. Roosevelt before he dies." [68]

On October 30 the First Lady's column commenced in this fashion:

> "Please 'Dod,' let the President be fat," so prayed a three year old girl the other night. The next morning the friend that was taking care of her and her sister, while the mother and father were away for the night, inquired why she wanted the President to be fat.
>
> "Because," said she, "then he won't never be hungry the way we were before he helped Daddy get a job." [69]

Happily Mrs. Roosevelt, with the passage of years, ceased using these rather dreadful little anecdotes. By the time of the 1938 elections she was confining her enthusiasm to such straightforward remarks as "I like to cast my vote in New York State for the candidates I believe in and whom I look upon as friends — Governor Lehman, Senators Wagner and Mead and Congressman [sic] -At-Large Caroline O'Day." [70] And in 1940, when her husband was again the Democratic nominee for President, her column contained scarcely any outright political references to the campaign.

The political techniques of "My Day" had, by that time, become in fact a good deal more sophisticated. Rather than using the transparent stratagem of talking about Franklin Roosevelt in the manner of a news commentator discoursing on a favorite personality, the column was beginning to act as a direct spokesman for presidential ideas and desires. An excellent instance of this is to be found in various of her remarks which clearly referred to the controversy involving her husband's plan to enlarge the Supreme Court in early 1937. The First Lady brought all of her verbal weaponry to the defense of FDR's position. Comments of the opposition press she found "most amusing." They appeared to her full of meaningless and irrelevant "fear" and "forebodings," and stemmed "largely from the same group which opposed much of the social legislation of the present Administration. . . ." She was, however, encouraged by letters which ridiculed such sentiments; and it seems worthwhile to reproduce one of them, which she quoted at some length:

People's fears are an odd thing anyhow. Here are these people all so scared of the Supreme Court, because it "protects our liberties." *Whose* liberties has it protected?

Here they are terrified lest the Constitution be interpreted as it was meant to be interpreted in each age according to that period's own ideas, instead of those of the past generation. It seems to me it would be more intelligent to be afraid of strangling democracy by letting a fossilizing process harden the Constitution into a cocoon which must be violently broken because it *could* not grow up with the life within. Life implies growth, and the Constitution was never meant to be used as the Bible was by our most Puritanical Puritians [sic].

"The letter killeth." Do these people really want to be ruled by a frozen document? If so, they are the ones who are going back on the American spirit, not we.

I do hope that there are enough men and women of vision in Congress who are not ridden by these fears, which seem most inappropriate ones in the mouths of self-governing people. It seems to me, it would be better to have less in the Constitution than more, because it has all got to stand interpretation and reinterpretation through the ages.

Suppose we fill it up with stuff about employers and labor, and two hundred years from now, we are all employing one another in cooperative fashion. All that instead of being fundamental law is really changeable human provision for certain conditions. There is very little actual fundamental law. Really only "love one another." The rest is all interpretation — even the Ten Commandments.

You know, I really hate to see even the Child Labor Amendment added, but I am working for it because it is not less inappropriate than others in the Constitution and there seems to be no hope of accomplishing the end otherwise.

Curiously enough I never thought very much about what could be considered fundamental law. If it is really "love one another," how woefully short we fall of New Testament Standards.[71]

This letter is enlightening, for it strikingly demonstrates the extent of Mrs. Roosevelt's anxiousness to forward the virtues of her husband's programs. That she had ever received the letter just quoted is, in fact, highly doubtful. The prevalence of the phrase, "It seems to me," the unfavorable mention of the Puritans as opposed to laudatory references to the words of Christ and the New Testament, the implied hope that "cooperative" employment would become the norm, and the whole tenor of the viewpoint expressed are too close to the First Lady's rhetoric and way of thinking to be coincidental. In all probability, Mrs. Roosevelt wrote the letter herself.*

* "It seems to me" was a favorite phrase of Mrs. Roosevelt's. For her unflattering opinions regarding the Puritans, see "My Day," Jan. 9, 1937 ("For sheer cruelty our old Puritan ancestors can hardly be beaten. . . .") and *This Is My Story* (New York, Harper & Brothers, 1937), pp. 192, 316; for her devotion to the principles of Christ see Chapter II of the present work. "Cooperation" rather than "competition" in economic life was a concept for which she propagandized diligently (see this work, Chapter IV, *passim*); her viewpoint concerning the inevitability — and desirability — of change and the "vision" (another favorite word) we must have as to what forms it should take can be found in "My Day," Feb. 19, 1937.

With respect to the use of the cited letter, Mrs. Roosevelt kept within the technical bounds of propriety. She did not say that she had "received" it, but that she had "come across" it. "My Day," Feb. 13, 1937.

So strong did the political linkage between the First Lady and the President appear to have become in the late 1930's that observers began to believe that the former's words presaged subsequent remarks made by FDR himself, an impression in no way dispelled when in 1939 Mrs. Roosevelt was not only at her husband's side during one of his press conferences but was prompting him as well. National magazines, taking notice of such occurrences, began to imply that the influence of the President's wife was second only to that of the Chief Executive, and even *New York Times* analyst Arthur Krock editorialized that "My Day" had emerged as a "connubial" political endeavor and must from that time forward be regarded as "required political reading." [72]

There can be little doubt that Mrs. Roosevelt increasingly found herself in the position of being what Grace Tully called "a preferred listening post" with respect to her husband's ideas. "In one or two instances," continued Miss Tully, "correspondents queried the Boss on the basis of a 'My Day' disclosure, forcing him either to disclaim any knowledge of whether she was right or wrong or to admit ruefully that he had just forgotten to tell her it was off the record." Mrs. Roosevelt herself contributed to the growing belief that her column might be a source of tips when, in answer to a query about whether she and the President discussed matters of national interest in their rare moments alone, she remarked: "Well, you don't just sit at meals and look at each other." Increasing precaution thus had to be taken against any possible leaks, and the President frequently wrote his wife direct instructions to this effect. "The real danger," stated one of FDR's unequivocal memorandums concerning oil shipments to Japan in 1940, "which you *cannot* use is that if we forbid oil shipments to Japan, Japan will increase her purchases of Mexican oil and furthermore, may be driven by actual necessity to a descent on the Dutch East Indies. At this writing, we all regard such action on our part as an encouragement to the spread of war in the Far East." [73]

Moreover, even as her influence as a columnist was growing, the First Lady was also called upon to enact a role which clearly illustrated the high estimate placed upon her political ability within Democratic Party circles. What she was asked to do resulted ultimately from the fact that, in the summer of 1940, her husband had accepted the Democratic nomination to run for a third presidential term. The reasons for his acceptance have traditionally been construed as stemming from the tense international situation and FDR's conviction that it was his duty to continue to serve as President since he was the most qualified person to deal with these developments. Nevertheless, as Bernard Donahoe points out, there were other forces which led to Roosevelt's decision, forces which lay principally in the liberal, New Deal wing of the Democratic Party. This wing, throughout FDR's second term, had struggled to gain ascendancy in party councils and affairs. Yet, by 1940, all their plans would have gone for naught had the Democrats nominated a relatively conservative individual like Farley, Secretary of State Cordell Hull, or Vice-President John Nance Garner. FDR appeared to the liberals to be the only man whose nomination could both overwhelm conservative pressures within the Democratic Party and defeat the Republicans in November. It was these liberals, according to Donahoe, who ultimately succeeded in convincing the President that he must accept the call for a third term nomination.[74]

Roosevelt's acceptance, however, left the Democratic conservative wing, which was substantial, in an astringent frame of mind. They felt they had been dictated to by certain of FDR's aides at the convention and were in a rebellious mood. When, therefore, the President indicated that Secretary of Agriculture Henry A. Wallace, who was anathema to party conservatives, was his choice for running mate on the ticket, the Democratic

convention at Chicago became an angry, snarling mass of delegates. The party, it seemed, was threatened with open schism.

Roosevelt himself would not leave Washington to make an appearance at the convention, but he remained in close touch with
proceedings there. He soon became convinced that, unless desperate measures were taken, Wallace would be beaten, a serious
potential rebuke to presidential leadership. Even his son Elliott
was prepared to second the nomination of Texas conservative
Jesse Jones for the Vice-Presidency.

To help mend the fissures which threatened to crack the convention wide open, President Roosevelt turned to the accomplished hands of his wife. The First Lady's own preference for
the nomination was Jones, not because she agreed with his philosophy, but because Wallace "doesn't impress people" while the
Texan "would bolster the ticket and win it business support. . . ." [75] But these were private sentiments, made only to
her husband or trustworthy friends. Publicly, in deference to
FDR's wishes, she delivered to the convention an exceedingly
effective speech which urged the wrangling delegates to compromise and close ranks. She did not specifically refer to the dispute
at hand, emphasizing instead the tremendous burdens of the Presidency at that dangerous time, and making it clear that the Chief
Executive must be trusted, supported and allowed to select
whichever individuals he thought could best assist him. She concluded with an exhortation in behalf of American unity so that
"this country can . . . bring the world to a safer and happier
condition." *

* Chicago *Tribune*, July 19, 1940. Oddly enough, less than three weeks before her own plea for unity, Mrs. Roosevelt had scorned Republican presidential nominee Wendell Willkie for his advocacy of the same thing. "In Heav-
en's name," she had exclaimed, "will anyone aim at anything else? Sometimes
I wonder if we shall ever grow up in our politics and say definite things which
mean something or whether we shall always go on using generalities to which
everyone can subscribe, and which mean very little." "My Day," July 1, 1940.

The First Lady's simple but high-minded approach managed, at least for a short time, to settle the turbulent atmosphere at Chicago. Many persons, Secretary of Labor Perkins among them, felt that this period of quiescence was critical in allowing the President's lieutenants to round up enough delegates to put Wallace over.[76] What is beyond question is the fact that Eleanor Roosevelt, by 1940, had achieved a political stature sufficiently impressive that it mandated FDR's choice of her as his political emissary in a crucial situation. That the delegates responded as hoped, according her a unanimously warm hearing, was probably due to a number of factors. She was, first of all, a woman; the reservoir of chivalry evident even at political conventions would have tended to work in favor of a comparatively courteous and hospitable atmosphere for her.* She was, in addition, the President's wife, and as such would receive much of the admiration felt for him. Also to be considered, however, was her own political reputation. She was looked up to; her "sense of politics" and keen political perceptiveness were valued. That such respect was well merited can be seen in the tactics she employed in her convention address. With apparent artlessness, she completely avoided the germane grievances of the delegates. She did not, for example, speak about the merits of Henry Wallace; she did not, moreover, engage in any discussion about whether or not delegates to a national political convention should be free to name their own vice-presidential candidate. Too politically shrewd for that, she based her approach on larger issues: the seriousness of the state of the world, the awesome responsibilities of the Presidency, and the necessity for Americans to be a unified people. She thus took a mundane political squabble and, imper-

---

* The subject of how women have made use of their peculiar advantages as a sex in American politics is too broad a one to be treated upon here; but it deserves much more attention than it has heretofore attracted.

ceptibly, transformed its terms of reference into those of high statesmanship and patriotic duty. She had gauged the atmosphere of the convention perfectly; and, accordingly, her approach enjoyed a startling success.[*]

That Mrs. Roosevelt was herself well aware of her matured sense of political sophistication was evidenced by a remark she made just before boarding the plane for her return journey to Hyde Park. Turning to Harry Hopkins, whose arrogance and lack of tact had caused so much of the convention's bitter climate, she smilingly observed, "You young things don't know politics." [77]

~

Eleanor Roosevelt's role, as it involved active support of the Democratic Party and of her husband, appears therefore to have been a very effective one. Through the media of speechmaking, writing, organizational work and direct reporting to the President she thoroughly fulfilled her side of a political "partnership." Nor did she hesitate, as instanced by her various recommendations with respect to FERA activities and her blunt advice to her husband concerning who should be his 1940 running mate, to make her own views clear.

It would be a mistake, however, to conclude that Mrs. Roosevelt was in any sense the "power behind the throne" or that she was invariably familiar with FDR's political plans. She did not, as John Dos Passos has claimed, "induce him to run for Governor of New York." [†] The extent of her "inducement" on that

[*] Senator George Norris, the old progressive Republican warhorse from Nebraska who in the 1930's sided mainly with the New Deal, subsequently wrote her: "When it seemed the battle [was] about to be lost, you came on the scene and what you said in that short speech caused men of sense and honor to stop and think before they plunged. Like Sheridan in the Shenandoah, you stopped the fleeing warriors." Quoted in Steinberg, *Mrs. R*, p. 274.

[†] The novelist, in an eight-page vignette entitled "Rover" (Mrs. Roosevelt's code name during World War II), managed among other things to (1) get the First Lady's birth date wrong; (2) misspell the name of her English boarding

score was merely to place a call (after repeated importunings on the part of Al Smith and other Democratic leaders) to her husband, then in Georgia, so that the reluctant FDR would at least speak with Smith. She herself left the room immediately after the telephone connection was made; she did not converse with him at all and did not find out until the following day that he had accepted the nomination. She then wired: "REGRET THAT YOU HAD TO ACCEPT BUT KNOW THAT YOU FELT IT OBLIGATORY." [78]

So it was also with many other aspects of her husband's political plans. She was not, for instance, cognizant of FDR's thoughts concerning how he would handle the Walker scandals in New York City during the early thirties, and often speculated with Howe and Ed Flynn about the matter. Even years later, when the influence of her daily column was being made so much of by observers, the indications are that she was by no means always privy to behind-the-scenes events and calculations. ". . . I wish I knew more of what really led to your refusal to renew [Hugh] Johnson's appointment [as a brigadier general in the Army Reserve]," she wrote her husband early in 1941. "I suppose there is some valid reason, but . . . to a great many people it looks as though you had simply indulged in annoyance because . . . Johnson has been attacking the Administration on its foreign policy. Some people think that you have [also] done that with Lindbergh. . . ." [79]

To cite yet another example, it has been implied that Eleanor Roosevelt "knew that the third-term issue was settled" by the end of 1939. [80] Available evidence, however, indicates plainly that she was neither aware of her husband's plans nor in any way instrumental regarding their final outcome. In the spring of 1939, after a lengthy discussion with the First Lady concerning the state of the nation, Harry Hopkins recorded that

school; (3) put Theodore Roosevelt in the White House at the wrong time; and (4) mistake the date of the U.S. entry into World War I. John Dos Passos, *Midcentury* (Boston, Houghton Mifflin Co., 1961), pp. 182–90.

Mrs. Roosevelt was greatly disturbed about 1940. She is personally anxious not to have the President run again, but I gathered the distinct impression that she has no more information on that point than the rest of us. She feels the President has done his part entirely. That he has not the same zest for administrative detail that he had and is probably quite frankly bored.

Furthermore James A. Farley, very much involved because he hoped to get the nomination himself, is explicit concerning the third term imbroglio. "I don't know whether you know it or not," he informed the First Lady in late July, 1940, "but the President never discussed his candidacy with me until that Sunday [July 7, 1940] I saw him at Hyde Park." "I never knew it either, believe me, until that afternoon," Farley quotes Mrs. Roosevelt as replying. "After you left, Franklin told me that he assumed he would have to run." She then told Farley she did not understand "why anyone would want to be President for the next four years." [81]

These sentiments accord perfectly with her other expressions on the question. She wanted her husband to retire. Soon after the ceremonies of the second Presidential Inauguration Mrs. Roosevelt, commenting upon the strain associated with such events, told her readers that her "only consolation was that there would never be another [in which she would have to participate]. . . ." Some two years later she noted in a memorandum to her husband the growth in certain circles of pro-third term expression. But she regarded such an attitude as "most unwise" and stated frankly to him: "You know I do *not* [orig. emph.] believe in it. . . ." Even after FDR was in fact nominated in 1940, she confided to a friend that she had "a real horror" of four more years in the White House. [82]

Before Franklin Roosevelt's political plans regarding a third term became known, there were occasional outcroppings of sentiment urging the First Lady herself to seek the Presidency. As far back as 1934 Louis Howe had half-jestingly announced to her: "Eleanor, if you want to be President in 1940, tell me now so I can start getting things ready." [83] By the late 1930's, in addition to the countless invitations Mrs. Roosevelt received requesting her to appear at local Democratic clubs, meetings and banquets, many of her husband's constituents beseeched her to continue the Roosevelt occupancy of the White House. One Los Angeles admirer admitted he would consider it a pleasure to announce the First Lady's candidacy. "I would also be glad to mamage [sic] your campaign," he generously concluded. A Nebraska voter wrote FDR that "it would be well to nominate Mrs. Roosevelt and set up as her opponent Mrs. [Robert] Taft," a suggestion interesting but somewhat chimerical.[84]

Mrs. Roosevelt recognized these sporadic gestures in her favor as wholly unrealistic and was inclined to treat them as something of a joke. Her own experience had shown her the widespread prejudice which still lingered against active female participation in the realm of politics. Bearing this in mind she had written in 1935: "Certainly, a woman can be elected President — in all probability, sometime a woman will be — but she *may* not, in my opinion be elected at the present time or in the near future." [85] Even, however, had conditions for women in politics been more propitious, the First Lady would herself have given public office a wide berth. She was apparently aware that the scope of her activities would be considerably diminished were she to accept an official position; in commenting upon suggestions that she seek the Presidency she wrote: "I cannot quite bring myself to believe that there is any service beyond that of being as useful a private citizen as possible which I can render my country." Later, she informed listeners at her press conference that "nothing would induce me to run for political office." *

* "My Day," Aug. 10, 1938; Joseph P. Lash, *Eleanor Roosevelt: A Friend's Memoir* (Garden City, New York, Doubleday and Co., Inc., 1964), p. 83. After

Mrs. Roosevelt nevertheless continued to exercise political influence, although at times this influence was difficult to pinpoint. It is known, for example, that she warned her husband against adding one of Al Smith's most illustrious aides, Belle Moskowitz, to his own staff after he was elected Governor of New York.[86] It is also a matter of record that Mrs. Roosevelt wrote, in March 1932:

> There are many women, I think, who would feel that the time has come for a woman to fill a place in the Cabinet . . . perhaps the best place to begin would be the Department of Labor as in that Department there are so many things in which the women are interested.[87]

FDR did, of course, both refrain from utilizing Mrs. Moskowitz's services when he was Governor and break with tradition by appointing a woman, Frances Perkins, to his Cabinet as Secretary of Labor when he became President. What is to be guarded against when confronted with such cases, however, is the *post hoc, ergo propter hoc* fallacy. FDR, in other words, may have quite possibly made up his mind about the solution of both these issues independent of his wife's outlook or before she made her opinion known. Still, it is difficult to refrain from the conclusion, in view of Mrs. Roosevelt's vital interest in political preference as it affected women, that her influence was a powerful factor in these decisions.

So, also, with the now-famous phrase, "the only thing we have

---

her husband's death, serious pressures were exerted upon Mrs. Roosevelt to seek political office. She was especially urged to run for the U. S. Senate in New York. Her refusals to officially enter politics, however, remained adamant; her views on this score had been confirmed by an unhappy tenure in a quasi-political position with the Office of Civilian Defense in 1941–42. She did, of course, later bend her rule to accept President Truman's offer to serve as a delegate to the United Nations; but that post contained only the most tenuous relations to "politics."

to fear is fear itself," from FDR's first Inaugural Address.*
Three months before Roosevelt took office, his wife wrote an
article in which the following statements appeared: "The worst
thing that has come to us from the depression is fear. Fear of an
uncertain future, fear of not being able to meet our problems,
fear of not being equipped to cope with life as we live it today."
Did the future First Lady's sentiments by chance implant themselves in the mind of Louis Howe from whence they would later
find their way into the Inaugural Address?†

We shall, in all probability, never know. There is simply no
way of proving either a negative or a positive conclusion in such
instances. What should be taken into consideration is that the
weight of available evidence distinctly indicates that Mrs. Roosevelt's role in the political "partnership" between her and her husband was a very substantial one. As Governor's wife and then as
First Lady she had gradually shifted her posture from one which
concentrated upon liaison work and reportage to one which emphasized her own social views, which, while they did not conflict
with those of her husband, were for a variety of reasons not
stressed by him. Neither of these functions were at fundamental
variance with her earlier outlook as it concerned the behavior of

* These words, which have since been given such heavy emphasis by historians, attracted very little notice at the time they were uttered. The *New York
Times* quoted the editorial reaction of over twenty major newspapers and forty
prominent national legislators to the Address as a whole; not one of the newspapers or the congressional leaders mentioned the "fear itself" phrase. *New
York Times*, March 5, 1933. See also Lorena Hickok, *Reluctant First Lady*
(New York, Dodd, Mead and Co., 1962), p. 103.

† ER, "What Religion Means To Me," *Forum*, LXXXVIII (Dec., 1932),
p. 323. Raymond Moley presents extremely convincing evidence that it was
Howe who inserted the "fear itself" phrase into the Address. It is also possible
that Howe got the phrase from a department store advertisement, as Moley
claims. Even so, it is not inconceivable that Howe grasped its possibilities because he had been subconsciously influenced by Mrs. Roosevelt's thoughts along
those lines. For the two of them — Mrs. Roosevelt and Howe — were very
close. See Raymond Moley (with the assistance of Elliot A. Rosen), *The First
New Deal* (New York, Harcourt, Brace & World, 1966), pp. 115-19.

a statesman's wife. Though she might preach the virtues of her own convictions, the doctrines she stressed did not basically war with those held by Franklin D. Roosevelt. As the thirties wore on, however, her beliefs on the score of what was proper conduct for "wives of great men" must have undergone a change; for, at least in private, she most assuredly did not follow the dictates of agreeing "never . . . to try to convince him on any point, whether regarding some stand already taken or upon some matter upon which he has not yet passed judgment." [88] Rather, she distinctly tried to influence him, sometimes subtly, as in the case of the type of correspondence and reading matter she placed by his bedside, or on other occasions more directly, as certain of her more forceful memorandums indicate. "I've just read the State Department report *to me* [this writer's emphasis] on their [sic] attitude on trade with Japan & the figures on that trade," she wrote her husband indignantly in 1940. "What you told me on scrap iron was incorrect & their [sic] whole attitude seems to me weak. We help China with one hand & we appease & help Japan with the other. Why can't we decide what is right & do it?" [89]

The simplistic approach and its implications of a belief in absolute values gradually became the dominant one in her private political relationship with her husband. As she told her friend Joseph Lash, she was "the agitator" while her husband was "the politician." Self-cast in the former role, she continually entreated him to do what was "right" instead of temporizing for the sake of public opinion. Presidential speechwriter Sam Rosenman was well aware of President's and Mrs. Roosevelt's conflicting viewpoints as regarded methodology when he observed:

> She had none of the give and take . . . that is one of the great essentials of a successful political leader. It was hard for her to compromise, and she frequently disagreed with the President when he was willing to. She advocated the direct, unrelenting

approach. If she had had her way, there would have been fewer compromises by Roosevelt, but also, I am afraid, fewer concrete accomplishments.[90]

Certainly, the testimony of virtually all Mrs. Roosevelt's contemporaries within government bears out the opinion that she was influential. Rosenman himself called her "very helpful on certain kinds of speeches," and added, ". . . we would try to get her ideas on the best general line of approach, and at times would show her drafts of a speech." Robert Sherwood has termed her "the keeper of and constant spokesman for her husband's conscience." "She was supposed to have influence at the White House," recorded Rexford G. Tugwell. "She was not only supposed to have that influence, she did in fact have it." Jesse Jones believed that "because of her many activities she might aptly have been termed Assistant President." [91]

Of her political influence more generally there can be little doubt. James A. Farley noted particularly her political accomplishments as they regarded women, saluting her as "one of the pioneers who helped establish for the feminine voters of the nation, at least in the Democratic Party, a positive and responsible part in party councils." In 1940, at a dinner attended by over five thousand Democratic women, she was honored by a testimonial signifying the occasion as "a mark of recognition for what she has done for the democratic way of life, for the Democratic Party, and for the cause of women in a democracy." [92]

More broadly still, her writings, which contained constant allusions to political matters, reached millions of readers; and on her reportorial trips for her husband she reached countless thousands more. That such trips included a considerable amount of effective "politicking" was attested to by the words of many of her auditors. ". . . we certainly like that glorious wife of [the President]," declared the head of the New York State Milk Producers Federation. ". . . she has the capacity of going out and finding what really is the trouble. She has been of more benefit to [FDR] than a thousand Farleys." [93]

In matters of political organization, Mrs. Roosevelt's talents were already highly regarded by 1936. In addition to her lengthy memorandum to Farley, which concerned campaign tactics and was prepared at the President's behest, her influence was reflected in telegrams such as "IF YOU AGREE [HAROLD] ICKES SHOULD MAKE SPEECH FRIDAY . . . KINDLY WIRE FDR IN MY NAME, SEEMS TO ME WISE BUT WOULD LIKE YOUR SLANT"; or, "DID YOU GET [MARRINER] ECCLES TO RECONSIDER FOR FORUM? IF NOT WHO IS TO TALK ON MONEY? VERY IMPORTANT. PLEASE WIRE ME WASHINGTON TONIGHT." [94]

It is this sort of evidence that causes skepticism concerning Mrs. Roosevelt's disclaimers of her political importance. Indeed, in taking account of her multifarious activities in this sphere, one can only conclude that, for a young woman who had begun her career as a politician's wife with virtually no background in that sort of endeavor, Eleanor Roosevelt had not only learned her political lessons well, but had employed them, in behalf of her party and her husband, to excellent advantage.

Perhaps it was Charles Taussig, prominent in Government youth programs and himself so often the beneficiary of Mrs. Roosevelt's good offices, who most aply summarized the First Lady's position. Writing to FDR to express his gratitude for numerous past favors on the President's part, Taussig concluded:

When you add to this fact that Mrs. Roosevelt actually gets into . . . and participates in our work, you put a human touch and a sense of your personal leadership into a large and complicated piece of government machinery, which I believe is unique in statecraft.[95]

IV

ADVISER TO A NATION

ADVISER TO A NATION

Not long ago someone sent me an article. . . . [which]
proved that, as a family, we all like publicity, for otherwise
we would not write so much and talk so much and do so many
things that put us in print, or in the public eye one way or
another. . . . I fear I must plead guilty to the writing and
talking, for I did both before my husband became President
and I hope I shall continue to do so after he ceases to be
President.
    . . . I think in some of us there is an urge to do certain
things and, if we did not do them, we would feel that we were
not fulfilling the job which we had been given opportunities
and talents to do.

"My Day," August 13, 1938.

I N ATTEMPTING to analyze Eleanor Roosevelt's influence in,
and contributions to, the political fortunes of her party and
her husband (see Chapter III), there always exists the temptation
to stray from consideration of distinctly political concerns into
those of the broader area of public policy. The point at which
such transference is made is necessarily blurred and uncertain; in
some cases the one cannot be examined without mention of the
other. Essentially, however, except for a limited group which
makes party organization and function its vocation, "politics"
mainly consists of the means for a presumably more successful
achievement of larger ends. It is the discovery and selection of
various methods by which men and women can be placed in positions of power in order to further certain social and economic

goals. In the final reckoning, however, it is the ends themselves which are usually of most concern to those who take an interest in public issues.

The importance of Mrs. Roosevelt's position as it involved many of the directions in which the New Deal (and, by implication, the country generally) tended to move has already received some notice. Her active role as it concerned governmental relations toward youth, American Negroes and women has been described. In her efforts to model administration objectives into a pattern more nearly similar to her own hopes and desires, it can be seen that she accomplished more solid results in some areas than in others. Even where she enjoyed comparatively limited success, however, she was almost invariably able to build up a nucleus of support for her ideas, both within administration circles and on the part of those who comprised her national audience.

The encouragement she received assumed a variety of shapes. Certain of her activities were looked upon favorably until inherent errors in their conception or execution became obvious. This was the case, for example, with her patronage of the American Youth Congress. Other objectives which she pursued met initially with either widespread opposition or apathy; but time and the course of events often convinced sizable numbers of Americans that Mrs. Roosevelt's position was a sound and just one. In such instances she gradually acquired more allies and was, at the least, able to establish a climate in which her ideas eventually implanted themselves in a large portion of the national consciousness. This was what occurred as a result of her labors in behalf of Negro aspirations. On still other occasions her advocacy of certain ideals met with such a hospitable response that they enjoyed rapid, tangible and permanent success; her work with women in the political process provides a striking example of this.

But Eleanor Roosevelt by no means confined her interests to the problems of youth, colored Americans, women and politics. Her energetic zeal and broad sympathies led her to preachments and activities concerning virtually every aspect of national life. Here again, her ideas and efforts were sometimes abortive; elsewhere, they appear to have made many converts and to have been instrumental in major reforms. This alone would render such ideas and efforts worthy of study. More than that, however, consideration of her outlook and activities regarding the varied problems facing America in the 1930's is essential to the understanding of Eleanor Roosevelt as a person and to her philosophy as a whole.

~

Perhaps the earliest venture in which Mrs. Roosevelt's role evoked spirited debate concerned the administration's program for subsistence homesteads. Her interest in this project began but a few weeks after she moved into the White House and reached its height in 1934; thereafter, although she remained favorably disposed, her active participation waned considerably. While her involvement lasted, it exemplified clearly both her strengths and her weaknesses. She intervened, as one of her strong critics said, "with the best intentions"; her generosity of motive was beyond dispute.[1] At the same time, however, her activities in behalf of homesteads displayed an appalling lack of practicality, of fiscal responsibility and of administrative sense.

The ideological roots of the early subsistence homesteads program were nourished by several related American traditions. Allen F. Kifer summarizes them as consisting of "recurrent agrarian nostalgia in the face of ugly problems inherent in the industrial revolution, the safety-valve theory described by Frederick Jackson Turner, and a heritage of communitarian life." The more immediate considerations leading to the policy were, he suggests, a "back-to-the-land" movement in vogue at that time, "a recognition of unemployment in the city and poverty in the country, and an old Congressional habit of making lands easily available to homesteaders." [2]

With many of these traditions, Eleanor Roosevelt had a surprising affinity. Though city-born, much of her early life was spent in the pastoral beauty of the mid-Hudson River valley; and she continued to retain a sincere attachment to rural surroundings in her later years. Sojourns in the country, she once said, made her "begin to feel that cities were never meant to be permanent habitations for men"; and, in a speech at Cornell University in the early 1930's, she declared:

> My own roots lie in the soil and the love of nature and country life, but [sic] perhaps that is why I feel so strongly that it is from our rural home dwellers that we must hope for vision and determination to bring against [sic] contentment and well being into the homes of our nation.[3]

Mrs. Roosevelt also repeatedly praised the virtues of "early pioneers," chiefly the "community spirit" which she felt had prevailed among them. This feeling of being "responsible for each other," she was convinced, must once again become the accepted norm:

> . . . one of the most important and violent of the "new ideas" necessary to mankind today is the realization that no civilization can last where even a small percentage of the people have to struggle against impossible social conditions.
> We cannot go on thinking of ourselves alone. . . . We must begin to think and plan for the race as a whole. . . .[4]

Such sentiments — the advantages of a country environment and a belief in eradicating "impossible social conditions" wherever they existed — were perfectly calculated to propel the First Lady's interest in the direction of the administration's homestead projects. For unquestionably there were certain Americans who, in the early 1930's, were being forced to endure conditions which were a national disgrace. And among such disadvantaged citizens were those who resided in minimally productive farm areas or in places where industry had simply dried up, leaving the inhabitants of the vicinity to a bleak and all but hopeless struggle for existence. Mrs. Roosevelt termed these unhappy locales "rural slums." [5] She, together with other individuals in the government who shared her concern, believed that if the administration could establish in such regions model communities based upon both farming and light industry, the original investment would be easily repaid. Opportunity for the now-deprived citizen would enable him to earn enough to make the costs of the projects virtually self-liquidating. Furthermore, these model communities would encourage "cooperation" and "community spirit," objectives upon which Mrs. Roosevelt placed a very high value.

According to Paul K. Conkin the government, after considering the problem, came up with three more or less distinct types of subsistence homestead projects. The first consisted of

> communities of part-time farmers near industrial employment. Secondly, there would be all-rural colonies for resettled submarginal farmers. Thirdly, there would be a few villages with newly decentralized industry. The last were to be the most experimental and the most controversial. . . .

Arthurdale, with whose fortunes Eleanor Roosevelt was to so vitally concern herself, came under the third heading.*

* Paul K. Conkin, *Tomorrow A New World* (Ithaca, New York, Cornell University Press, 1959), pp. 104–05. Arthurdale was originally called the Reedsville Experimental Community; it shall be referred to here by its more popularly-known title.

Mrs. Roosevelt made her initial tour of the coal mining region around Morgantown, West Virginia, during the summer of 1933 in the company of Clarence Pickett of the American Friends Service Committee. The President's wife was deeply moved by the desperate conditions she observed there, notably at a place known as Scott's Run where the mines had been almost entirely inoperative since 1920. Complete absence of plumbing, lack of bedding, inadequate food, shanties of the most dilapidated sort, typhoid epidemics — all were daily experiences for the residents of the stricken area. Mrs. Roosevelt later recalled a gentleman of substance who had accompanied her on a Scott's Run trip and pled with her to accept "any money you want" to help remedy conditions if only he could discontinue the visit; the sights he witnessed were making him physically ill. The First Lady herself considered the situation in the West Virginia hill country so critical that "if there had been a leader . . . a revolution could have easily started." [6]

The Division of Subsistence Homesteads was organized by the government in August, 1933. The administrative hierarchy within which it was placed reflected the President's predilection for splitting authority and responsibility in New Deal agencies. The parent agency for Homesteads was the NRA, which was headed by General Hugh Johnson. But the public works aspects of NRA were put in charge of Secretary of the Interior Harold L. Ickes. Under Ickes, Milburn L. Wilson was theoretically head of the Division of Subsistence Homesteads. Each project of the Division had an Executive Committee; in the case of Arthurdale it was comprised of Wilson, Mrs. Roosevelt, presidential assistant Louis Howe, and Bushrod Grimes who, as extension agent for the University of West Virginia, was to represent "local interests" and act as Resident Director. Clarence Pickett was made Wilson's assistant, a staff job. Subcommittees were set up under the Executive Committee:

Mrs. Roosevelt was chairman of the Committee on Admissions, which included Grimes and Silliman Evans [of the Post Office Department]. Evans and Howe were the Industrial Committee. Howe *was* the Electrification Committee, all by himself. Eleanor *was* the Population Committee.[7]

This administrative morass was to handicap the entire enterprise from the outset.

But it was Howe who made the first of the overt blunders which were to typify Arthurdale. After the old Richard M. Arthur estate had been purchased to provide land for the project, Howe began boasting on the radio and in the press that suffering families in the area would be in their new $2,000 homes by Christmas. In order to implement this prognostication, he thereupon ordered fifty prefabricated houses, dwellings soon to be notorious for their light summer construction as well as because they did not fit their foundations. The presidential assistant was beginning to get nervous about the whole scheme and, in something of an understatement, mourned that "I have a disturbed feeling about it."[8] His confident predictions concerning cheap electric power likewise turned into mirages. Meanwhile, the Bureau of the Budget was raising strenuous objections to the decentralized corporate structure under which Arthurdale operated, objections which led to a change embodying Ickes' formula for a central corporation with separate project managers. As a result of this M. L. Wilson resigned in a huff.

It was at this juncture, in January, 1934, that Mrs. Roosevelt began the most active phase of her labors on behalf of Arthurdale. She was filled with extravagant visions of what the experiment might presage. According to one close student of the project, her view was that it would not only rescue the miners from poverty,

[but] it was to point . . . to a new way of life . . . for all America. It was to show the way to a solution of the problems

of stranded populations, was to promote industrial decentraliza-
tion, and was to show what social and economic planning might
accomplish if given a chance. . . . She wanted Arthurdale to
. . . [be] visited by 50,000 to 100,000 people each year. She desired a national research center in subsistence homesteading at
West Virginia University, since Arthurdale would be the first
project of its kind in the world . . . it would be the focal
point for the regional planning and development of the Upper
Monongahela valley.[9]

Possessed of such grandiose notions, the First Lady naturally
regarded talk of excessive expenditures as somewhat irrelevant.
She selected the architect, one Gugler, to redesign Howe's prefabs to fit their foundations; but the new design was found to be
unworkable, and the foundations had to be revised as well. She
then arbitrarily announced that the costs of Howe's error would
"not be borne" by the homesteaders. She procured the services
of her friend, Nan Cook, to help design the homes' furniture and
interiors. The furniture included beautiful and expensive pieces
made of maple, pine and poplar which, according to the Washington *Star*, "possess[ed] considerable elegance"; the interiors
were graced with linen, curtains and tapestry. So that the mounting expense of these now-impressive dwellings would not be
overly criticized, Mrs. Roosevelt wrote: "For the first experiment [one hundred and twenty-five] families will be very carefully chosen. Both the husband and wife and the children and
their ancestry will be considered. . . ." This, however, was not
of her doing. She had opposed the "background selection" system in favor of a representative group but was overruled.[10]

The First Lady also assumed direction of the educational plans
for the community and, to assist her, called in the well-known
progressive educator, Miss Elsie Clapp of the Ballard Memorial
School near Louisville, Kentucky. Together, they planned a
school system which was to have six buildings and twenty-one

faculty members for a colony of no more than two hundred families. Miss Clapp "lived in a specially constructed house and directed the unusual school program which was to begin before a child was born and was to continue throughout his life. Pre- and post-natal instruction was given by the project nurse and doctor." The nursery school, where the children went when they were two or three years old, was one of the happier aspects of the experiment; its procedures of learning with wooden blocks and creative painting became widely accepted. The elementary grades, where there was to be a "new economic and social freedom" and where there were no examinations or formal teaching, and the high school, which failed to secure accreditation in the state, were somewhat less successful. As Clarence Pickett sadly recorded, the leaders in this educational pioneering perhaps "assumed more experimental-mindedness among the homesteaders than had yet developed." The majority of homesteaders seem to have feared their children were not getting as good an education there as they could elsewhere, and so transferred them to more orthodox institutions. The Arthurdale school was turned over to the Preston County school system in 1936.[11]

Mrs. Roosevelt's initial effort to procure light industry for Arthurdale took the form of a request to manufacture certain items for the Post Office Department. Because this involved a government contract, the Arthurdale plan came under a closer scrutiny by Congress than might have ordinarily been the case. Debate concerning the project arose in the House of Representatives in January, 1934, when Representative Louis Ludlow, Democrat of Indiana, presented an amendment to a postal appropriations bill. This amendment would have blocked authorization of an Arthurdale contract along the lines of Mrs. Roosevelt's proposal. It was Ludlow's contention that a venture of this sort would injure private concerns then engaged in the manufacture of similar items for the Post Office Department. In order to escape that possibility he suggested, in an amendment which was passed by a voice vote on January 26, that no government-sponsored manufacture of such items be permitted outside Washington, D.C.[12]

The bill, as amended, reached the Senate the following month (February) where Kenneth McKeller, Democrat of Tennessee, introduced an amendment which would have effectively scotched the one passed by the House. Referring to McKeller's action, Senator Arthur Vandenburg, Republican of Michigan, asked his colleague from Tennessee whether the latter's "rather cryptic amendment" was proposed for the reason that the administration wished "to make this experiment [i.e., manufacturing items for the Post Office Department] in a new subsistence center. Is not that the fact?" queried the Michigan senator. "I am inclined to think that is the fact," replied McKeller, whose amendment was nevertheless passed.[13]

Debate thereupon switched back to the House. Congressman Jennings Randolph, Democrat of West Virginia, read into the *Congressional Record* an article from *Labor*, the official publication of the Railroad Brotherhoods, which referred to the attempts to gain a contract at Arthurdale as "Mrs. Roosevelt's plan" and accused Representative Ludlow of trying to protect the Keyless Lock Co. of Indianapolis, termed "one of the worst anti-union plants in the country" by *Labor*. All this Ludlow denied; the House then rejected the Senate amendment, whereupon the latter body agreed to "recede from" its previous position.[14]

It is interesting to note that in spite of the rejection of Mrs. Roosevelt's program to bring industry to Arthurdale on the strength of a government contract, the vast majority of the members of both houses of Congress seemed favorably disposed toward the homesteads plan as a whole. Even Ludlow himself saluted "the humanitarian purpose back of this project" and paid special tribute to its sponsors who, he declared, were moved by "high altruistic and humanitarian purpose." There were few members indeed who sided with the Republican senator from Minnesota, Thomas D. Schall, who likened the homesteads program to a "commune." Schall appeared to have followed the line of that misguided zealot, Dr. William A. Wirt, who had termed subsistence homesteads "communistic," a charge which the First Lady naturally denied with vigor.*

The ultimate failure of the Arthurdale experiment can hardly, therefore, be attributed to Congressional hostility or to a deluded rightist minority. The blame must rest instead upon visionary expectations, administrative chaos, and truly fantastic costs. Soon after Congress refused Arthurdale the contract to manufacture supplies for the Post Office Department, Mrs. Roosevelt persuaded Gerard Swope of the General Electric Co. to set up a vacuum cleaner assembly plant in the area. Legal complications involving the formation of a private association which could lease the factory were eventually overcome; nonetheless the financial loss suffered by the operation was sufficiently heavy that within one year the company cancelled its contract. Later ventures were also unsuccessful. Mrs. Roosevelt's plans underwent a further setback when Louis Howe, now thoroughly frightened by the unfavorable publicity the experiment was beginning to receive, vetoed the First Lady's plans for community gardens and herds.[15]

* *Congressional Record,* 73rd Congress, 2nd session. For Ludlow's remarks see Jan. 25, 1934, p. 1359; for Schall, May 1, 1934, p. 7738. Rep. Randolph read Mrs. Roosevelt's denial of Wirt's charge into the *Record* on April 23, 1934, see p. 7186.

Dr. Wirt had founded the Gary, Indiana, school system. During a series of trips to Washington in 1933 he had acquired the notion that a group of "brain trusters" were deliberately delaying the return of prosperity in order to foment a revolution, and that they were successfully manipulating the President for this purpose. FDR, Wirt alleged, was merely "the Kerensky of the revolution"; when conditions were ripe for the overthrow of American institutions he would be replaced. *New York Times,* March 24, 1934; New York *Herald Tribune,* March 27, 1934.

The Arthurdale imbroglio drove Harold Ickes frantic. Even taking into consideration the fact that the entire three volumes of the Interior Secretary's *Diary* are rife with his imaginings of supposed conspiracies being hatched against him, there seem grounds for sympathy with the problems he faced in this particular case. Generally, his opinion of Mrs. Roosevelt was favorable; he had found her "really a very charming woman, natural, simple, and friendly." By the autumn of 1934, however, certain doubts began to beset him. "Of course, the Reedsville project is just one big headache," he wrote. After Howe had bungled with his prefabs, "Mrs. Roosevelt took the . . . project under her protecting wing with the result that we have been spending money down there like drunken sailors — money that we can never hope to get out of the project." The Curmudgeon's misgivings were apparently shared by the President, whom Ickes reported as having told him that "she wants to build these homesteads on a scale . . . we can't afford because the people for whom they are intended cannot afford such things." And, according to Ickes, FDR added: "My missus, unlike most women, hasn't any sense about money at all." [16]

By December the Secretary had convinced himself that Mrs. Roosevelt was part of "an active cabal working against me," and traced her animosity to the Arthurdale experiment. She "practically took hold of Reedsville herself. . . . She took to Reedsville a temperamental architect from New York who spent money lavishly. . . . Finally I had to ride roughshod over him. . . ." She maintained "a great dislike" for Ornan Smart, the general project manager, and had tried to have him fired. Recently she had interfered with the Interior Department's functions on a broader basis, opposing E. K. Burlew, one of Ickes' assistants, as a "stand-pat Republican." She was responsible for an Ernest K. Lindley newspaper article which charged Louis Glavis, another Interior employee, of disloyalty to the New Deal, wiretapping, and general terrorization of the Department's workers.* She had written a letter to one of the members of the Secretary's engineering staff "in which she had urged favorable consideration of a grade-crossing elimination project in a New Jersey city because a woman there who was 'a good Democrat' was interested and had written to her about it. . . ." All this "annoyed me exceedingly," Ickes recorded with some heat. "Soon I will expect Sistie and Buzzie [two of the Roosevelt grandchildren] to be issuing orders to members of my staff. Fortunately they can't write yet." Shortly after FDR's 1936 reelection, Ickes continued to lament that "I still am of the opinion that I do not stand in too well with Mrs. Roosevelt." The scars of the Arthurdale project, the Secretary seemed to feel, were a long time in healing.[17]

The First Lady remained steadfast in her defense of the West Virginia experiment. She continued to laud it in her daily column, saying among other things:

> If you are interested, any of you, in visiting Arthurdale, I think you will want to see these people at work, to see their homes and their gardens, and you will get an idea of what this homestead project may mean to many people if it spreads throughout the country.

Though admitting that there had been "mistakes and drawbacks" connected with the plan, she emphasized what she regarded as its positive aspects, claiming in 1938 that "there is a greater sense of solidarity and security among the homesteaders than ever before," and that the project "will give the 200 families there real security and will, therefore, give more courage to those in other homesteads all over the nation." [18]

This type of defense was anchored firmly in the middle of the liberal stream. Mistakes were secondary if "good" were accomplished. As the First Lady declared in a newspaper interview:

---

* Glavis' zeal had also been the subject of controversy in the well-known Ballinger-Pinchot affair during the administration of William Howard Taft.

. . . over and over again, I have felt that all the money that some people have said was foolishly spent [at Arthurdale], or even wasted, is well expended if it brings some happiness to those who need it, some security where before the future held nothing but terror.[19]

But surely this line of argument did little to help clarify the issue. It tended instead to force the opposition into something of a contrived corner. It implied that those who criticized extravagance and waste were somehow wicked and heartless. Such an intellectual device was closely akin to the ancient shibboleth that the liberals possessed a sole monopoly on humanitarianism because they alone were concerned with human rights while their opponents confined their interests to the upholding of property rights. Mrs. Roosevelt was very near this misleading "good" versus "evil" proposition when, in a later reminiscence about Arthurdale, she primly concluded: "Oh, yes, the human values were most rewarding, even if the financial returns to the government were not satisfactory."[20] Such a dichotomization refused to recognize that there might be an increasingly diminishing return upon needless monetary largesse, that unsatisfactory financial results to the government in the long run were harmful to the citizens at large; its terms did not admit to the existence of a middle ground of reform without incompetence. It was a rationale which in reality could often lead to the fallacious position of making a virtue of mistakes.

That the Arthurdale project aided many families who had lived under the most deplorable conditions is hardly open to doubt. The area itself, when finally completed, was assuredly attractive; and portions of the experiment, such as the nursery school, achieved high praise. The cost of these improvements was, however, astronomical. A 1939 accounting by the Farm Security Administration reckoned overall expenses to be $16,377 for each family unit or $8,665 for each dwelling plus outbuildings in a region where a two-story brick home with thirty-five acres of farm land was selling for $5,000. Nor did these figures take into account the thousands of private dollars spent by Mrs. Roosevelt and friends of hers like Bernard Baruch.* In spite of all this, by 1940 the homesteader family income at Arthurdale averaged only $467 annually.[21]

Further, Mrs. Roosevelt's championship of the project ironically helped to work an additional hardship upon it. Having made promises and being unable to deliver, the Division of Subsistence Homesteads, and later the Rural Resettlement Administration under which Arthurdale was placed in 1935, felt that with the spotlight of publicity on them they must come through. This encouraged such absurdities as entwining trellises with wild grapevines (which promptly died) and spending several hundred dollars to import rhododendrons (in an area where they already flourished) to impress the public at dedication ceremonies.[22] The houses, the inn, the gas station, the barns, the forge, the gristmill, factories, educational plant, barber shop and stores were all ultimately sold at great loss. When the last of the assets were finally liquidated in 1946, the government, in Professor Conkin's words, "at last relinquished one of the most embarrassing experiments in its history." [23]

To this embarrassment the efforts of Mrs. Roosevelt had contributed not a little.

~

A prominent aspect of the homesteads program was its emphasis upon a revival of craftsmanship as opposed to the dehumanized mass techniques of manufacturing associated with the industrial revolution. To many of Arthurdale's principal backers the

* Baruch, although apparently having very little faith in the concepts which motivated the Arthurdale experiment, wrote a check for $22,000 for the school, interested the Guggenheims in backing dental clinics for the children, and promised Mrs. Roosevelt aid in buying a pottery kiln. See Margaret L. Coit, *Mr. Baruch* (Boston, Houghton Mifflin Co., 1957), pp. 452–53.

introduction of handicrafts was one of the experiment's most attractive features. It was believed that such vocations as metalworking, pottery and weaving would stir the long-absent emotion of individual pride in one's work.

Eleanor Roosevelt was emphatically of this view; her sentiments on the matter in fact antedated by a good many years the onset of the New Deal homestead projects. Indeed, Mrs. Roosevelt had been so thoroughly persuaded of the desirability of decentralized manufacturing and restoration of pride in craftsmanship that she had participated in a private scheme along such lines in the 1920's. Her enterprise, called Val-Kill and located on the Roosevelt grounds at Hyde Park, had its inception in 1925. Its beginnings actually were more social than commercial. Mrs. Roosevelt, in company with her close friends, Marion Dickerman and Nancy Cook, had found it disappointing that Sara Delano Roosevelt closed her big house on the Hudson every winter, for the three women had enjoyed getting together on the Hyde Park property. They thereupon persuaded FDR to allow them to construct a cottage on part of the acreage; furthermore, he agreed to give them this section of land with the proviso that upon the death of the last survivor the said property would revert to the estate. The cottage, a somewhat primitive affair at first, was opened January 1, 1926. Nan Cook, who possessed exceptional woodworking skills, designed the furnishings, and the ladies came up with the idea that this talent might be utilized for commercial purposes. Eventually another building for a factory was added, each of the women investing a portion of the capital for proposed operations.

The shop had two purposes, the first of which was the reproduction of famous Early American pieces; the second, the off-season employment of rural farm youth. Mrs. Roosevelt was in charge of promotion and sales; Miss Cook oversaw production; Miss Dickerman helped wherever she was needed. Later, according to the *New York Times*, Caroline O'Day also participated in the venture.*

Insofar as aiding the local populace by providing off-season employment, the Val-Kill furniture factory was not entirely successful. Nan Cook's standards were meticulous, and unskilled farmers were not often able to meet them adequately. Hence, as Mrs. Roosevelt put it in 1930:

> . . . we were obliged to hunt until we had located American citizens who had learned from their fathers and their grandfathers in the old world the secrets of handcraftsmanship and the need for patient labor, young men filled with the old ideas of craftsmanship. It took some time to make them realize that this new American spirit of getting everything done in the quickest way possible was not what we wanted in our Shop and that we were interested in beauty, not in speed, and in good workmanship rather than in mass production.†

In addition to its somewhat limited success in employing farm workers during the off-season, the profit-making capacity of the company as a whole has never been clarified. Mrs. Roosevelt was able to open wide avenues of publicity for the venture; but the pieces were elegant and highly expensive, two endowments certainly not calculated to appeal to a large clientele after 1929. In any case, the Val-Kill furniture factory closed its doors soon after Mrs. Roosevelt became First Lady.‡

---

* *New York Times*, May 17, 1927. For the rest of the above information this writer is indebted to Marion Dickerman (interview, May 25, 1965).

† ER, copy of a radio interview, Nov., 1930, "ER, Speeches and Articles," Box 1, FDRL. At its height of production the factory employed about twenty skilled workmen.

‡ Basically, there are two accounts of why Val-Kill shut down. The first is that of Joseph P. Lash, who received it from Mrs. Roosevelt's secretary, Malvina Thompson. "Tommy" told Lash that the cottage was originally built because of Sara Delano Roosevelt's dislike for Nancy Cook; such a refuge provided, in other words, the only way Eleanor Roosevelt, Nan Cook, and Marion Dickerman could get together on the Hyde Park property. As for the furniture

The importance of the Val-Kill project is in the further illumination it sheds upon Eleanor Roosevelt's viewpoint concerning the economic organization and structure of society. There was a good deal of William Morris in her outlook — a belief that man should strive for excellence of product and that his heart should be in his work, and that modern, industrial methods of production tended to degrade and vulgarize these aspirations. Recapturing the older atmosphere, she felt — and here again her thinking paralleled that of Morris — would lead to a fellowship and joy of living presumably not present in a system dominated by the machine.*

Moreover, Mrs. Roosevelt held the belief that Americans must re-embrace the virtues of the "early pioneers," the "more simple ideals and more simple ways of living." In 1934, while addressing members of the Rural Homecrafts Project, an organization which represented these objectives, she declared:

> Home industries will constitute a busy part of a new rural life in America. The result, if predictions are true, will . . . get the worker out of the congested cities into the country, and who

---

factory, the Lash-Thompson version is that "it did not show a profit. Friends of Mrs. R. suggested she get a business-minded person to manage the enterprise. Miss Cook objected and they decided to dissolve the partnership. Mrs. R. thought the furniture factory was hers. The process of dissolution was not pleasant." See Joseph P. Lash, *Eleanor Roosevelt: A Friend's Memoir* (Garden City, New York, Doubleday and Co., Inc., 1964), pp. 141–42.

To all this Miss Dickerman takes vehement exception. FDR's mother, she maintains, was fond of Nan Cook; as to the company, it made a profit and ceased operations only because the volume of orders and work were becoming injurious to Miss Cook's health (interview, May 25, 1965). Miss Dickerman's version is similar to that of Eleanor Roosevelt in *This I Remember* (New York, Harper & Brothers, 1949), p. 24.

The profitability of the Val-Kill factory will in all likelihood remain a matter of speculation. Miss Cook burned all the records before her death (confidential source to this writer).

* William Morris (1834–96) was an English poet, artist, craftsman, and socialist who urged a return to the spirit of the medieval artisans. Although no existing evidence indicates that Mrs. Roosevelt was acquainted with Morris' philosophy, there was, nonetheless, a startling similarity of outlook between the two.

[sic] with his rural neighbor will not only cultivate land but will develop handcrafts eventually to grow into small industrial plants as part of the economic and industrial settlement.[24]

Ideas of this nature did not augur, on the First Lady's part, an overly-receptive attitude toward large capitalistic enterprise. "We cannot do away with the machines," she lamented, ". . . they are here to stay. . . . But we must ask ourselves are we happier and better off today because of them?" While admitting that "the machine which seems to be responsible for so many of our troubles is not wholly bad for it gives us leisure and greater plenty," she was yet concerned "that we learn how to make it serve us." [25] To an innate suspicion of the mass production complex itself, Mrs. Roosevelt thus appeared to be additionally anxious concerning the manner by which such potential would be controlled.

She was not happy about the rise of large business combinations:

> Because of our complicated modern civilization, we have tended to do away with the independent small business man and to combine and re-combine until the real power has come to lie in the hands of a few people and much of the money, which has been a symbol of power in this country, has been concentrated in a few hands.

Like her Uncle Theodore, however, she believed that there existed both "fair-minded" and "unsocially-minded" manufacturers. The former, in her view, were those businessmen who always placed priority on "the human side" of the decisions they made.[26] With this in mind, she occasionally lent verbal encouragement or even outright praise to members of the industrial community. Referring in her column to one of her husband's speeches to Congress in 1936, she called it "an encouraging message" because it voices a faith in the ability of business organizations to really get together and work for re-employment. This could not be done unless they were genuinely willing to consider human values . . . . It is a challenge to the common sense and good will of American business people and I feel confident they will succeed.[27]

On another occasion the First Lady announced herself as "thrilled" over the testimony (before the Senate Unemployment Committee) of meat packing company president J. C. Hormel during the course of which he suggested a guaranteed annual wage. She was further pleased by Mr. Hormel's assurance that his company would retain a full-strength payroll even during periods of business downturn, for as he stated: "That is what we do with our vice-presidents." "Good logic," the author of "My Day" applauded, "but I wonder how many heads of business have given it much thought." [28]

But references favorable to business did not emanate from the First Lady with great frequency. Such instances, when they did occur, were almost invariably because a particular concern, like that of Hormel, showed itself friendly toward labor; or, as in the case of her early leanings toward Jesse Jones for the Democratic vice-presidential nomination in 1940, because of political considerations. Rather, her attitude toward business was in the main characterized by the combination of a certain distrust together with a lack of comprehension, each of the two elements perhaps feeding upon one another.

It has been pointed out that Eleanor Roosevelt's perspective with regard to business was influenced by misgivings about the size and scope of large-scale manufacturing enterprise as well as doubt concerning the alleged blessings of modern machine-dominated industrial economies. Moreover, it is quite probable that whatever latent suspicions she held on these scores would only have been increased by the apparent inability of business leadership to prevent and then to successfully weather the Depression. Her theories on the origin and course of that disaster contained elements both of insight and of ignorance. The United States had, she asserted, learned little from the lessons of the World War, and with its termination had plunged into an orgy of speculation while simultaneously allowing the agricultural segment of the nation to "sink lower and lower." This sensible statement was followed by the puzzling declaration that the "sinking standard of living in part of our country [i.e., agriculture] meant that fewer goods were needed by other sections of our country." [29]

It is true that these statements were made *ex post facto* — in 1932 — for Mrs. Roosevelt, like the vast majority of her countrymen, had not in the 1920's foreseen many of the danger signals which indicated the shallow premises upon which the then-current prosperity was based. "We are less apt today to have panics because of the Federal Reserve Act," was her opinion. In the political arena, she was in fact forced to campaign, like so many Democrats of that era, on the issue that both good and bad times were the result of normal economic cycles, and that the Republican administrations therefore had very little to do with the prevailing prosperity:

> Economists say that prosperity goes in cycles; that no party can claim entire responsibility for it; that it is the result of economic world conditions. Of course, any party may contribute towards it by its policies and its help but it would be foolish to contend that the government alone is fully responsible.

To emphasize her point Mrs. Roosevelt quoted with implicit approval President Calvin Coolidge's view that

> it would be unfortunate if . . . the impression should be gained that it is the obligation of the government to furnish the people

with prosperity. They are entitled to such an administration of their affairs as will give them every fair opportunity, but if their [sic] was to be prosperity they must furnish it themselves.[30]

If Mrs. Roosevelt later used hindsight in her analysis of some of the factors having to do with the Depression's origins, she could also justifiably claim that she had issued early warnings concerning certain other policies which later contributed to the economic collapse. This was especially true as it involved the area of tariff planning. As early as 1924 she stressed "the close connection of our economic situation and the stabilizing of our international relations," and called for a tariff that would provide "not only foreign markets but markets which are again able to pay for what we [sic] need." In 1928 she advocated a tariff commission which would take schedule-making "out of politics" and would "scientifically determine where our Tariffs are too high [and] where they are too low after fully [sic] consideration of the interests of both the manufacturers and the consumers." Although the proposed Smoot-Hawley Tariff provided for such a commission, Mrs. Roosevelt clearly indicated the other weaknesses of the bill:

> I am against the bill not only because of the higher rate of living which it will bring but because . . . I also believe that the continued prosperity of a country depends upon the prosperity of all countries. I do not see how we can shut out goods from nations which owe us great sums of money and expect them to prosper.[31]

Similar to this clearheaded thinking regarding the tariff were her remarkably accurate remarks concerning certain of the weaknesses of the businessman-engineer par excellence, Herbert Hoover. Occasionally, it is true, her utterances on this subject were in the nature of orthodox political sniping, as when she declared that Hoover's nomination in 1928 was due to the fact that "he has [as Secretary of Commerce] . . . the most tremendous political machine of employees scattered throughout the United States that has ever been gathered together under one head with the exception of the Presidential Post Office patronage itself." Generally, however, her criticisms were much more in harmony with her own misgivings about the modern capitalistic spirit, and they scored Hoover's public shortcomings with decided insight:

> . . . he has exhibited an almost fanatical interest in investigation of causes. On things material and commercial he has conducted endless researches, he has prepared yards of charts and reduced statistics to the last decimal point but on the great fundamental human problems of life he shows no such interest, perhaps because they cannot be charted and reduced to figures. He has indeed the engineer's mind and problems which cannot be solved by algebra and mathematics do not attract him.[32]

Occasionally when speaking of Hoover, Mrs. Roosevelt even produced what was for her that extremely rare commodity of a genuinely humorous remark. "It was a Republican worker," she related to one audience, "who stated . . . that the life of a consistent Republican was hard, [because] first he must for seven [sic] years be enthusiastic over an ice-berg and now he must transfer this enthusiasm to an adding machine." [33]

Aside from her comments upon the tariff and upon certain of Hoover's defects, however, Mrs. Roosevelt's observations concerning the Depression were not notably acute. She appeared in part to have embraced something like a pseudo-religious interpretation of the economy's decline, at one time saying: " 'Whom the Lord loveth, he chasteneth,' and perhaps he knew that only great disaster would open our eyes." Elsewhere, she seemed to abandon such gloomy views, advocating in their stead a vacuous optimism. "We must have faith that better times are coming," she exhorted her listeners in a speech accompanying the presentation of an award in the National Smiles Contest. "There was a

war song that I wish we could get this country to sing again —
'Pack up your troubles in your old kit bag, and smile, smile,
smile.' " [34]

After she became First Lady, Eleanor Roosevelt did not devote a large portion of her attention to the subject of business.
This was possibly because she felt uncomfortable in dealing
with it; not only did she harbor misgivings about the industrial
and commercial sectors of the economy, but her own words suggest that she found the workings of business and economics in
general a trifle bewildering. Modern business "with all its complicated ramifications" appeared to her "a bit like the Mad Hat-
ter's tea party," and she pled for a "little simplification" in that
sphere which "would be the first step toward rational living. . . ." [35] Thus, from time to time when her better judgment deserted her and she felt constrained to offer her audience
advice pertaining to the overall business or financial situation, her
counsel made somewhat peculiar reading. At one juncture, for
example, she urged a kind of nationwide white sale, in which the
retailer and consumer could purchase goods at cost so that the
economic cycle could be got moving again. The campaign
theme for this idea, called "People come before profits," was, she
ventured, "a good slogan, and a wise man knows that only when
you think of people first, can you ever make profits." [36]

Her thoughts were ever centered upon the "human element"
— i.e., the consumer — a commendable enough attitude in itself,
but one which seemed invariably to leave the businessman or
banker in a sort of economic limbo. The latters' interests she
never consulted; she appears to have thought them unassociated
with consumers. She constantly excoriated banks for supposedly
demanding too much collateral for their loans; some idea of what
she considered proper can be gathered from her advocacy of a
government agency which would lend money on a basis of the
borrower's "character" alone.[37]

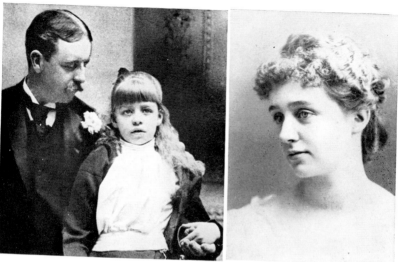

Left. Eleanor Roosevelt and her father, Elliot, about 1889. He was, she later testified, the "great love" of her early life.

Right. Contributor to a complex: Anna Hall Roosevelt, whom her daughter called "the most beautiful woman I have ever seen."

The diffident young matron with her awesome mother-in-law, Sara Delano Roosevelt.

Mrs. Roosevelt's interest in children never flagged. She is
seen above working with New York City schoolchildren, and
below, at the Brooklyn Jewish Hospital.

Mrs. Roosevelt's well-meant enthusiasm for youth groups occasionally led her to aid movements from which she might better have withheld her support. Above she is shown with leaders (*left to right*, Jack McMichael and William Hinckley; Mrs. Hinckley is partially shown at far left) of the Communist-infiltrated American Youth Congress. *U.P.I.*

Mrs. Roosevelt's value as a political asset was immense. She had begun her political labors in the 1920's, and appears (*top*) at one of the typical Democratic conclaves of that period. By the 1930's an indefatigable campaigner, she often accompanied the President on his "swings around the circle." (*bottom*)

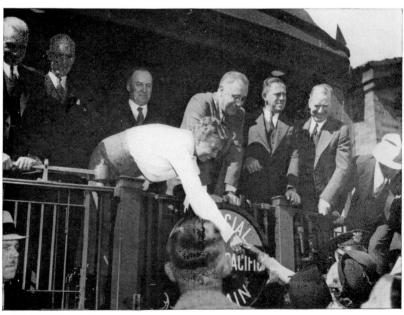

Mrs. Roosevelt at the Democratic National Convention, 1940.

"Charting Mrs. Roosevelt's travels," stated *Life* Magazine in 1940, was "a map maker's headache." By that time she had visited every state but South Dakota, and had gone overseas as well. An unceasing champion of air travel, she flew wherever and whenever she could.

Mrs. Roosevelt visited Puerto Rico and the Virgin Islands in 1934, and examined conditions there (*above*).

Below, she is seen with the Indians at the Golden Gate International Exposition in San Francisco in 1939. *Newsart Photos, San Francisco*

Anna Eleanor Roosevelt in 1940.
Bradford Bachrach

On yet another occasion, when the United States was beginning actively to assist Nazi-beleaguered England with war materials and supplies, the First Lady proposed that "the best minds in the country should be occupied at the present time with determining how it can be made equally certain that capital, wherever possible, is drafted for the use of the country in just the way that lives are drafted." [38] In commenting upon this idea, economist Ralph Robey was moved to point out that conscription of income already existed in the form of taxation, but that what Mrs. Roosevelt was advocating was conscription of capital. If such a scheme were adopted, Robey believed,

> . . . our system of private enterprise will necessarily come to a dead end. There will be no supply of private savings with which to go ahead — no private wealth out of which to make the investment necessary to create jobs — no private capital for even the replenishment of present productive facilities. Everything, from top to bottom, will have to be government.

The economist concluded his remarks with the opinion that Mrs. Roosevelt did not recognize the implications of her proposal. Rather, "like so many others, [she] has simply been led astray in her thinking by a phrase which has the ring of social fairness." [39]

It is certainly possible that the First Lady was unaware of what the "draft capital" plan might ultimately mean. She had oftentimes mistakenly supported causes, notably those associated with youth, in part because of the high-sounding "social justice" rhetoric with which those causes surrounded themselves. At the same time, however, it can hardly be denied that Mrs. Roosevelt maintained no real affection for or understanding of business and financial enterprise. She continued to be suspicious of the motives which she felt activated decisions in such quarters. Thus, though she was willing in 1940 to admit that the Du Pont interests did not want war, her reason for this opinion was that "they

are making plenty of money now." And, characteristically, she
added: "Of course one can't be sure of any corporation if a huge
sum of money should be placed before it." [40]

Distrust remained the keynote of her thinking as it regarded
business, a distrust that was anything but typical of the approach
she displayed in other areas of her concern. She reached this position because of a multitude of factors: her predisposition to the
country life and a semi-rural economy, her observation of the
failure of a business-dominated society to either withstand or
overcome an unprecedented depression, and a lack of training in
economics and business matters which rendered her vulnerable
to suspicions of the profit motive.* To these sources of influence, however, must be added one other element — and one that
weighed greatly upon the scales of her perspective. That element was Mrs. Roosevelt's attitude toward labor.

~

It was natural that, given Eleanor Roosevelt's inherent sympathy for the "underdog," she would display much interest in
the problems of labor in America. Perhaps "laborer" would be a
better word, for the origin of her concern — which again
squared with her philosophy in other matters — centered chiefly
upon the industrial worker and his problems rather than upon
the labor movement as a more abstract concept. Involvement
with the one, however, necessarily led Mrs. Roosevelt to enter-
tain certain concepts about the other; and these concepts can be
fairly summarized as embodying a distinctly "pro" attitude regarding labor's aspirations.

Her position had doubtless been reinforced as a result of her
work during the 1920's for the Women's Trade Union League,

* The effect of her husband's equivocal disposition toward the business community upon Mrs. Roosevelt's thinking cannot at the present time be accurately
gauged.

an organization which, according to its constitution, was dedicated to protecting

> the women wage earners of America from an inadequate wage
> and extreme work hours; to insure them a voice in the adjust-
> ment of industrial conditions by establishing self-government in
> the workshop through trade-union organization; to create a pub-
> lic opinion which really understands the labor movement; [and]
> to further the enactment of such legislation as will benefit the
> workers.[41]

Although activity in an organization of this nature led Mrs.
Roosevelt to occasional forthright statements in behalf of the laborer — she lashed out, for example, at New York's Governor
Nathan Miller for his alleged "cynical indifference to the perils
of long working hours for women and children" [42] — her initial
well-publicized campaign for unionization of a particular group
did not occur until 1930. In that year she made the first of her
many proposals for the unionization of domestic servants, a project she dropped only when World War II rendered the practice
of hiring domestic help virtually obsolete in America.[43]

By the time she became First Lady, however, Mrs. Roosevelt
was prepared to advocate unionism on a broader scale. During
her husband's first presidential term she began her exhortations
to the women of America to buy only such goods as bore a
"union-made" label. Many labor organizations, well aware of
the immense propaganda value of the First Lady's efforts in this
regard, gave prominent space in their bulletins to her endorse-
ments.[44]

An example of Eleanor Roosevelt's pro-union partisanship at
this time can be seen in her attitude toward an establishment in
New York City called Emergency Shelter, Incorporated. Customarily, the First Lady extended to others the benefit of every

doubt, as in the case when the leaders of the American Youth Congress assured her that they had no connection with the Communists and she thereupon "decided to accept their word, realizing that sooner or later the truth would come out." [45] Even in instances where she knew she was being taken advantage of, she nonetheless persisted, if she believed the cause was worthy, in lending it her energetic aid. She once somewhat ruefully reprinted in "My Day" a letter in which a job applicant — who had evidently gotten his envelopes crossed — had written to a friend: "I am trying to get me a PWA job through Mrs. Roosevelt and they are checking up on me so don't say nothing, don't know nothing"; but such examples of chicanery did not deter her from continuing to act as a one-woman employment office for almost everyone who wrote to her. [46] The case of Emergency Shelter was, however, different, and she appears to have immediately gotten the notion that it constituted a threat rather than a potential source of assistance to causes in which she believed. Hence, her attitude became untypically guarded and mistrustful.

What happened was that in late 1933 the Director of Emergency Shelter, Walter D. Britt, wrote the First Lady a flattering and polite note in which he requested any helpful suggestions she might have concerning the Shelter's program:

> Your kindly interest in unemployed girls and women has come to my attention, also your desire to make it possible for them to help themselves during their period of unemployment. Your well-known hand of sympathy has been felt throughout this entire nation, and you have been a blessing to many poor souls with your proposed activities. . . .

Britt then explained that his wife had undertaken a program of help for unemployed women in which they would be "taught the art[s] of lace-making, hooked rugs, various types of tapestries, and needlecraft." In this way it was hoped that women participating in the program could become independent of charity: ". . . those [women] interested will take their work home after instruction, finish same and return it to us to be sold, they to receive all monies earned above the cost of materials." The director concluded his letter by saying that he would welcome "any suggestions you may have in mind in the furtherance of helping unemployed girls and women, and I assure you we would be happy were you to pay us a visit." [47]

Here was a letter, in brief, whose tone and whose ideas — helping women keep off the charity lists, stressing handicrafts, etc. — might have been expected to appeal greatly to Mrs. Roosevelt. Somewhat surprisingly, however, her reaction to it appeared to be one of distinct suspicion. She did not reply directly, but the tenor of her thoughts was conveyed in a letter written by Ellen Woodward, Director of Women's Work for the Federal Emergency Relief Administration. In contrast to the sympathetic note struck by similar missives to others, this one was obviously curt: "Mrs. Roosevelt has referred me to your letter of November 4. We are very much concerned . . . All such projects are the responsibility of the [FERA] State Administrator and it would be wise for you to communicate with [him]. . . ." [48] To the State Administrator himself Miss Woodward wrote at the same time: "The [enclosed copy of a] letter from Mr. Britt was forwarded to us by Mrs. Roosevelt, who suggested that this project might be in competition with labor and it might involve sweatshop work and she suggested that it might bear looking into." [49]

From this correspondence it seems plain that Mrs. Roosevelt did not apply the same standards to private programs devised by others that she applied to those who wrote to her directly asking for jobs. To the latter she appeared invariably anxious to please; her lack of distrust in such cases being demonstrated by the fact

that of those applications for jobs examined by this writer for
which she gave a positive recommendation to FERA, over thirty-
five percent were fraudulent; that is, the applicant was found not
to be in need of work.* By the same token, she showed no disposition to oppose government-sponsored competition to private
business, as exemplified by her proposal for the authorization of a
contract to manufacture supplies at Arthurdale for the United
States Post Office. Contrariwise, even at the bottom of the Depression Mrs. Roosevelt's pro-union and pro-government leanings caused her to react unfavorably to an enterprise which she
felt might compete with union labor or the activities of a government agency.†

The First Lady, however, by no means confined her pro-labor
sentiments to the eyes and ears of government friends, such as
was the case in the Britt matter. She wished to create a more

* As further evidence of the First Lady's zeal to procure a government job
for virtually anyone who appeared to need it without first checking into the
applicant's ability, Alfred Steinberg indulgently relates the story of one man
who, after conversing with Mrs. Roosevelt, was recommended by her to the
Post Office Department. The man, it turned out, was insane. By means of a
further investigation to account for such an occurrence it was found that the
individual had first approached Representative Florence P. Kahn, Republican of
California. Congresswoman Kahn later explained that she "thought he was insane, but the only way I could get rid of him was to send him to Mrs. Roosevelt." Alfred Steinberg, *Mrs. R* (New York, G. P. Putnam's Sons, 1958), p. 219.

† Mrs. Roosevelt's misgivings concerning an establishment such as Emergency
Shelter, Inc., might have seemed somewhat farfetched to her had she taken the
time to check its reputation in a manner similar to what she claimed to have
done with other entities to which she lent her assistance. Consultant Rolfe Andersen of that organization, while admitting to a personal dislike of Britt (since
deceased), told this writer that Emergency Shelter was the only private charitable corporation in the Bowery with sufficient funds to feed those desperate
enough to seek its aid during the early years of the Depression. Andersen further unqualifiedly maintained that no hint of anything like the suspicions Mrs.
Roosevelt harbored had ever been connected with Britt, and seemed genuinely
shocked that she might have felt as she did. Interview with Rolfe Andersen,
Emergency Shelter, Inc., 69 St. Mark's Place, New York City, May 15, 1965.

It is interesting to note that the 1933 letterhead of the organization bore the
names of such sponsors as Robert W. Morgan of the New York Stock Exchange, Albert H. Watson of the New York Cotton Exchange, General J. Leslie Kincaid, and other luminaries, names that, given Mrs. Roosevelt's outlook,
were not calculated to lessen her sense of distrust.

hospitable climate for labor on a national scale, and to further this objective she once again relied heavily upon her newspaper column. She tried earnestly to be fair in some of these articles dealing with business-labor controversies; although this displayed her good will, it could not really conceal her bias. She at times pleaded the case for unionization with a superbly simple dignity and truth — such instances presented the First Lady at her most straightforward and conscientious best. Citing the example of six young girls who were unemployed, probably because they belonged to a union, she wrote:

> Their demands are not such unreasonable ones — a wage which will make it possible to live in New York City, perhaps even enough to contribute two or three dollars a week to help the families at home or with whom they live, a forty hour week, a definite period of notice before lay-offs take place and the eradication of a number of other conditions which would probably right themselves with these three basic things settled.[50]

Mrs. Roosevelt appeared also to realize that some cases were not of a "black versus white" character. In commenting about a letter she had received from a skilled mechanic who was much upset because the union was trying to interfere with work he obtained as an independent operator, she made clear that the blame for this situation rested in her opinion more with the vexations of modern society than with any individual or group: "I believe so strongly in unions and their value as a protection to the workers," she declared, "and yet, in these individual cases, I have a sympathy, too, for the man who is caught at the point of change between two philosophies. . . . the pioneer philosophy and the philosophy of machine civilization." Adhering as she did to so much of what she believed was represented by the former, the First Lady was yet compelled to recognize the necessities, such as unionization, demanded by the latter. Her perplexity was therefore often evident when she was forced to make a choice between the implications of the two. She proposed no "spot solutions," having instead to seek refuge in such phrases as "Why can't we sit down together with a board of arbitration, honestly state our difficulties, and try to work out a sane method of procedure?" or, "all we can do is to . . . try to solve our problems by better co-operation." [51]

Still, Mrs. Roosevelt on occasion seemed to maintain a "defensive" attitude about unionism, employing a *tibi quoque est culpa* rationale when alleged mistakes of unions reached her attention. Thus, in noting an article in which an industrialist had asked for more "cooperation" in labor-management relations, the First Lady stated that this was something "that comparatively few of the business men of today have thought through, so one cannot blame labor if it has not done so, either." Then too, there occasionally crept into Mrs. Roosevelt's stand on behalf of labor the melancholy notion that the liberal, pro-union side represented all that was virtuous while the opposition was the incarnation of greed and selfishness. In this vein were her comments on a letter from a woman irate about the tactics of the "sit-down" strikers in Michigan:

> The writer is a woman and I searched my files to find if this same woman had written me any protest on the matter of intimidation of labor by spies . . . .
> On this subject the lady has been silent so far as I can discover, so I must decide that, for her, property rights are all important. Human rights mean so little . . . . A strange feeling for a woman.[52]

The subconscious mental process by which Mrs. Roosevelt reached the above opinion seemed to be something like the following: (1) this correspondent has written me a letter condemning what she regards as the illegal violation of property rights by strikers; (2) I shall not take cognizance of that allegation; (3) I shall instead infer that because she had not troubled to write me about company spies she does not object to company spies; (4) this implies on my correspondent's part a double standard — that is wrong; (5) it also implies that she is not interested in human rights — that is "strange" and, inferentially, wicked.

This logic — or lack of it — typified many of Mrs. Roosevelt's pronouncements and showed her at her muddled and disingenuous worst. Her comments were (1) evasive — because they did not deal with the correspondent's complaint; (2) unfair — because they imputed something about the correspondent not warranted by the evidence; (3) hypocritical — because they employed a *prima facie* double standard, a procedure they had already unfairly implied about someone else; (4) arrogant — because they clothed themselves in a moral and philosophical righteousness which was, essentially, artificial and not germane to the facts.

Despite these written evidences of strong pro-labor leanings, Mrs. Roosevelt, in her actions, tried to cultivate among those who followed her activities the fanciful impression that she was scrupulously neutral in disputes where unions and management were involved. The device she adopted, that of not crossing a picket line, appeared somewhat mysterious as an aid to furthering a posture of nonpartisanship; moreover, in at least one case of a strike, she actively intervened in behalf of the workers.

The dispute in which Mrs. Roosevelt took a hand in March, 1940, concerned the Aunt Martha's Box Lunch Service, a small enterprise which supplied box lunches to customers in the New York City area. The First Lady had met several of Aunt Martha's delivery boys at a Youth Congress convention; they told her they were making an average of only twenty-three cents per day and were planning to strike for a daily wage of one dollar. Mrs. Roosevelt thereupon wrote the Soda Fountain and Luncheonette Employees Union, of which the boys were members, and indicated her interest: "From what I know of conditions under which they work, I feel they need the protection your organization can give them." She expressed the hope that some arrangement might be worked out whereby the strike would be settled and the boys enabled to earn a living wage.[53]

Eleanor Roosevelt thus acted instinctively, as was her wont whenever she was confronted by a touching story. It is also to be noted, however, that she entered the controversy after having heard only one side of it. Charles J. Corbetoff, owner of Aunt Martha's, subsequently claimed that his delivery boys in fact made over one dollar per day if their earnings in tips were included. He further stated that he was unable at that time to increase his pay rates without bankrupting his business, and produced his books in order to show this.[54] That Mrs. Roosevelt herself had some second thoughts on the matter, that she seemed to realize that Mr. Corbetoff might not be able to meet the strikers' demands, can be inferred from her own words:

> [Recently] I had a rather pathetic experience. The poor little couple who run Aunt Martha's Box Lunch Service, felt I had harmed their business and asked to be allowed to tell me their side of the controversy with the lunch box boys. Mrs. Corbetoff was voluble, Mr. Corbetoff was silent, but it was quite evident that they needed a mediator with plenty of time to verify the statements made by all sides, to look over their business and give them sound advice and a little courage. He must see too, that the boys get a fair break, so they will have enough interest really to build up the business. I left them feeling very sorry for everyone concerned . . . .[55]

This bland account illustrated very clearly the First Lady's predisposition toward labor. She had plunged in full tilt on the side of the striking boys and had lent the prestige of her name to their cause. Only later did Mrs. Roosevelt adopt the use of such phrases as "be allowed to tell me their side of the controversy," and "a mediator with plenty of time to verify the statements made by all sides." The introduction of the term "mediator" and the notion that he might "look over their business and give them sound advice" were concepts employed by Mrs. Roosevelt *after* she had in effect already demonstrated her partisanship by her letter to the union. It wasn't that Mrs. Roosevelt did not want to be generous to both sides; it was that she so often acted impetuously on behalf of only one when her prejudices were aroused. It was not that she did not wish to be genuinely fair; frequently, however, her biases kept her from being so.

~

The First Lady's concern with the plight of the worker was also sharply evident in areas other than those of the private sector of the economy. She was particularly enthusiastic in her support of various government agencies whose tasks were centered upon alleviating unemployment. In addition to her interest in the CCC, the NYA, FERA and Subsistence Homesteads, she devoted much of her efforts to propagandizing the virtues of the Works Progress Administration (WPA). While her column lavished praise on the latter agency in general terms — citing its personnel, its exhibits, its accomplishments in the field of construction, and the spirit of hope it seemed to infuse all over the country[56] — Mrs. Roosevelt developed a special interest in those of its branches that affected the arts.

Eleanor Roosevelt's artistic tastes were in the main traditional; they appear to have been a product both of her wide acquaintance with the classics and the Victorian atmosphere in which she was raised. As a young woman, such influences tended to narrow her attitude concerning anything of an artistic nature which bordered on the "modern" and therefore possibly on the risqué. "I am reading a . . . book by Anatole France," she wrote her mother-in-law while on her honeymoon, "but he occasionally disgusts me so that I have to stop, and yet it is a mild and proper book for the French. . . ." [57]

Even much later her own literary preferences contained a noticeable aura of the conventional. She always numbered David Grayson's *Adventures in Solitude* and *The Countryman's Year* and Edna Ferber's *Nobody's in Town* among her favorite works of prose; in the field of poetry she was partial to the epic, especially Stephen Vincent Benét's *John Brown's Body*. The play with which she was happiest was *Claudia*, a rather emotional drama by Rose Franken. On the other hand, in one of the very few adverse notices she ever publicly gave an artistic venture, Mrs. Roosevelt professed disappointment with Clare Boothe's *The Women*. This production had left the First Lady with an "unpleasant impression," and she hoped that Miss Boothe would some day write a play "about real people and the cleverness will not be just superficial turns of word and phrase, but there will be depth and meaning and understanding." [58]

As to music, which one gains the impression she enjoyed without having any deep emotional attachment to it, she preferred Chopin. Bach, because "I always feel that he belonged to a life very different from the one we lead now. . . . leaves me dissatisfied." Of painting and sculpture she also said little; she did dutifully note her appreciation of Michelangelo, albeit with the somewhat obscure comment that he exemplified "a great soul [who] may go down to the depths, but . . . can also soar to the heights." [59]

Eleanor Roosevelt thus appeared to retain a substantial residue of the "message" approach to artistic judgment. She seemed to value artistic works not so much for themselves or for their innate merit, but because of the sentiment they inspired. This concept had been the norm in her youth, and she never completely abandoned it.

Personal experience and a variety of contacts, however, broadened Mrs. Roosevelt's area of artistic appreciation perceptibly. Two decades after her prudish reaction to Anatole France, she gratefully acknowledged a present from a friend: "I love [Baudelaire's] 'Les Fleurs du Mal' and a thousand thanks. . . ." Similarly, in the 1930's, expressing pleasure over the fact that New York's Governor Herbert Lehman had vetoed a bill which would have subjected certain plays to censorship in his state, she declared: "No one can quarrel with those who 'desire to maintain the theatre on a proper moral plane,' but there is too much effort in the world today to regulate too minutely by law the lives and morals of whole groups of people." In a manner much like the one she held regarding youth, she was determined to be open-minded — by the time she was First Lady she apparently felt, as a close friend put it, "an obligation to encourage the new and experimental." Moreover, in addition to this alteration in her own viewpoint, the spectacle of countless thousands of artists thrown out of work by the Depression seemed to her to mandate furthering the arts for social and humanitarian reasons as well as for personal ones.[60]

Mrs. Roosevelt therefore became a great booster of administration agencies which employed artists. There were four such projects established under the WPA in August, 1935; each concerned, respectively, musicians, dramatists and actors, writers, and painters and sculptors. The First Lady was a zealous propagandist in behalf of all of them: she wrote favorably about and lent her presence to the painters' and writers' projects; she broadcast on radio the virtues of government-sponsored musical programs; she hoped that

perhaps the day will come when artists as a whole — whether they are painters, sculptors, musicians, actors or singers — may look for appreciation and assistance not from individual patrons or foundations which some rich and cultured individual has established, but may actually feel that the Government, which is really the people as a whole, is the place to turn for assistance and understanding.[61]

She seemed particularly pleased by the accomplishments of the Federal Theatre Project. Of Irwin Shaw's *Bury the Dead,* a savagely ironic pacifist play written originally for the New Theatre League, she wrote enthusiastically: ". . . the thoughts hit you like hammer blows . . . a great performance. . . . [It] will long be remembered by anyone who sees it." The entire production reinforced Mrs. Roosevelt's conviction that "there are two great waves of thought and feeling sweeping over us today — one is the desire for peace — the other is the determination that life shall be made more worth living for the masses." [62]

Many of these Federal Theatre productions seemed almost tailored for the First Lady's favorable reception. They were experimental, they were government-sponsored, they provided artists with employment, and their "message" was obvious. Of the "Living Newspaper" drama *One-Third of A Nation* by Arthur Arent, which dealt with slum conditions, evil and malicious capitalistic landlords, and the necessity for government's taking over the housing complex, Mrs. Roosevelt noted that although "some situations [in the play] may not tell the whole story. . . . too much explanation might have weakened the main points. . . . we [sic!] couldn't have shown it more truthfully and dramatically." *

Plays of this persuasion — seldom revolutionary, but pro-New Deal and often vaguely collectivist — were much in fashion during the 1930's. Mrs. Roosevelt praised them highly,

---

* Hallie Flanagan, *Arena* (New York, Duell, Sloan and Pearce, 1940), pp. 155, 222; "My Day," March 4, 1938. The "Living Newspapers" presentations by the Federal Theatre Project were "a series of stark, kaleidoscopic scenes that translated social problems into gripping dramas." See Ray Allen Billington, "Government and the Arts: The WPA Experience," *American Quarterly,* XIII (Winter, 1961), p. 469.

whether they were government-backed or not. Of the International Ladies Garment Workers Union production *Pins and Needles*, for example, she wrote that "no one could be disappointed by this entertainment. I hope," she added, "[that] the last scene, 'We've Just Begun,' is prophetic, for the Labor Stage has none of the restrictions and obstacles which have to be surmounted by other producers." [63]

Aside from propagandizing in behalf of the "underdog," especially the American worker, the First Lady took part in pro-labor activity on a more direct level. In the late 1930's she herself became a member of a union, the American Newspaper Guild, whose main purpose was to improve the working conditions and the pay of newspaper employees. That Mrs. Roosevelt joined such an organization, which consisted of fellow journalists, would have under ordinary circumstances seemed entirely proper. The difficulty in this case was that the Guild, especially the important New York chapter to which she belonged, was allegedly Communist-dominated. In the summer of 1940 her membership began, therefore, to be subject to heavy fire from certain quarters, notably from Westbrook Pegler. The acerbic columnist slapped at Mrs. Roosevelt for supposedly "consorting" with Communists and for her "hypocrisy" in not resigning from the Guild as she had done in the case of the DAR.[64]

There appears in this instance to have been some substance to the allegations of Communist influence in the Guild. Hugh T. Lovin is convinced such influence existed, citing especially the powerful role of party-liner Milton Kaufman, who was executive secretary of the New York chapter. Bess Furman Armstrong, herself a working journalist and an intimate of Mrs. Roosevelt's, told this writer in unequivocal terms that there were a number of Communists active in the Guild at that time. Even the First Lady obliquely admitted that there was something to the charge. She would not resign from the organization, she declared, but she "meant hereafter to take an active part in guild affairs and to do what she could to see that it is conducted in accordance with its avowed purpose and not to forward any 'party line.' " [65]

Nor was her membership in the Newspaper Guild the only undertaking relative to American labor in which Eleanor Roosevelt's identification with leftist causes became the target of hostility. She had over the years taken a marked interest in education; and certain of her theories in this field were, as has been noted, somewhat unconventional. She appears always to have been attracted by cloudy humanitarian rhetoric like that which accompanied such experiments as Black Mountain College, an institution whose mission, according to its literature, aimed at turning out a type of individual

> who will know and *feel* that life is essentially not competitive but calls for co-operation everywhere, and that, lest humanity perish, men must cease spending most of their energy scheming how to harm one another and begin looking toward a goal, toward something they wish to become and make of this world.

The First Lady, evidently much impressed by this manifesto, called it "one of the best statements I have ever seen on the aims of education," and added that though she knew nothing about Black Mountain College, ". . . if any type of education can give its students a real understanding such as this, we will have made a stride in solving the problems of the present day, which, so far, our education does not seem to fit us to do." [66]

This bent for educational novelty, particularly if the novelty's purpose were couched in expressions of hazy goodwill, disposed Mrs. Roosevelt to view favorably programs concerned with "workers' education." Such projects, she believed, were "particularly vital" in order that "the workers . . . have an opportunity to study the labor movement and the economic problems of the day." She generously lent encouragement to all such endeavors, from praising the "bright and intelligent faces" of the young teachers in WPA worker education camps to speaking in behalf of the Communist-tinged Pioneer Youth Organization, which she described as "a trade union organization looking towards the development of children of the workers." [67]

Among the many enterprises of this kind to which Mrs. Roosevelt gave her support was, for example, an institution which called itself the Highlander Folk School. Located in the mountainous eastern region of the state of Tennessee, the school was founded in November, 1932, its purposes being to train workers for cooperative rather than competitive life and "to prepare rural and industrial leaders for a new social order." It also helped in union recruitment in the area, organizing WPA workers into locals of the Workers' Alliance, the latter a powerful union of the unemployed led by David Lasser. Highlander's curriculum featured short intensive courses in such subjects as labor history, economics, workers' problems, and strike tactics.[68]

There is a kind of dated charm in the school's activities if the institution's newspaper, *The Highlander Fling*, can be relied upon. "Singing of labor songs after supper was part of the daily program," that organ informed its readers, and among the theatrical projects were creations such as " 'Stretchout,' a product of the students' collective action in drama class." The *Fling* added gratefully that "reports from the Amalgamated [Clothing Workers] leaders are that several new members joined up as a result of the meeting and program that night." The staff members were openly on record as opposing capitalism and substituting a worker-run society.[69]

Beginning in 1937 Eleanor Roosevelt, without checking on the aims or personnel of the school, had donated one hundred dollars annually to Highlander "to be used as a scholarship for some deserving member of the Southern labor movement." This impetuous gesture, especially after the signing of the Nazi-Soviet pact in 1939, brought about a host of complaints about the First Lady's conduct. As a rule, unfriendly comment was directed toward the totality of Mrs. Roosevelt's support of leftist movements rather than her contributions to the Highlander enterprise alone. Her patronage of the American Youth Congress, for example, was often also unfavorably mentioned. Then, too, she was criticized for sending a personal check to Alan Shaw, secretary of the Oklahoma City local of the Communist Party, for the purpose of aiding Oklahoma Communist Robert Wood, at that time (autumn, 1940) appealing a ten-year sentence for advocating the violent overthrow of the U.S. Government.[70]

As was often the case, Mrs. Roosevelt's misguided beneficence toward left-wing causes evoked a strong hue and cry from equally myopic elements of the political right. Joseph Kamp, who possessed an unenviable record of supporting bigoted causes in the guise of patriotism, was quick to raise the specter of the First Lady's participation in what he termed "The Fifth Column in the South." More balanced criticism, however, also appeared, as exemplified by a worried Oklahoma citizen who, in citing evidences of Mrs. Roosevelt's misled zeal, urged the President "for God's sake" to "stamp out the Bund, the Nazis, [and] the Communists." [71]

The First Lady was, in any case, forced to take notice of this hostility; and in September, 1940, her secretary wrote to Hilda W. Smith: "Will you tell Mrs. Roosevelt what you know about the Highlander Folk School. . . . Mrs. Roosevelt gave them some money and has since received many complaints about their activities. Are any of the instructors Communists?" Miss Smith, a WPA specialist in Workers' Education, returned an effusive letter of recommendation for the school; notwithstanding, expressions of discontent continued. Mrs. Roosevelt eventually held a conference with a school official, James Dombrowski, in late 1941; opposition to Communism had somewhat diminished by then due to the Nazi invasion of Russia the previous summer, and Mrs. Roosevelt was apparently satisfied with what Dombrowski told her.[72] She did, however, refuse further aid to the Oklahoma Communist group, although her reasons for doing so were extraneous to the fact that its members were Communists.[73] Eleanor Roosevelt apparently was still reluctant to face the harsh realities of Communist objectives.

Face them, however, she was increasingly forced to do. Events necessitated such a confrontation. The myths of the Popular Front approach, which centered upon assertions that the Soviet system was a kind of social-democratic experiment and that Russia and the western democracies were proceeding toward goals essentially not incompatible, had been subject to severe stresses all through the latter 1930's. The purges, the Russo-German peace pact, and the Soviet invasion of Finland had, each in its respective turn, opened the eyes of large numbers of European and American liberals to the actualities of Communist practices. Mrs. Roosevelt, distinctly a member of this once hopeful liberal coterie, perhaps retained her illusions about Communism longer than many of her like-minded friends. Fascism abroad and hard-core pockets of reaction at home reinforced her predilection to view events in terms of black and white, good and evil. The frightening successes of the Nazi war machine, however, with which the Soviet Union was at that time still allied, forced her to reappraise her attitude of tolerance toward all left-wing movements and to reexamine her previous notions that such movements represented, ultimately, the side of the angels. And, in negotiating this change of outlook, the First Lady would shape for herself an almost entirely new set of concepts regarding the United States and international developments as well.

~

For many years before the rise of the Axis menace Eleanor Roosevelt was inclined toward pacifism. The word "inclined" must be stressed, for though in the early 1930's she was an adamant believer in the campaign to abolish military toys for children, and though in 1935 she was condemned by Mrs. O. D. Oliphant, past National President of the American Legion Auxiliary, as the country's "Number One Pacifist," she never adhered to the dogmatic belief that there could exist no conceivable circumstance which would render fighting a necessary and just course.[74] Rather, she bent her energies in the direction of support for reason and understanding in international problems, and for arbitration whenever and wherever it could be applied. As early as the mid-1920's she urged women to back United States membership in the World Court. "This should be a crusade," she declared. "Cannot the women rise to their great opportunity and work now, and not have the double horror, if another war comes, of losing their loved ones, and knowing that they lifted no fingers when they might have worked hard?" [75]

Mrs. Roosevelt had a genuine horror of war. "Another war such as the World War," she believed, "could certainly eventually cause the wiping out of our civilization." The central problem of her time appeared, accordingly, to be the achievement of a peaceful world. This could only come about, she contended, if mankind embraced the teaching, "Love thy neighbor as thyself." Christ, the great Jewish teachers, and Buddha "all preached it. Their followers forgot it." Thus, lasting peace could best be secured by a revolution in the hearts and minds of men:

> . . . I think too little stress is laid on the preparedness of thought for a future for real peace. . . . The first requisite for bringing about peace is a state of mind, when people are thoroughly convinced that international difficulties are not settled by force, they will put their full weight into having difficulties settled by reason. Then we will have peace.[76]

These concepts were not at variance with the Wilsonian heritage absorbed by many members of both political parties who had served under the twenty-eighth President during the World War. Peace was God's way; war His antithesis. Man could follow the one and renounce the other by an inner spiritual and moral change. Mechanisms could then be established wherein reason prevailed. Such, in brief, was Wilson's great rationale for bringing peace and understanding between nations. Mrs. Roosevelt, in essence, did not deviate from it.

Further, it had been President Wilson's view that the United States, in its own institutions, had shown more progress than had other nations toward the realization of these goals. Hence, it was this country's duty to lead the rest of the world to a similar appreciation of the values of persuasion and negotiation, reason and compromise. With this formula Eleanor Roosevelt was also as one with Wilson. She never abandoned an internationalist, as opposed to an isolationist, outlook. Unlike her husband, who curtailed his Wilsonianism in exchange for the votes controlled by the journalist Hearst at the 1932 Democratic convention and who during his early presidential years took comparatively slight interest in European diplomatic complexities, the First Lady retained a commendable sense of the necessity for U.S. leadership in world affairs. "You may not care what happens in Europe or Asia," she told an audience during the height of the isolationist mania in 1935, "but you feel here at home the result of anything which happens in other parts of the world. . . ." And, again, in the same year: "It is a fallacy to consider that we are really isolated from the rest of the world." John Gunther suggests that Mrs. Roosevelt was worried about FDR's lack of concern with international events; early in his first term she asked Anne O'Hare McCormick to a White House dinner and requested the latter to "try to get the President more interested in foreign affairs." [77]

Certainly, the First Lady was discomfited by administration policy regarding the Spanish Civil War in the late 1930's. "Like most liberal Americans," notes her friend Joseph Lash, Mrs. Roosevelt's sympathies "had been passionately engaged upon the Loyalist side" of that conflict. She praised the Loyalist legions as representing "a democratic form of government"; she loved to hear the "Six Songs of the International Brigade," and for many years kept on her desk "a little bronze figure of a youthful Spanish militia-man in coveralls that was a symbol of the Republican cause." She accepted, in addition, a set of Goya prints inscribed "A Remembrance from the People of Spain" from the Loyalist Ambassador, Señor Ferdinand de los Ríos. Publicly, she expressed relief when hostilities in that unhappy country ceased; despite the victory of the Falangist forces, she was glad the bloodletting was over. Privately, however, her gestures indicated distinct disapproval of her husband's past acquiescence in a course of nonintervention. She had tried to prod him into overt measures with respect to certain events during the struggle, as when she telegraphed: "JUST RECEIVED WIRE SIGNED EINSTEIN, DOROTHY THOMPSON, ETC., ABOUT IMPORTANT LEADERS TRAPPED IN MADRID. ARE YOU OR STATE DEPARTMENT DOING ANYTHING?" She reportedly told Leon Henderson in FDR's presence: "You and I, Mr. Henderson, will some day learn a lesson from this tragic error over Spain. We [the pro-Loyalist contingent within the administration] were morally right, but too weak." Then turning in the direction of the President, she emphatically stated: "We should have pushed *him* harder." [78]

It will be noticed that Mrs. Roosevelt's desire for some sort of U.S. aid to Loyalist Spain did not comport exactly with a posture ostensibly pacifistic. The Spanish Civil War, however, was possibly the last struggle in recent times which could be regarded by many observers in the western democracies as a clear-cut conflict between the forces of freedom and those of totalitarianism. That such a viewpoint contained numerous oversimplifications and distortions does not alter the fact that contemporaries did indeed consider the Spanish upheaval as, basically, an encounter between good and evil. It was so looked upon by the First Lady. A cause which seemed so uncomplicatedly right apparently overcame her sincere compunction as to the inherent risks in the country's taking sides with respect to it.

This metamorphosis in Mrs. Roosevelt's thought had not taken place without a good deal of soul-searching. Even considering her attachment to the Loyalist position, she had not recommended active U.S. aid in its behalf until 1939, almost three years after the conflagration had originally begun. In 1936, her approach to problems of foreign policy in general continued to stress the awesome human costs of war and the advisability of employing reason and negotiation to nullify the possibility of military conflict. She explained her attitude in this respect as it related to the ominous moves of Nazi Germany:

> I have always felt that in a tense situation, if time could be given for everyone to discuss what was going on before they actually went to war, we might come to our senses. Most of us were taught as children to count to thirty before we opened our mouths when we were angry, and that same lesson should apply to nations.
>
> No one denies that the Versailles Treaty was unjust in many ways and that revisions should be made. It is quite evident, however, that Germany has ignored the agreements under the Locarno Pacts, but it seems more profitable to talk this over than to fight it out. . . .[79]

The following year she echoed these sentiments, reiterating her conviction that men would ultimately resort to reason if only they could resist the temptation to act impulsively:

> The news from Europe seemed very distressing last night, but today there seems to be a return to a calmer attitude which will allow everybody to explain the why and wherefore of what seemed to be at first inexplicable occurrences. Like so many

things in life, if we have a little time to think, we are apt to be
calmer. I wish twenty-four hours, a good night's sleep and a day
spent in the open air could always elapse before any government
officials take action on matters of grave importance.[80]

Throughout the summer of 1937 Eleanor Roosevelt continued
to propound her belief in the efficacy of reason and tolerance in
international affairs. Declaring that differences between nations
were "fairly normal and healthy," she claimed that the absence
of arbitration machinery constituted "the real trouble" in the
matter of why the world did not remain at peace. Most nations,
she appeared to feel, were in accord on general objectives; conferences fell apart due to disputes over a lack of procedure and
methods which had been agreed upon. "Temporary expedients"
which attempted to solve international disagreements were
therefore worthless; what the situation obviously called for were
"permanent ways of dealing with troubles." [81]

Nonetheless, it is at about the same time that one begins to
notice a certain hesitancy, a lack of confidence, and a new and
unwelcome note of bewilderment in the First Lady's comments
regarding foreign complexities. She did, it is true, make it quite
clear that her definition of pacifism did not include an uncompromising posture of surrender to force:

> There seems no question to me that being a pacifist means that
> you do not seek a fight, that you use every means in your power
> to prevent a fight, and that this includes giving all the assistance
> you possible [sic] can, short of military assistance, to other na-
> tions which are honestly trying to keep out of war. It also means
> you do not try to impose your opinions on other people nor
> force them to grant you anything they do not wish to grant.
> But if war comes to your own country, then even pacifists, it
> seems to me, must stand up and fight for their beliefs.[82]

But this statement was, at the same time, somewhat perplexing.
It seemed to suggest that the First Lady would limit any United

States commitment of an international nature to a kind of moral support, or perhaps to an offer of good offices for the purpose of mediation. It did not include as a necessity material aid, even short of military assistance, because any commitment was to be confined solely to other nations which were at peace. Moreover, it implicitly went far in the direction of complete appeasement; not only should a country's policy not ". . . try to impose [its] opinions on other people," but also it should not "force them to grant . . . anything they do not wish to grant." Carried to their logical conclusions, it is difficult to see how such sentiments could render any nation which held them much more than an international cipher.

It appears safe to surmise, however, that Mrs. Roosevelt did not really intend that her statements embrace appeasement. Her rhetoric can quite as easily be interpreted as merely the residue of past emphasis upon accommodation, international leadership in trying to find methods to keep the peace, and a general tolerance of the aspirations of others. Of primary importance, really, was her explicit admission that overt force might, in certain cases, have to be utilized. Whether abject passivity under any circumstances had ever been a genuine part of her philosophical equipage is questionable; be that as it may, she had by the summer of 1937 consciously rejected it.

Events of the succeeding twelve months seem to have further toppled Eleanor Roosevelt's former sense of optimism concerning man's essential rationality. The *Anschluss* in Austria, the increasing barbarism which accompanied the fighting in Spain, and the Japanese rape of Nanking deeply depressed her. Absent by 1938 were her once-customary declarations of faith in the mechanism of arbitration, in the motives of national statesmen, in the capacity of humankind to solve their problems by reason and good will. She felt "positively disgusted with human beings" who were "such fools as to go on senselessly taking human life."

Why the women in every nation, she lamented, "do not rise up and refuse to bring children into a world of this kind is beyond my understanding." Planning, she inferred, was useless: ". . . trying to project ourselves too far in the future is a rather unprofitable business. We might better deal . . . with situations as they are at the moment and leave the future to look after itself." If she were living in certain foreign nations, she concluded, "I think I would develop the philosophy of Omar Khayyam and live for the day and its pleasures." [83]

Eleanor Roosevelt's concern was, as always, first and foremost with the tragic human ramifications of war. The incredible deprivations suffered by children as a result of military holocaust caused her severe anguish. It made no difference which side was in the wrong: "the children are not responsible." Just as this country had fed the youth of every nationality during World War I, the First Lady hoped that "we will feed, clothe and educate any children who need it at the present time." She "adopted" (in the sense of becoming responsible for their physical needs) war-orphaned Spanish and Finnish children; she headed the Advisory Committee of the (Jewish) Youth Aliyah, and sponsored the Paderewski Fund for Polish Relief; she urged that Americans should "facilitate in every way" the reception of refugee children from England.[84]

Feeling as strongly as she did about children uprooted and stricken by the ravages of war, Mrs. Roosevelt put aside all political considerations by proposing that Herbert Hoover, who had been in charge of European relief programs during and after the First World War, be named coordinator of a similar understaking in the Second. This suggestion of Hoover's appointment to high position was in contrast to the attitude of her husband who, according to Raymond Moley, feared that "only Hoover among the notables of the Republican Party possessed the massive convictions and intelligence to provide an alternative to the New

Deal," and for that reason refrained from asking him to serve in any public capacity. Whatever the case may have been, Mrs. Roosevelt's suggestions came to nothing; and the ex-President formed, as he had done a generation earlier, his own private organization to help deal with European famine and displacement.[85]

The First Lady's area of concern extended to adult refugees as well; here again she did yeoman work in attempting to open the gates of U.S. hospitality to those whose position rendered their continued European residence dangerous. She exerted her influence in behalf of the transportation to America of Socialist leaders stranded in Europe; when the President, who seemed "somewhat impatient over the request," balked, she nonetheless pressed her case to a successful conclusion. Karl Frank (Paul Hagen), who had been active in the German Socialist underground against Hitler, was later able to write her a grateful letter concerning the friendly support of the State Department: "I know it is due to your interest." So, too, she tried earnestly to have citizenship papers granted to former Loyalist fighter Gustav Regler; and although she was unable to accomplish getting Regler into this country, her influence was decisive in the matter of persuading the Soviet Union to release to the United States the wife and sons of writer Louis Fischer.[86]

Much of Mrs. Roosevelt's help to refugees took place, of course, after the outbreak of European hostilities. Before that event became an actuality, however, the First Lady had tried, despite her growing pessimism with respect to the European situation, to retain a vestige of faith in the possibility of a peaceful outcome to European tensions. Most people tend, as in the cases of close personal contacts and treasured material objects, to cling to convictions built up and cherished over a great many years. Eleanor Roosevelt was no exception to this. Wherever a gleam of hope appeared across the dark international waters, the First

Lady made fast in its direction. Although unhappy about the fate of Czechoslovakia, she nonetheless considered that the English Prime Minister, Neville Chamberlain, had done "a fine thing" in seeking to negotiate with Hitler. In the spring of 1939, she believed that the entire foreign milieu was "becoming much less tense"; by August of that year she was even beginning to piece together some of the shattered fragments of her confidence in long-range planning, negotiation, and tolerance:

> . . . no one goes beyond the immediate necessity and talks about the final elimination of the difficulties which have thrust the various powers into their present situation.
>
> Why can't we get around a table and face the fact that Germany and Italy have started this whole performance because it was the only way in which their people could exist? It hasn't been a very good existence and I don't imagine the German and Italian people look forward to war any more than we do, but desperation is desperation wherever you find it. . . .[87]

The remnants of Mrs. Roosevelt's faith in a peaceful solution to the international dilemma were, of course, wiped away soon after she wrote the above. Although subsequent to the Nazi invasion of Poland she expressed the conventional wish that the United States might stay out of the conflict, her own mental struggles over the question of when and if the use of national force was necessary and proper were all but over. She was henceforth to become increasingly militant.

While it is true that Mrs. Roosevelt had debated earnestly with herself the complicated moral questions which the use of military force involved, and while it had been, as she put it, "very difficult for me to think this situation through," [88] her growing belief in the necessity of giving all possible assistance to the Allied powers was not, after the outbreak of the war, as sudden as it might at first have appeared. Her devotion to the cause of Republican Spain had, after all, eventually led her to a point where she was convinced that America should forswear its posture of neutrality with respect to the struggle there. By a similar process of reasoning she became certain, early in 1939, that her country must oppose Hitler and Mussolini. Detachment, in her opinion, was simply no longer possible. "Let us," she wrote, "examine our present situation. We are the leading democracy of the world. Do our sympathies lie with the other democracies or do they lie with the totalitarian states?" Moral opposition to the Fascist nations and a concomitant sympathy for the democracies were, moreover, not enough:

> People awaken rather slowly to the appeal of the Oxford Movement or to any other type of spiritual awakening which would bring about moral rearmament. The danger today seems to lie in certain very definite places where this appeal makes slower headway than anywhere else. So, when I say that it cannot stand alone, I mean that much as we may dislike to do it, it may be necessary to use the forces of this world in the hope of keeping civilization going until spiritual forces gain sufficient strength . . . .[89]

The First Lady seemed to be well aware that her audience included substantial numbers of Americans who were wedded to the idea of nonintervention. Thus, more and more, she assumed her husband's view; namely, that peace could best be preserved through strength. She scorned those who opposed administration attempts to end neutrality legislation as "aiding and abetting" the position of the totalitarian nations; the United States, she believed, must take a stand. "If war comes as a result we must endure it, but we do not want it and in standing for what we believe is right, we are doing what we can to preserve peace and justice in the world." She actively opposed the Ludlow Amendment, which called for a national referendum before this country could go to war, commenting that although "neutrality might be safe, I am not sure that it is always right to be safe." [90]

Once the European war began, Mrs. Roosevelt stepped up her exhortations for U.S. aid to the democracies. Her position in the early months of the conflict was that the United States was justified in refraining from overt participation since Americans could then "throw our weight as best we can toward a speedy termination" of the struggle. That "weight," however, would count for nothing if the Allies were thoroughly defeated. "Hundreds of thousands of men, women and children are dying," she pointed out. "Are we going to think only of our skins and our own pockets? We have a right to stay at peace, only if by doing so we render a greater service to a war-torn world." By April, 1940, although she guardedly saw "no reason for entering the war — as yet," she soon thereafter totally renounced all hope of "sweet reasonableness" where Hitler's Germany was concerned. In one of the most remarkably perceptive utterances she ever made, Eleanor Roosevelt summarized her position with respect to the European imbroglio in July, 1940:

> I have a letter today from a young university woman who makes the following suggestion: "If America, instead of pouring all her wealth into armaments and waiting to be attacked, would begin a positive program of relief to all, but no aid to either army, giving repeated promise of technical and material aid to both sides in the event of an equal negotiated peace, if the United States would do this, I believe we would undercut all loyalty to, and power of Hitler before he could endanger our own welfare."
>
> This is the best example of wishful thinking that has come to me in some time, and that is why I am giving it to you today. Many of us would like to feel that this role was possible. It would be, if there was not one strong victorious nation which already has in her power many other weaker nations, and to whom "equal" peace would mean complete control for herself alone.
>
> There never would have been a war if the sweet reasonableness for which most of us have been hoping for [sic] in international affairs had existed. Under the present circumstances, all

that we can hope for is to keep alive in our own nation a desire
to establish this kind of peace on earth, but to realize that a vic-
torious force with a philosophy in back of it such as is preached
in "Mein Kampf" can never be vanquished except by equal
force.[91]

As might have been expected, the First Lady's increasingly pro-
Allied sentiments were received with some animosity in various
quarters. That her opinions were recognized as highly influential was borne out by the fact that certain German newspapers
took strong exception to her line of thought. The Nazi press did
not attempt directly to answer her charges regarding Axis aggression; instead they attacked her on extraneous issues. The
Berliner Nachtausgabe, for example, dredged up the hysterical
allegation that the blockade against Germany during World War
I had killed thousands of women and children and that, since
Mrs. Roosevelt had not opposed the measure, her denunciations
of white outrages against the Negro were hypocritical. Another sheet in the same city, the *Lokal-Anzeiger*, added that she
should confine her attention to U.S. unemployment, child labor
and alleged public immorality.[92]

Mrs. Roosevelt's pronouncements on foreign policy were the
subject of controversy in America as well. One Nevada citizen
rudely wrote her that her views of the Ludlow Amendment
would be different "if you and your kind had to do the fighting." Columnist Dorothy Dunbar Bromley, otherwise well-
disposed toward the activities of the First Lady, felt that the latter, insofar as her growing pro-interventionism was concerned,
was being "less searchingly honest than [she] usually is with herself." Former supporters, such as New York's left-leaning congressman Vito Marcantonio, now vigorously opposed her stand
in behalf of a greater American arms buildup.[93]

Changing political alignments were, of course, very much a
part of the immediate prewar years in the United States. The

issues of aid to the Allies and the possibility of ultimate intervention played havoc with conventional liberal and conservative
groupings. Rightist spokesmen like Charles A. Lindbergh
clasped hands in the cause of nonintervention with liberal leaders
such as Chester Bowles. Prominent pro-administration figures
like Pennsylvania's Democratic Senator Joseph Guffey were glad
to join forces in behalf of a more vigorous stand with nominally
conservative individuals such as disillusioned ex-New Dealer
Lewis Douglas. Eleanor Roosevelt's shifting audience of opposition and support was thus merely the reflection of a widespread
national trend.

The First Lady, it is true, sometimes tried to mollify certain of
her former backers by attempts to assume a nonpartisan pose.
Such, for example, was the case when, after being asked to contribute a chapter to a book on neutrality by such erstwhile followers as John L. Lewis, Norman Thomas, and Democratic
Representative Jerry Voorhis of California, she was responsible
for the preposterous dictum that "while she is in the White
House she does not feel that she can write on international matters." [94] Devices of this kind were so patently absurd, however,
that she soon gave them up.

Mrs. Roosevelt's break with some of her onetime adherents
also had causes less directly related to her stronger pro-Allied
position. Such a stance inferentially required a certain opposition
to the Soviet Union, with whom Germany had signed a non-
aggression pact in August, 1939. Numerous left-wingers, such
as the leaders of the American Youth Congress, opposed aid to
"imperialist" nations like Britain and France. Hence, Mrs. Roosevelt's attitude came to be in open conflict with that which was
held by pro-Russian sympathizers.

Eleanor Roosevelt was greatly disillusioned by Russia's course
of action. She had always harbored doubts about Communism;
as has been pointed out, however, she shared the 1930's-liberal

proclivity to excuse Communist extravagances and misunderstand Soviet aims. As her friend Joseph Lash recalled, ". . . until the Nazi-Soviet pact she had looked upon Russia as a positive force in world affairs, a nation from whom we could learn much." Success of the Soviet experiment, she felt, "would have had a vast influence upon thinking in our country." By late 1939, on the other hand, the actualities of Russian conduct led her to publicly endorse aid to Soviet-invaded Finland; soon afterward, she verbally scored the Russian take-over of Latvia, Lithuania and Estonia. "Power," she believed, had "gone to [Stalin's] head"; Nazism and Communism "amount to the same thing in that they stifle individuality and instead make the individual dependent upon a leader. . . ." [95]

Mrs. Roosevelt accompanied her hostility toward totalitarian "isms" by a simultaneous advocacy of greater democratic reform in America. National defense of a military nature, she urged, must not be used "as an excuse to enable us to ignore the equally vital national defense of having people devoted to democracy and feeling that democracy meets their need[s]." She did not spell out in detail what reforms she believed necessary except to state that they should aim unmistakably in the direction of "a minimum standard of security" for democracy's citizens and "an economic level below which no one is permitted to fall." So strong were her exhortations for "more democracy" that one gains the impression she was almost trying to soothe her own conscience in order to ease what might have been a still not altogether comfortable posture of militance in international affairs. "Wake up every one of you," she ejaculated, "to the two fronts on which our defense must be built!" Outbursts of this kind indicate that the First Lady may have found it easier to adapt herself to an essentially uncongenial air of martiality by simultaneously trumpeting with renewed vigor the familiar choruses of domestic liberal reform. [96]

Certainly her grandiose visions, perhaps to a degree self-induced, of postwar world conditions render such a theory tenable. She seems to have cultivated the notion that her belief in the risks of war was due, ultimately, to the fact that after the defeat of Hitler a sort of super-New Deal could be ushered in all over the globe. Poverty would be abolished; disarmament would be complete; the Four Freedoms* would become a reality everywhere. She was especially enthusiastic over Harold Laski's *Where Do We Go From Here?* in which the British Socialist called for an end to "the vested interests of privilege" and for a postwar "revolution by consent." These programs comprised part of Professor Laski's "strategy of victory," and they were ones with which the First Lady professed herself in complete accord. She had a difficult time, she complained, explaining such matters to people like Harry Hooker, the President's conservative former law partner who, though he very earnestly favored increased defense measures and Nazi defeat, did not know what Mrs. Roosevelt was talking about when she introduced her social and economic panaceas. "I don't know if he ever will [understand]," she concluded sadly, "for he wants to preserve the economic system. I do too if life can be made better by so doing but I don't care if it has to go because my main object is a better life for all." [97]

~

So it was, really, with all the problems to which Eleanor Roosevelt addressed her manifold energies. "A better life for all" remained the objective from which she never deviated.

* Freedom of speech and expression, freedom of every person to worship God in his own way, freedom from want, and freedom from fear. President Roosevelt called for these freedoms in his annual message to Congress, Jan. 6, 1941. See Edgar Eugene Robinson, *The Roosevelt Leadership 1933-1945* (Philadelphia and New York, J. B. Lippincott Co., 1955), pp. 267-68.

Sometimes, in the pursuit of aims which she believed productive of this goal, a certain self-righteousness led her to be
guilty of unfair tactics; she was never, insofar as this writer is
aware, consciously cruel or mean. When her benign intentions came to grief, it was most often due to ignorance, an ignorance which was emphasized by her impulsive generosity.
Though she constantly exhorted others to "think things
through," she rarely followed her own advice in this regard.
Thus, an effectively recited sob story immediately moved her
to an attempt, by the most direct means possible, to eliminate
the causes of her petitioner's distress. Often, particularly
where individual cases were concerned, Mrs. Roosevelt's
efforts were successful; on the other hand, when the issue
claiming her attention was more complicated and the First
Lady continued to view it in simplistic terms, her zeal frequently resulted as much in confusion and obfuscation as it
did in gaining a logical and coherent solution.

Mrs. Roosevelt's preachments and her actions reflected a
fundamental lack of appreciation for the necessity of hard,
sustained study of complex issues. Impatient of subtleties, she
reduced intricate problems to "blacks" and "whites," and in
so doing, often radically distorted them. Since, however, she
did think in such uncomplicated terms, and since she was a
genuinely good and kindly woman, it was natural for her to
place herself always, as she saw it, on the side of the forces of
light.

It was in attempting just this that Eleanor Roosevelt became
able to justify a conventionally non-liberal, "tough" international line. By the rationalization that such a posture would
be the means to the ultimate achievement of long-sought, humanitarian ends, she could face the possibility of risking involvement in a war, the accompanying horrors of which were
essentially repugnant to all her instincts. This mental legerde-

main, however, when viewed within the context of her social outlook as a whole, was hardly surprising. Possessed of an uncommon empathy with suffering wherever it existed, Mrs. Roosevelt could not consciously embrace a policy which she knew would entail so much sorrow and pain without the solace that from it would arise a heretofore undreamed-of totality of human happiness. This viewpoint may have been unrealistic; it was not, however, ignoble.

V

REFORMER AT LARGE

REFORMER AT LARGE

Wise and naive, rational and impulsive, determined and
uncertain, compassionate and occasionally misguided. . . .
                    Characterization of Eleanor Roosevelt
                    by her son James.

RESULTS OF A GALLUP POLL taken in early 1939 demonstrated that a substantial majority of American citizens
"approve[d] . . . of the way Mrs. Roosevelt . . . conducted
herself as First Lady." Although the science of poll-taking was
still in a somewhat primitive state, the survey indicated such top-
heavy sentiment in favor of the President's wife that only her
most implacably stubborn and purblind opponents could continue to deny the fact of her popularity. Sixty-seven percent of
those interviewed declared themselves well disposed toward her
activities; this was a figure that exceeded by 9 percent the one
which indicated approval of her husband.[1] In addition, this reservoir of good will appeared to spread itself over the boundaries
of sex, income group and political affiliation. *Fortune Magazine*,
which in May of 1940 conducted a poll and obtained results similar to Gallup's of the year before, suggested that

> . . . Mrs. Roosevelt's incessant goings and comings . . . have
> been accepted as a rather welcome part of the national life.
> Women especially feel this way. But even men betray relatively
> small masculine impatience with the work and opinions of a very
> articulate lady . . . the rich, who generally disapprove of Mrs.

Roosevelt's husband, seem just as friendly toward her as the poor . . . even among those extremely anti-Roosevelt citizens who would regard a third term as a national disaster there is a generous minority . . . who want Mrs. Roosevelt to remain in the public eye.[2]

Reflections of the First Lady's popularity could be seen frequently in the press; although the news media often criticized her stand on specific issues, their overall treatment of her activities ranged from forbearance to distinct sympathy. Perhaps this was only to be expected from such quarters as *The Nation* and *The New Republic* where there was general agreement with her viewpoint. What is surprising, however, is the amount of editorial tribute given her by several of the country's more neutral-oriented journals as well. High circulation magazines, many of which on occasion expressed opposition to the policies of the President were on the whole consistently generous to Mrs. Roosevelt and commented favorably about her peregrinations and her influence. *Newsweek* believed that by 1937 "Eleanor Roosevelt [had] turned into an idol, second only to her husband in popular fancy"; while *Time*, in a 1939 cover story, hailed the First Lady as "the world's foremost female political force . . . a woman of unequaled influence in the world . . . a self-made influence [which] rests upon thousands of small activities. . . ." *

The "thousands of small activities" which *Time* mentioned were in good measure the result of Eleanor Roosevelt's immense energy, a part of her makeup which assumed truly phenomenal proportions. The incredible "busyness" which characterized her activities appears to have stemmed from a multitude of sources, among which were a lively sense of curiosity, a humanitarianism which impulsively responded to virtually any hard luck story,

* In 1940 *The Nation* gave Mrs. Roosevelt the first of its annual awards for "distinguished service in the cause of American social progress." The magazine opinions cited above are from *Newsweek*, X (Oct. 4, 1937), p. 14; and a cover story, "Oracle," in *Time*, XXXIII (April 17, 1939), pp. 21-22.

and a desire for, as she phrased it, "the privilege of being useful." [3] This combination of factors along with a robust constitution, led Mrs. Roosevelt to what sometimes seemed an almost compulsive activism.

Eleanor Roosevelt was herself well aware of the remarkable pace she maintained and often made reference to it. "How do you do all the things you do? If I am asked that question once, I am asked it hundreds of times!" she prefaced one of her radio broadcasts, while her columns were generous in their use of such expressions as "This has been a full day," or "a busy day," and variants thereon. Her readers must have felt that she was a kind of human whirlwind. ". . . I did most of my exercise before breakfast," she informed them on one occasion, "starting with a ride at seven-thirty and a swim afterwards." She did not walk during her daily round of activities, she "dashed." When she was about to embark on one of her countless trips it was with the breathless notation that "I have no idea where I shall be tonight and am not very sure where I shall be tomorrow." If she actually enjoyed a pause in her fantastically active schedule, it was mentioned as "that rare thing for me, an evening of leisure." One of her biographers quotes her as saying, after an impatient wait at a New York hospital while her daughter-in-law gave birth to a granddaughter: "Well, I've just got to get into action. I've just got to do something. I can't stand this inaction." *

What one observer referred to as her "torrential energy" [4] was important to Mrs. Roosevelt's career in two notable ways. The first was that it gave her the capacity to personally involve

* ER, radio broadcast entitled "Making the Wheels Go Round in the White House," spring, 1935, copy in "ER, Speeches and Articles," Box 6, FDRL; "My Day," July 3, Nov. 25, 1936; April 12, 20, June 2, 1937; July 1, 1938; Alfred Steinberg, *Mrs. R* (New York, G. P. Putnam's Sons, 1958), p. 255.

The press at times seemed flabbergasted at the First Lady's inexhaustible goings-about. In June of 1935 one Washington, D.C., newspaper ran a headline on its society page which read: "Mrs. Roosevelt Spends Night at White House." William E. Leuchtenburg, *Franklin D. Roosevelt and the New Deal 1932–1940* (New York, Harper & Row, 1963), p. 192.

herself in an enormous number of "causes." The publicity attendant upon the First Lady's efforts in behalf of those causes was often sufficient to render them the subjects of attention by administrators and lawmakers who otherwise might have given them but scant consideration. The severe deprivation and suffering of the West Virginia miners, for example, might never have made an impact upon the national consciousness unless the wife of the President of the United States had made her services available to them. Mrs. Roosevelt's vigor enabled her to extend her interest to a variety of similarly disadvantaged groups, groups whose plight justifiably merited the concern of public officials.

The second effect of her wide-ranging interests was perhaps less happy in its ramifications. Individuals who occupy positions of influence customarily devote themselves to a comparatively circumscribed range of issues over a given period. They appear to realize that there are limitations on the number of subjects with which the human intelligence can effectively grapple at any one time, and they are aware that to violate these is to dissipate the capabilities that otherwise might be brought to bear on the problem at hand. They believe, in other words, in the conventional injunction of "not spreading yourself too thin."

This notion seldom seems to have crossed Mrs. Roosevelt's mind. Few unwelcome barriers arose to block her vista. Instead, her gaze went virtually unimpeded across the landscape of what she believed to be America's ills. To whatever point her vision led, there she herself hastened straightaway to attempt repairs. And while Mrs. Roosevelt's interest and good will often resulted in much that was necessary in the way of ameliorative measures, it should be remembered that truly remedial actions were seldom based upon her recommendations. One does not have to look far to find the reason for this. It was because Mrs. Roosevelt's proposed solutions were often farfetched and unrealistic. Thus it was in her relationship with the Arthurdale community. No one did more to point up the horrors of the mountaineers' existence; no one, at the same time, did more to befuddle the attempts to solve the vexing problems inherent in the subsistence homestead concept. Deep and sustained analysis was simply not the First Lady's strong suit. One of her "greatest faults," she admitted, "was that I seized the main points and anything colorful about a subject and didn't really dig down deeply enough to have my foundations firmly placed on facts." She was adept, she told Joseph Lash, at "skimming the cream off a person's ideas," but she "had never learned to deal with ideas analytically." [5]

To this weakness Mrs. Roosevelt's abundant vitality only added. Preoccupation with a multiplicity of issues made it even less likely that she would be able to find time to devote thorough investigation to any. Thus it was that the beneficent effects of her generous impulses in recognizing and calling attention to various inequities were not always matched by her proposed solutions to the problems with which she came into contact.

The strength of Eleanor Roosevelt's energetic drive led her, to a greater or lesser extent, to concern herself with an exceedingly wide variety of questions. Some of this interest resulted in various positive accomplishments. She appears, for example, through her friendship with Secretary of the Interior Franklin K. Lane, to have been able to exert some influence in behalf of materially improving conditions at Washington's St. Elizabeth's Hospital for the insane during the years of World War I. Similarly, when she became First Lady, she followed in the tradition of Woodrow Wilson's first wife by denouncing the abominable living conditions of the so-called "alley dwellers" whose hovels were within a few minutes' walk of the Capitol. Her exertions in this regard seem to have been instrumental in the introduction of a slum clearance project for the blighted area. [6]

In certain other cases, the results of Mrs. Roosevelt's vast curiosity and unbounded zeal were primarily funny or, perhaps, ludicrous. One cannot help but smile, for instance, at her sober reports of a 1920's expedition through which she and several fellow members of the Woman's City Club ventured, "as participants rather than investigators," to inform themselves on the prevailing climate of New York dance hall emporiums. Happily, the good ladies found that despite "the fascination [and] the dangers" of such nefarious haunts, there was withal "[a] surprisingly low percentage of disaster to the girls around them." Occasionally her comments with respect to the existing morality were somewhat injudicious. ". . . the average girl of today faces the problem of learning very young how much she can drink of such things as whiskey and gin and sticking to the proper quantity," was her unfortunately phrased declaration in the course of one of her radio talks in December, 1932. Since Prohibition was still theoretically the law of the land, Mrs. Roosevelt's statement was the subject of some consternation. Similarly, the First Lady's auditors were surprised to learn that anyone facing starvation acted quite properly in stealing as much as he could; that Bruno Richard Hauptmann, the kidnapper of the Lindbergh child, should not be sentenced to death on the strength of circumstantial evidence; and that it was a national indignity that a woman's sculptured head did not adorn the face of Mt. Rushmore.[7]

It is probable, however, that no matter what form Mrs. Roosevelt's observations might have assumed, the very multiplicity of her interests would have been sufficient to attract wide and varying general comment. For it was not only the kinds of causes she embraced, but the outspoken exuberance with which she stood for them which constituted such a novelty. Other First Ladies, particularly in the twentieth century, had exercised a strong influence on their husbands' careers. Both Helen Herron Taft and Florence Kling Harding were active in overcoming their husbands' reluctance to become candidates for the presidential nomination; and the second Mrs. Woodrow Wilson was, for a while, practically the only channel through which her husband might be reached.* But whatever the degree of influence wielded by these women, it was influence exercised on a *sub rosa* level; and the country at large had little knowledge of it at the time. Opinion on the First Ladyship continued to hold that the position was an innocuous one, that "the President's wife must be a silent partner . . . the unwritten law is that the First Lady gives no interviews, makes no public statement." [8]

Eleanor Roosevelt changed all this. Although as late as the autumn of 1932 she remained in apparent accord with the conventional attitude on how the wives of Presidents should conduct themselves, her humanitarianism and energy, when combined with the appalling disasters which accompanied the Depression, soon caused her to overcome her tradition-minded outlook.

The resultant plethora of activities in which she engaged could not have come as an undue surprise to anyone who had followed her earlier career. Although she had occasionally given conscientious lip service to the idea of moderating her activities,† she was never able to follow up such a concept. An examination of *New York Times* citations discloses that during the years 1924 through 1927, when her husband neither held nor ran for any public office, Mrs. Roosevelt was cited forty-eight times. In the

---

* See Henry F. Pringle, *The Life and Times of William Howard Taft*, 2 vols. (New York, Farrar and Rinehart, Inc., 1939), I, pp. 313–18; Samuel Hopkins Adams, *Incredible Era* (Boston, Houghton Mifflin Co., 1939), pp. 121, 125–126; Gene Smith, *When the Cheering Stopped* (New York, William Morrow & Co., Inc., 1964). Smith makes too much of Edith Wilson's influence, but there can be little doubt that she occupied a critically strategic position with respect to what opinions gained her husband's ear during his illness in 1919–20.

† For example, her statement in 1928 that she would give up all political speechmaking and her hope that "there will be no speechmaking at all, for I do not enjoy making speeches." Diana Rice, "Mrs. Roosevelt Takes on Another Task," *New York Times Magazine*, Dec. 2, 1928, p. 5. See also *New York Times*, March 5, 1933.

same period Mrs. Alfred E. Smith, wife of the New York Governor, received but thirty-eight citations. Between 1929 and 1932 *Times* references to Mrs. Roosevelt were just barely fewer in number than those which pertained to Mrs. Herbert Hoover, then First Lady of the Land. In 1932, references to the activities of the former far outran those directed to Mrs. Hoover.[9]

As impressive as the numerical ratio of these citations are the subjects to which they refer. As regards Mrs. Smith and Mrs. Hoover almost all of them concern personal tidbits or social or ceremonial affairs. "Will go to Florida," "Christens new municipal ferry-boat," "Pinkie, pet dog, runs away" (and, later, "Pinkie found") are representative of the subject matter pertaining to Mrs. Smith, while "Entertains Girl Scout officers," or "Receives a Japanese doll" are not untypical examples of the publicity attendant upon Mrs. Hoover. Releases concerning Mrs. Calvin Coolidge were similar — "Plans . . . lawn parties," "Attends First Congregational Church," or "Remains until end of World Series game" are indicative.

Contrast these with most of the citations regarding Mrs. Roosevelt: "Advocates child labor plank in New York State Democratic convention," "Speaks for R. F. Wagner in NYC debate," "Hits Woman's Party for supporting Hoover," "Urges support of emergency bond issue" — the tenor was entirely different, and was a harbinger of the novel activity which she was to bring to the White House.[10]

Mrs. Roosevelt's unique concept of the role of First Lady, together with her remarkable capacity for taking on an ever-increasing amount of tasks, was nowhere better illustrated than in the various commercial contracts into which she entered during the 1930's. "My Day" was, of course, the most noteworthy of these enterprises; but there were other ventures as well, and they included stints with magazines, radio and the movies. Many of these engagements, particularly the earlier ones, seem to have had little relevance to public affairs; rather, they were the gossipy, female-oriented sorts of undertakings usually to be found in the women's sections of many newspapers. Immediately following her husband's election to the Presidency, Mrs. Roosevelt commenced a three-month series of radio broadcasts for the Pond's Co. (women's toilet articles) which were concerned almost exclusively with what she called the "homely subjects" — marriage, the home, children and similar themes. At about the same time she became editor of Bernarr Macfadden's *Babies, Just Babies,* whose journalistic level was unfortunately nearly as infantile as its subject matter. In August, 1933, she began a two-year association with *Woman's Home Companion,* writing a column called "Mrs. Roosevelt's Page." By February, 1935, she was back on the radio for a weekly broadcast sponsored by the Selby Shoe Co. Previously she had squeezed in engagements for the Simmons Co. (mattresses) and Johns-Manville (building materials). By 1940 she was featured on "Sweetheart Toilet Soap Presents Eleanor Roosevelt," and the same year made a Fox-Movietone short plugging the radio show, "Hobby-Lobby." Over and above this activity were a spate of books, a substantial output of individual articles, and innumerable speeches and lectures, not to mention her daily newspaper column.[11]

The commercial aspect of the First Lady's career occasioned, as might have been expected, widespread comment. Initially, criticism of such ventures centered around the allegation that they lowered the dignity of her husband's position. That Mrs. Roosevelt paid scant heed to this type of censure is obvious from the fact that she maintained a number of such efforts for as long as she was in the White House. On the other hand, she did become more discriminating in her choice of employers. The advice of friends was sufficient, for instance, to lead her to terminate her connection with the sensation-seeking publicist Macfadden by the spring of 1933.[12]

A second angle of attack concerned the inference that the First Lady was money-hungry. Partisan critics seized upon the example of certain of the Roosevelt children and chided their mother for having an equal desire to make an easy dollar. This charge, which was fundamentally unjust, continued to plague Mrs. Roosevelt throughout the 1930's. In fact, she made very little in a monetary way from her various endeavors. The vast majority of the fees she received were donated to the American Friends Service Committee.[13] Mrs. Roosevelt did, however, give the somewhat misleading impression that she donated *all* her earnings from commercial work to various charities.[14] During the course of each of her broadcasts for Selby Shoes, an announcement was made to the effect that the First Lady's fees were "paid by the Selby Shoe Company not to Mrs. Roosevelt, but to a charity designated by her." [15] But this was not exactly the case. Of the per-broadcast stipend of $4,000, a hefty $3,000 went to the Friends; but Mrs. Roosevelt's agent Myles F. Lasker received $1,000, and of the latter amount, $400 went to her friend Nan Cook. It was also true that the First Lady was, for a while, something of a special case with respect to the manner in which she paid her taxes. There was nothing in the nature of malicious intent about the fact that she wrote off all her income from commercial ventures without first paying taxes on it; on the other hand, the Internal Revenue Bureau had plainly ruled that 15 percent was the maximum allowable write-off. The First Lady's generosity was thus depriving the government of revenue. After New York Republican Representative Hamilton Fish pointed out this discrepancy, Mrs. Roosevelt changed her tax deduction methods accordingly. Some time later, a reporter quoted her as admitting "quite honestly . . . that she has not given away all the money she earned." *

* *Congressional Record*, 75th Congress, 1st Session, July 19, 1937, A1823–24; Kurt Singer, "Eleanor Roosevelt," *The Negro*, III (July, 1946), p. 77. Con-

One might note, also, that despite the undoubted good accomplished by Mrs. Roosevelt's charitable donations, the way in which the sums for them were originally accumulated could not have helped but appear unjust to some people. It is difficult to refrain, for instance, from a certain sympathy for the president of Honorbilt Products, Inc., a mattress manufacturing firm, who wrote FDR that Honorbilt had "been cooperating with your administration wholeheartedly from the very beginning even to our own hardship," and that "it certainly does not seem fair that the First Lady should use her influence and assist any one manufacturer to promote his products over that of another." Attached to his letter was a large newspaper advertisement by the Simmons Mattress Co. which confidently predicted that "While Listening Tonight to Mrs. Franklin D. Roosevelt over WJZ at 9:30 P.M. You'll Probably Make Up Your Mind to Own A Simmons 'Beautyrest' Mattress." The consensus with regard to this letter was, simply, that it should not be answered.[16]

Yet another form of criticism of the First Lady's written and spoken efforts concerned the banality which they allegedly contained. Why, many people wondered, should Eleanor Roosevelt be paid large sums for journalistic and broadcasting products which all too often seemed so intellectually barren? Was it fair, they asked, that she should utilize such a vast amount of magazine, newspaper and airwave space merely because she was the wife of a famous man rather than because of the intrinsic merit of her ideas? These detractors evidently felt that the First Lady's efforts lacked the distinction which was customarily required of similar endeavors from others who did not enjoy her position.

This line of criticism contained a good deal more substance

---

trary to some interpretations, notably that of John M. Blum, Rep. Fish's comments about Mrs. Roosevelt's tax procedure were moderate in tone, his ire being directed toward former Internal Revenue Bureau General Counsel Robert H. Jackson. See *From the Morgenthau Diaries: Years of Crisis* (Boston, Houghton Mifflin Co., 1959), p. 336.

than those which stressed either Mrs. Roosevelt's alleged lack of dignity or her monetary greed. Careful study of her rhetoric leads one to believe that it was often not only stylistically embarrassing but also singularly lacking in both originality and intellectual content. Instead, many of her oral and written efforts were characterized by trivia, platitudes, *non sequiturs* and emotive declarations which set forth hazily desirable long-term objectives in the guise of concrete proposals on how to reach those goals.

Mrs. Roosevelt appears always to have had difficulty in avoiding clichés. Her descriptive vocabulary, dating from the years of her youth, was almost unrelievedly confined to the words "interesting," "amusing," and "lovely." Later she was to embellish almost every pronouncement she made with Heywood Broun's well-worn "it seems to me" or her own "although I'm not sure," and (in what must have been especially desperate moments) to decorate her sentences with such phraseological horrors as "oh, gentle reader." * In addition, her writing was further burdened by the fact that she was a poor speller and never learned the rudiments of correct punctuation.

Of greater moment was Mrs. Roosevelt's proclivity for sententious expression in preference to analytic exposition. "A vote is never an intelligent vote when it is cast without knowledge"; "There is in every man, I think, the eternal boy"; "youth and beauty will not get you very far permanently, unless you have a few more solid qualities behind them"; and "no problem is ever

---

* For the stylistic tone of her early writing, see those of her letters quoted in Elliott Roosevelt (ed.) and James Rosenau (asst.), *F.D.R. His Personal Letters 1905–1928* (New York, Duell, Sloan and Pearce, 1948); for later examples, almost any citation will do, although see especially "My Day," June 6, 1939. Heywood Broun, with whom Mrs. Roosevelt was personally friendly, had called his column "It Seems to Me," and the First Lady later used this phrase for the title of one of her books: ER, *It Seems to Me* (New York, W. W. Norton & Co., Inc., 1954).

solved till you try" were some of the Edgar Guest-like items with which her prose was liberally strewn.* Sometimes she stooped to the downright silly. "People who do not sleep should not worry about it," she advised. "They should lie there and rest and think about pleasant things." Or, "A man who trains horses will usually understand people. . . . He will be interested in watching the development of a personality, and, as a rule, he himself will be an interesting personality." This, however, was only normal, for "people are the most interesting things in the world." [17]

Mrs. Roosevelt also often made it a practice to sunnily conclude a lengthy monologue on some vital and complicated issue with a commonplace remark which begged the entire question she had been discussing. Thus, she ended her discussion of mandatory college training for government service with the observation: "There are great possibilities for good in this idea but dangers also, and it must, I think, be carefully considered." Similarly, she would wind up a protracted exposition concerning the difficulties of youth with the proposition that "It looks to me as though we can not relax in the study of the general problems which face us all, for there is the nut which must be cracked." [18]

The verbal detritus which characterized Mrs. Roosevelt's writing was evident in many of her radio broadcasts as well. Her well-imbursed efforts for the Selby Shoe Co. in 1935, for example, included such topics as "The Wife of A Public Official" ("There are rewards and compensations but it is far from being always a bed of roses") and "Keeping House on A Budget in the White House" ("Oh, Mr. Hoover, can you tell me anything about the financial side of running the White House?").[19] In

* ER, *It's Up to the Women* (New York, Frederick A. Stokes Co., 1933), p. 191; "My Day," April 1, 9, 1937; Sept. 12, 1938. Edgar Guest (1881–1959) was a popular American rhymester.

the case of radio broadcasting, moreover, the intellectual poverty of the First Lady's orations was matched by a high-pitched, creaking delivery which became the source of much merriment on the part of both her friends and antagonists.

From the time when she first began her public speaking career, Eleanor Roosevelt had always had a certain amount of difficulty controlling her voice. Louis Howe had remonstrated with her in the early 1920's about a tendency, during the course of her remarks, to giggle for no apparent reason.[20] She managed to overcome this habit, but until well into the 1930's she continued to speak in a quavering treble disconcerting to her listeners. She was perfectly well aware that this peculiarity rendered her speaking efforts vulnerable to ridicule, but took the majority of such mimicry with good grace.[21] Certain of these performances — which Mrs. Roosevelt fortunately did not witness — were, however, conducted in a spirit of malice. Dorothy Thompson, who caustically described Mrs. Roosevelt's remarks at a dinner in 1935 as "footling," could not help but remember an earlier occasion when "Alice L." imitated her. "Alice is cruel, of course," noted the journalist. "Still, she was right." *

Immense, not to say indiscriminate energy, commonplace verbiage, pedestrian ideas, and a speaking style easy to mock were the characteristics of the First Lady which most often became the targets of her detractors. Frequently her critics were moved to write irate letters to FDR on the subjects. "I voted for you," stated a Pennsylvania complainant. "I really thought you were President and able to handle . . . things yourself, but if you are not, please put me on the list which your wife calls on: — I need it." From a Fort Wayne constituent, who announced himself as

* Vincent Sheean, *Dorothy and Red* (Boston, Houghton Mifflin Co., 1963), p. 264. "Alice L." was Alice Roosevelt Longworth, Eleanor Roosevelt's cousin and the daughter of the twenty-sixth President.

being "for you 100%," came the opinion that the First Lady "would be rendering her country a far greater service if she would but uphold the dignity of the White House," while "A Friend, A Democrat" commiserated, "Your friends feel sorry for you." Certain of the correspondents seemed scarcely able to contain their indignation. ". . . is it not humanely [sic] possible to muzzle that female creature, known to the world as your wife?" asked a New York woman. A Philadelphia voter, after loosing several choice phrases to the effect that Mrs. Roosevelt should cease "gadding about the country and butting into matters that are no concern of hers," seemed to experience some sort of collapse in his search for an adequate vocabulary. "My God, what a woman!" was all he could manage to splutter by way of conclusion.[22]

There was, of course, public opposition as well. The New York *Post*, for example, worried about Mrs. Roosevelt's "seek-[ing] . . . accolades just because her husband has been elected to something." The *Post* "consider[ed] her course very bad," and was concerned lest "small-minded Republican politicians" make political capital of her varied activities. One could almost hear their "chuckling glee," that newspaper concluded: " 'Sure! Let her keep it up. She's certain to wreck the new Administration.' "[23]

But critics of the First Lady appeared to be in a decided minority. Letters to her husband which praised her activities far outnumbered those which expressed disapproval. Correspondents friendly to Mrs. Roosevelt lauded the very things her antagonists derided; they believed that her energetic investigations and the pronouncements she made on public issues were welcome developments for the country at large. "Back in New York state I heard so much about her good deeds," stated an Ohio resident. "I have always admired her work for the needy class of people."

"An American Citizen" paid tribute to her "fine courage and moral integrity," while an Illinois woman wished to tell the President "how very much we enjoyed Mrs. Roosevelt's visit with us. And what a sweet talk she made to us." A Negro citizen in Philadelphia commented on the fact that in that city, "Both White and colored enjoyed her speech on selfishlyness, God must have controled her mind in that speech. Selfishlyness has destory the true love for their fellow travler, the world is in a uproar," concluded that perspicacious observer. The sentiments of such correspondents were perhaps best summarized by Representative Fred H. Hildebrandt, Democrat of South Dakota, when he declared:

> I have no patience with those who complain because [Mrs. Roosevelt] is active in public affairs. It is a blessing that at last we have a President's wife who goes into the homes of the people, learns their problems, burdens, and troubles and finds out how to cope with them.[24]

Surprising quarters of the press, which as has been noted was generally friendly, shared these views. ". . . character with a great big C," was the opinion of John S. Knight, a newspaper publisher not otherwise known for his undue attachment to New Deal policies. Columnist David Lawrence, who was to become a bitter critic of FDR, approvingly sent to presidential secretary Steve Early an editorial he had found in the Buffalo *Express* which asserted:

> We admit to some skepticism we felt when at first she started her all-enveloping activities. We subscribed to the place-in-the-home theory. But the White House isn't much of a home; and Mrs. Roosevelt has made her home in every corner of the country. Like a bird, she is restive. As to a bird, we salute her gay contributions.

And in 1938 another columnist, having viewed Mrs. Roosevelt's activities for over five years, set forth in unequivocal terms his conclusions with respect to them:

> It had been another routine day in the life of one who is stingily described as the "most remarkable" and "most energetic" woman of her time in this country, but who deserves more than that. I think we can take the wraps off and call her the greatest American woman, because there is no other who works as hard or knows the low-down truth about the people and the trouble in their hearts as well as she does.
>
> And for what reason? Mrs. Roosevelt doesn't give a damn about politics in the partisan sense. Profit? She is one member of the family who will not have a dollar of profit to show for eight or more years of banging around the country in a schedule that would break the body and mind of an old-time circus trouper. . . .
>
> Mrs. Roosevelt has been with us five years now. We know her better than any other woman, and she knows the country better than any other individual, including her husband, and the profit is all on our side.

Since the author of this tribute was, astoundingly enough, Westbrook Pegler, it should be sufficiently clear that, indignantly vocal critics notwithstanding, Eleanor Roosevelt was during the 1930's the object of widespread affection and respect on the part of large sections of the American press and people.*

* John S. Knight in the Akron *Beacon Journal*, undated but probably Nov., 1937; Buffalo *Express*, Nov. 12, 1939; see also covering letter of David Lawrence to Steve Early, Nov. 17, 1939, "President's Personal File #2," Box 2, FDRL; Westbrook Pegler, "Fair Enough," *San Francisco Daily News*, March 17, 1938. Pegler was on friendly terms with Mrs. Roosevelt throughout most of the 1930's; there is a well-known picture taken during those years which shows him and the First Lady, seated side by side and smiling jovially, at a softball outing in upstate New York. *The Wisdom of Eleanor Roosevelt* (a compilation of her columns done for *McCall's Magazine*) (New York, n.d.).
Just when or why Pegler's views later underwent such a violent shift is difficult to say. Mrs. Roosevelt hinted that it was because her husband never of-

~

In spite of the generous treatment accorded her by a sizable portion of the press and the handsome endorsement given her conduct by a majority of American citizens, Eleanor Roosevelt frequently reexamined those areas of her own activities toward which criticism seemed most heavily aimed. She was well aware that to take a stand on public issues was to invite enmity from various sources, but she by no means contemplated a timid withdrawal for the purpose of heading off such an eventuality. She would continue her "writing and . . . talking"; to halt her efforts along such lines would mean a craven abandonment of "the job which [some of us have] been given opportunities and talents to do." [25]

Yet, the First Lady appears to have been of the opinion that she could adopt measures which might neutralize some of the antagonism directed toward her. She seems from time to time, for example, to sincerely have wished to cut down on the immense scope of her interests. It has been noted that she hoped to restrict her speech-making efforts after her husband was elected Governor of New York in 1928. Following his first inauguration as President a few years afterward she continued to think in the same vein, saying that in the future she planned to slacken her pace, to "do a lot of reading," and to give herself more time for such leisurely diversions as horseback riding and visits with her friends and family. A decade later, she told a reporter somewhat sadly that what she really wanted in place of her enormously varied activities was "just a little job in a simple category,

---

fered the columnist an official position in the administration, but she presented no evidence to back up this opinion (*The Wisdom of Eleanor Roosevelt*, p. 91). At any rate, Pegler began attacking her in the summer of 1940 because of her association with the Newspaper Guild; and she in turn began to sarcastically refer to him as "my kindly fellow columnist" ("My Day," Aug. 9, 1940). From that time on the relationship, mainly on Pegler's part, grew increasingly acrimonious.

where I can see something I want to do, and judge for myself what progress I am making." Mrs. Roosevelt occasionally appears, in brief, to have realized that the very multiplicity of the causes in which she participated tended to render that participation not only more vulnerable to her critics but generally less effective than it might have been had she confined herself to a more restrictive list of concerns.*

The First Lady, either because of the force of circumstances or because she was constitutionally unable to refrain from an incessant activism — or both — was unsuccessful in limiting the horizon of her interests. Her manifold causes and the stands she took on them thus continued to be subject to the criticism of her opponents. She demonstrated more skill, however, in frustrating the detractors of other of her characteristics. She ceased to write for such puerile journals as *Babies, Just Babies;* she gradually made her daily newspaper column into more of a vehicle for serious news commentary and less of a podium for Sunday school homilies; and she struggled manfully to be objective — somewhat unsuccessfully as when her subject matter embraced America's industrial-financial complex, but with rather better results when it dealt with such topics as the South and the mental outlook of many of that region's inhabitants. She was also able to communicate to the bulk of her audience the fact that she herself made virtually no economic profit from her commercial endeavors but instead gave most of her earnings to charity.[26]

Similarly, she sought to improve her awkward speaking style and delivery. In 1938 Miss Elizabeth von Hesse, a New York City speech teacher, saw the First Lady at Chautauqua, New

* Diana Rice, "Mrs. Roosevelt Takes Another Task," *op. cit.,* p. 17; *New York Times,* March 5, 1933; Kathleen McLaughlin, "Mrs. Roosevelt Wants 'Just A Little Job,'" *New York Times Magazine,* Oct. 8, 1944, p. 16. Even some of the First Lady's strong supporters, such as Frances Perkins, harbored doubts as to the ultimate effectiveness of her activities because of their very number. See Tamara K. Hareven, "The Social Thought of Eleanor Roosevelt" (unpublished Ph.D. dissertation, Ohio State University, 1965), p. 2.

York, "lose an audience of 5,000 within ten minutes," an occurrence which, in Miss von Hesse's words, "just made me ill." She thereupon wrote to Mrs. Roosevelt, and the latter agreed to take some speech lessons. Recalls Miss von Hesse:

> Mrs. Roosevelt stayed in town two weeks and did nothing but study . . . forty-four hours in all. She was one of the best students I ever had. We lowered her voice four major notes. . . .
>
> I taught her to walk well, to overcome her mincing walk that she had learned at girl's school. She [learned to walk] like a thoroughbred. . . .
>
> Her hands [were] small. She was inhibited and didn't use them. She became free with gestures.
>
> In her purse when she left my studio was a little card which she always carried with her when she traveled. On it were my words: "The Creator has never as yet made a woman who can talk and laugh at the same time becomingly." [27]

Miss von Hesse's efforts were evidently productive of a certain improvement in the speaking techniques of her illustrious pupil. A close student of those techniques, writing in 1941, numbered among the First Lady's assets as a speaker: (1) a pleasing change of pace ("rapid in narration; slow delivery of theoretical material"); (2) commendable variation of emphasis ("greater degrees of force are used . . . [in] the main lines of reasoning; comparatively unimportant material requires only slight degrees of force"); and (3) an articulation both "clear cut and that of a cultured Easterner." Nonetheless, Mrs. Roosevelt, according to this commentator, had not yet completely overcome her previous oratorical defects:

> Her voice often ranges into falsetto which produces irritation on the part of the listener. She uses little variety in resonance, and attempts to lower tones produce a strained effect. Steps and inflections are used indiscriminately and recur in such regular patterns that they become monotonous.

Even so, suggested this critic, the shortcomings present in the First Lady's speaking endeavors were frequently more than off-set by "the warmth, sincerity, and earnestness prevalent in her voice." [28]

Two further characteristics of Mrs. Roosevelt's rhetorical efforts are worthy of note — brevity and simplicity. She seems to have picked up these habits from Alfred E. Smith in the 1920's, and she seldom thereafter deviated from them. Governor Smith, she had then stated, was the only leader in New York "who has made complicated questions of government simple and interesting, so that everyone may understand [them]. . . . He has taken the most abstruse questions and put them in language which means something to the average voter. . . ." Many years later she was to urge a large gathering of Democratic women in Washington, D.C., to "for heaven's sake . . . say things you mean in very simple words. . . ." She had often wondered, she said, "if it would ever really dawn on people that simple things don't require a tremendous amount of verbiage." [29]

It is entirely possible, however, that Mrs. Roosevelt did not fully comprehend the lesson inherent in Smith's remarkable ca-pacity for simplification. For the New York Governor did not intend, as Mrs. Roosevelt would have had it, to convey the no-tion that "an intricate governmental problem" could be "put . . . into words so simple that any child can understand it." Indeed, Smith knew that governmental problems were anything but simple. His genius, as Felix Frankfurter pointed out, lay mainly in his ability "to enlist popular understanding of the *tech-nical means* [this writer's emphasis] by which alone social poli-cies can be realized." This was a radically different concept than what Mrs. Roosevelt understood it to be. For the First Lady's concern was with ends, goals and objectives; hers was the clarion voice which pointed to that toward which her listeners should strive; and too often she neglected means altogether — or if she did not neglect them, she confused them with the ends themselves. Her métier lay in inspiring rather than teaching, in exhorting rather than analyzing. Thus, at the Washington dinner cited above, immediately after propounding the belief that "simple things" need only "simple words," she launched into a discussion of a very *unsimple* subject ("making democracy work") with the statement: "Now if you really mean to make democracy work, and you are the people who have got to make democracy work, there is less and less opportunity for anybody else to make democracy work today, so it is a pretty heavy responsibility for all of us." Although later in her address she seems to have warily approached and even made contact with her subject, comments to the effect that in a democracy all should abide by the majority decision and dissenters should not be put into concentration camps could hardly have been viewed as startling or even very meaningful. They showed, instead, an unfortunate proclivity to not merely simplify but to drain many of her statements of viable content. Facetiously paraphrased, they amounted all too often to "simplicity running riot." *

Whatever misinterpretations Mrs. Roosevelt may have placed upon Al Smith's use of simplicity of statement, there can be little doubt that she was powerfully affected by his method as she understood it. But the "Happy Warrior" was by no means either the sole, or even the strongest, influence on her techniques or outlook. Much more profound were the early examples

---

* ER, "Seconding Speech of Mrs. Franklin D. Roosevelt [nominating Alfred E. Smith as candidate for President]," Democratic State Committee meeting (New York), April 17, 1928, "ER, Speeches and Articles," Box 1, FDRL; Frankfurter quoted in Raymond Moley, *27 Masters of Politics* (New York, Funk and Wagnalls Co., 1949), p. 18; ER, address to the National Institute of Government, Washington, D.C., May 4, 1940, excerpts of which were read into the *Congressional Record* by Senator Alben W. Barkley, Democrat of Kentucky, 76th Congress, 3rd Session, May 15, 1940, A2959–60. Associate U. S. Supreme Court Justice Benjamin N. Cardozo stated in A.L.A. Schecter Corp. v. U.S., 295 U.S. 495, that the authority exercised by the President under the National Industrial Recovery Act amounted to "delegation running riot."

(again, as she saw them) of individuals like Mlle. Marie Souvestre and her Uncle Theodore. The latter, especially, her memory molded into a hero of epic proportions. ". . . here was a man," she believed, "who practiced what he preached and inspired many others to do the same." Hypocrisy, calculation, the eye on the main chance — all, in her opinion, had been anathema to him. "There never was a moment in his career where he would have hesitated to espouse a cause he thought righteous because he felt it meant personal defeat." Indeed, the dominant characteristic in her somewhat idealized portrait of the twenty-sixth President was courage, which "was a cardinal virtue [to him] and the lack of it intolerable." [30]

The necessity of possessing courage was emphasized even further to Eleanor Roosevelt by her recollections of her father. Elliott Roosevelt, as she pictured him, remained throughout her entire life the apotheosis of all that was best in humankind. Her memory preciously reconstructed every detail of the comparatively few occasions they had been together; and although she never doubted that she had "stood first in his heart," one of her most persistent remembrances was of his annoyance whenever she seemed to display symptoms of cowardice. Not to do so in later life therefore became a virtual obsession with her. To her friend Joseph Lash she often spoke of "her despair at not being as brave as her father wanted her to be." In the late 1930's, during the course of a discussion with her husband about a book whose plot involved the betrayal of a friend because of Nazi pressure, the First Lady could not refrain from wondering aloud whether she, too, might not have acted in the same dishonorable way. "It was a theme," continued Lash, "to which she would revert frequently. Was she standing up firmly enough for what she believed in? she would ask. How would she behave if put to the test of torture for her convictions?" [31] Such preoccupations lead the historian to wonder whether Mrs. Roosevelt's stubborn and tenacious adherence to unpopular causes was not in part the result of a subconscious determination to convince herself that she too in fact possessed some of the qualities of bravery and intrepidity she so much revered in others.

If Mrs. Roosevelt worried lest her courage might fail her at some critical juncture, she seems otherwise to have been confident — privately — that she possessed a number of attractive and even laudable traits. It is true enough that she often affected a veneer of modesty in presenting herself to the public. She wrote, for instance, of an emotional gentleman in Oklahoma who, after having received her autograph, could not help informing her that " 'when I think of you people, it makes the tears come to my eyes.' " Similarly, there was the "delightful experience" she had undergone in a basket-making shop:

> No one was in the shop at first, but finally a lovely old lady with white hair appeared. My host murmured to her that I was "Mrs. Roosevelt." At first she said little, [then] suddenly she took a deep breath and said: "I must kiss you." I have rarely been paid as sweet and spontaneous a compliment. . . .

Although both of these accounts are followed by a disclaimer to the effect that such demonstrations "have nothing to do with me personally" but are "meant largely for the President," [32] one gets the impression that such remarks are not really relevant. What remains in the mind of the reader is the affection shown the First Lady, and the phrases which follow the narratives of the events themselves appear principally as covering devices which tone down the obvious but slightly.

For Mrs. Roosevelt, in her mature years, was not an excessively modest woman. There was, after all, no real reason why she should have been, given her record of many-sided accomplishments. A true self-evaluation on her part would have sounded like the following:

[Eleanor Roosevelt] is a woman of much simplicity and charm. She is unusually well qualified for the position of "First Lady" of the United States. Through a long line of foremost Americans, her ancestry goes back on her mother's side to Chancellor Livingston. . . . On her father's side, she inherits the strength and brilliance of the old Roosevelt family. . . .

She fulfills her duties . . . in a manner that leaves no doubt as to her housewifely training and her social graces.

At the age of fifteen, she was sent abroad to complete her education in the school of Mlle. Souvestre in England. During the next few years she travelled extensively in Europe and acquired all that was best in the education and culture of the Continent.

Despite her distinguished background and position, she is a woman of such friendliness and directness of manner that one seldom thinks of her except in terms of her own personality. She has escaped the devitalizing superficial dignities of high office and remains herself with a simplicity that is charming.

There are more of the same sentiments in this summation, but the above quotation should be enough to convey the general tenor. That Mrs. Roosevelt found the conclusions in it appropriate can be appreciated by an accompanying note from her secretary which reads simply: "Dear Miss Joseph: I am enclosing Mrs. Roosevelt's article which she has personally rewritten. She hopes it will be what you want. . . ." *

On yet another occasion Mrs. Roosevelt, without referring to herself by name, plunged into an obviously autobiographical passage in which she declared:

I knew a child once who adored her father. She was an ugly little thing, keenly conscious of her deficiencies, and her father, the only person who really cared for her, was away much of the time; but he never criticized or blamed her, instead he wrote her letters and stories, telling her how he dreamed of her growing up

* ER, draft of an untitled article, n.d. but 1932, in "ER, Speeches and Articles," Box 5, FDRL. "Miss Joseph" was Nannine Joseph, a literary agent of FDR's around 1932; the secretary who sent her the cited note is not further identified.

and what they would do together in the future, but she must be truthful, loyal, brave, [and] well educated, or the woman he dreamed of would not be there when the wonderful day came for them to fare forth together. The child was full of fears and because of them lying was easy; she had no intellectual stimulus at that time and yet she made herself as the years went on into a fairly good copy of the picture he had painted.[33]

From evidence like this, it might fairly be concluded that Eleanor Roosevelt, far from being unduly modest, regarded herself in most ways as having lived up to the high example of her father.

Another individual whose tutelage was of vast import in Mrs. Roosevelt's life was Louis Howe. It was he, more than anyone else, who encouraged her interest in politics in the 1920's, and she never failed to acknowledge her debt to him. In the mid-1930's, when the wizened little presidential adviser moved into the White House, she constantly attended to his needs, buying his clothes and other necessities as well as acting as a combination nursemaid and sister during his increasingly long and severe periods of illness. She seemed to find in the hard-boiled ex-newspaperman a capacity for tenderness which escaped many others; and when he died in April, 1936, she wrote:

There were few people for whom he really cared, but those who had the privilege of calling him their friend knew that he could always be counted upon. There never was a more gentle, kindly spirit.

He hated sham and cowardice, but he had a great pity for the weak and helpless in this world and responded to any appeal with warmth and sympathy.*

* ER, *This I Remember* (New York, Harper & Brothers, 1949), p. 30; Steinberg, *Mrs. R*, pp. 229-35; "My Day," April 20, 1936. Both Edward J. Flynn and Raymond Moley, among others, have commented on the close relationship between Mrs. Roosevelt and Howe. Edward J. Flynn, *You're the Boss* (New York, The Viking Press, 1947), p. 144; interview with Raymond Moley, May 26, 1965.

Mrs. Roosevelt had not been particularly fond of Howe when she first met him, but the two had grown increasingly friendly with the passage of years. Such, however, was not always the case with her relationship to other individuals within government circles. Her feelings toward Harry Hopkins, for instance, followed a far different course. The interests of Eleanor Roosevelt and the relief administrator were very similar; and, even early in the New Deal, the First Lady informed one of her audiences: "I know what Harry Hopkins worries about from morning to night." With time, their mutual esteem became even stronger; when Hopkins was ill in 1937, the President's wife generously told him that "if it would make his mind any easier, he should put a clause in his will designating her the guardian of [Hopkins' daughter Diana] in the event of his prior death." * Later, following Hopkins' recovery, Mrs. Roosevelt wrote:

> It was good to see Mr. Harry Hopkins yesterday and to have him spend the night with us. He is one of the few people in the world who gives me the feeling of being entirely absorbed in doing his job well. . . . He seems to work because he has an inner conviction that his job needs to be done and that he must do it.[34]

But sometime thereafter — one cannot be certain exactly when — a distinct chill set in between the two. As Hopkins' star rose his way of life seemed to change. Instead of being "entirely absorbed in doing his job well" he began to associate with a gay crowd who patronized liberally the race tracks and elegant night spots of Long Island. His conduct at the Democratic National Convention in 1940 was cavalier in the extreme; he did not seem to know, as the First Lady put it, "how to make people happy." Clarence Pickett of the American Friends Service Committee re-

---

* Hopkins was at this time also socially close to James Roosevelt, and there were expectations in some quarters that he would marry Anna Roosevelt after she divorced Curtis Dall. Louis W. Koenig, *The Invisible Presidency* (New York, Rinehart and Co., Inc., 1960), p. 306.

called a discussion among himself, Hopkins and Mrs. Roosevelt during August of that year wherein "Harry was opposing feeding [French children], because it would relieve Hitler of responsibility and actually might assist him in his war effort. I had seen a good deal of Harry when he was making his ardent pleas for the underprivileged of the United States," Pickett continued, "and this opposition to feeding in France seemed to me a new role on his part. It was as if political expediency had overcome human impulse. . . ." The apparent change in Hopkins was not calculated to appeal to the First Lady, and in November Harold Ickes gloatingly noted that she was "off of Harry." When the United States became more firmly committed to aiding the fight against the Axis, a struggle in which Hopkins assumed a vital role, he was heard to refer to many of his erstwhile friends as "goddam New Dealers" who in his opinion were too much concerned with trivial matters of domestic reform. According to Joseph Lash, "Mrs. Roosevelt would never admit it . . . but she had been Harry's staunchest advocate, having him to lunch and dinner with the President and then when he was close to the President, he dropped her." Mrs. Roosevelt therefore considered Hopkins personally disloyal and his conduct abominable, and so the intimacy between them accordingly came to an end.[35]

The First Lady's opinions of other important administration personnel varied widely. She was an admirer of Henry Wallace's ideas — he believed that "instead of each person being out for himself for what he can get . . . they [sic] [should] think 'what will be the effect not only on me, but . . . on those around me' " — but she was politically realistic enough to be aware of the fact that "people just don't become enthusiastic about him." Much more straightforward was her endorsement of Wallace's early New Deal assistant M. L. Wilson, of whom she wrote: "You cannot be with [him] and not feel a kind of strength . . . [he] faces situations and thinks them through, looks realities in the face and finds a way out." She felt an especial warmth, also, for Bernard Baruch whom, although he did not hold an official government position, she regarded as "a wonderful person." "I count as one of my blessings your friendship," she wrote him. "There are few people who one trusts without reservation in life and I am deeply grateful to call you that kind of friend." Mrs. Roosevelt also retained her friendship with Jim Farley despite the latter's unhappiness over her husband's third term candidacy in 1940.[36]

For others on whom her husband depended her regard was not nearly so high. Although she continued to like and respect latter-day brain truster Benjamin Cohen, she entertained a deep mistrust for his close associate, Thomas G. Corcoran. The latter, she felt, was witty and clever, but "did not know when to keep quiet" and "seemed to get pleasure out of manipulation and would do things deviously that could just as well be done openly." In addition, the First Lady was annoyed by the fact that Corcoran had used his charm on FDR's secretary Marguerite ("Missy") Le Hand, charm to which Miss Le Hand was apparently vulnerable. Her opinion of John Nance Garner was, if anything, even worse. Although the flinty Texan had been impressed with Mrs. Roosevelt as "a mighty sensible woman," she distinctly did not reciprocate; and, privately, she threatened to campaign against him if he became the Democratic standard-bearer in 1940. Concerning her opinion of U.S. diplomats little is known, although she reportedly held a low opinion of one-time Ambassador to Russia William C. Bullitt. She preferred Bullitt's successor Joseph E. Davies, apparently because of his thoroughness in reporting on the Soviet purges.*

---

* Koenig, *The Invisible Presidency*, pp. 276, 294; Joseph P. Lash, *Eleanor Roosevelt: A Friend's Memoir* (Garden City, New York, Doubleday and Co., Inc., 1964), pp. 86, 170; Garner to Farley, Sept. 2, 1932, quoted in Frank Freidel, *Franklin D. Roosevelt: The Triumph* (Boston, Little, Brown and Co., 1956), fn., 329. Mrs. Roosevelt's praise of Davies' dispatches was unjustified;

It is interesting to observe that the First Lady's friendships were by no means necessarily based upon political compatibility. Her warm relationship with Bernard Baruch, for example, could hardly have rested upon mutually held political beliefs; for Baruch, although he materially assisted various of her projects, was a man of basically conservative instincts. On the other hand, Hopkins, with whom she broke, essentially shared many of her social and political views. But Hopkins' private conduct had displeased her. Furthermore, he had in Mrs. Roosevelt's opinion been disloyal, something that she could not abide. In this she was as one with FDR; both were possessive of their friends and demanded absolute loyalty from them. With respect to their viewpoints on friendship, however, there were more differences between husband and wife than there were similarities. The First Lady summarized those differences by saying that while she

> . . . had to have contact with people she loved . . . [the] President seemed to have no such bonds to people. Not even his children. He was completely occupied by politics and his public duties. . . .
>
> [Mrs. Roosevelt] could never get accustomed to his lack of real attachment for people. Except for Louis Howe, she could never conceive of the President doing a reckless thing for a friend because of personal attachment. . . .
>
> [Although many persons imagined that they were] indispensable to the President. . . . All would be surprised at their dispensability. The President uses those who suit his purposes. He makes up his own mind and discards people when they no longer fulfill a purpose of his.

And, according to a somewhat wistful remark in her memoirs, Mrs. Roosevelt considered herself "one of those who served his purposes." [37]

~

they were often highly misleading. See Joseph E. Davies, *Mission to Moscow* (New York, Simon and Schuster, 1941), pp. 155–204, 259–280.

Observations of this kind have given rise to the belief in certain circles that Franklin and Eleanor Roosevelt did not enjoy, in
the sense usually conveyed by that homely phrase, a "close family relationship." Those who incline toward this view cite as further supporting evidence the fact that the First Lady and the
President were so often physically apart that any normal domestic intimacy between the two was rendered impossible. They
share the opinion that Mrs. Roosevelt's peregrinations signified,
as one blunt correspondent put it, that the presidential couple
"can't be very happy together." [38] And they buttress their conclusions by inferring that FDR was dominated by his mother,
that Eleanor Roosevelt was physically unattractive while her
husband was handsome and buoyant, that the First Lady annoyed the President by her crusading zeal, and, finally, that
Franklin Roosevelt was enamored of another woman.*

How much truth is there to this belief? Does the available evidence as it concerns each component of the allegation — mother-
in-law domination and interference, lack of Eleanor's personal
attraction as compared to FDR's exceptional physical magne-
tism, husbandly self-containment — justify the gravamen of the
accusation? Did Eleanor Roosevelt's supposedly resultant unhappiness lead to her seeking an outlet by embracing a multitude
of "causes"? How much is fact and how much is fancy as regards Franklin Roosevelt's relationship with a woman not his
wife?

While what follows does not pretend to be in any way a final

---

* Many of the constituent parts upon which rests the opinion that Franklin
and Eleanor Roosevelt did not have a thoroughly happy marriage have seldom
appeared forthrightly in public print. The present assemblage of them is thus
gathered from a myriad of works which, while they do not pose the charges,
indirectly infer them by attempting to answer them. Furthermore, this writer
can state unequivocally that, in the many conversations he had with people,
here unnamed, who either knew the Roosevelts or were students of the Roosevelt era, he found the "unhappy relationship" theory to be held by a surprisingly
large number of individuals — several of whom were staunch admirers of both
the President and his wife.

answer to these perplexing questions (for, indeed, matters of this
nature seldom lend themselves to anything approaching a final
answer), it is hoped that a brief review and analysis of such evidence as is available may help dispel some of the foggy notions
that have beclouded the entire subject. And it is to be hoped,
also, that the tentative judgments given might aid in presenting a
clearer picture of Eleanor Roosevelt's domestic environment and
her actions with respect to it.

To begin with, it can be stated with assurance that Franklin D.
Roosevelt's mother was a domineering and willful woman who
doted upon her only son. Young Franklin's father, a considerably older man,* died when the boy was eighteen; and from that
time on Sara Delano Roosevelt, in the words of Frank Freidel,
"concentrated everything on Franklin." [39] She moved up to
Boston to be near him when he was at Harvard; later, after he
had graduated and fallen in love with his distant cousin Eleanor,
she tried to dampen his ardor by taking him on a Caribbean
cruise. She wanted her boy to remain with her for a few years
anyway.[40]

The youthful Franklin, however, refused to be dissuaded; and
when his mother recognized this fact she gave in with overt
pleasantness. "[A]n added joy to have Eleanor now," she wrote
concerning a Hyde Park weekend shortly after the young couple's engagement.[41] One suspects, however, that Sara Delano
Roosevelt's sporting surrender was not unmixed with a certain
sense of calculation. She appears, in other words, to have recognized the possibility that the timid, shy and uncertain girl might
be easily dominated. By exercising the reins on Eleanor, she
seemed to believe, she might be able to maintain a vestige of control over Franklin as well.

Certainly her subsequent actions lend credence to this theory.
She procured a house for the couple in New York City, just

---

* He was fifty-three when Franklin was born in January 1882.

three blocks from her own; later, she built them a second that was actually attached to the one in which she lived. Mrs. Roosevelt, Sr., also dictated how the grandchildren should be brought up and where the family should spend their vacations. Later, when infantile paralysis struck her son, she was almost successful in her campaign to get him to abandon public life entirely. Even during the White House years Eleanor Roosevelt had to make constant adjustments to meet her mother-in-law's whims. Jim Farley quoted the First Lady as telling him, following his resignation as manager of the 1940 presidential campaign: "She [Sara Delano Roosevelt] doesn't like the idea and is going to tell you so. You must brace yourself for a letter telling you what she thinks; the old lady does not understand anyone refusing a request from the Roosevelts." [42]

The President's mother had, in the beginning, been right in her appraisal of her daughter-in-law. Extant letters between the two reveal, on the girl's part, an almost pathetic eagerness to ingratiate herself and an abject thankfulness for Sara Roosevelt's direction of familial affairs. ". . . I know just how you feel and how hard it must be," she wrote her mother-in-law shortly after the engagement, "but I do so want you to learn to love me a little. You must know that I will always try to do what you wish for I have grown to love you very dearly. . . ." Her letters from Europe where she honeymooned in 1905 displayed a clamorous affection and sense of gratitude. "Thank you so much dear for everything you did for us. You are always the sweetest dearest mama to your children . . ."; "We are so glad [about the house] and think you have done wonders for us, in the way of a good bargain . . . we will get settled so much sooner than if we waited to choose a house on our return"; "goodbye dearest and a thousand thanks and kisses. I feel as though we would have such long arrears of kisses and cuddly times to make up when we get home!" were typical expressions. [43]

Later, of course, Sara Roosevelt's ubiquity and interference began to pall. Realizing her dependence, Eleanor tried to interest herself in leisure activities to which her husband was devoted. But golf, horseback riding and driving an automobile were all attempted without success. Frustrated beyond endurance, the young matron seems to have experienced periods of mild emotional difficulty. But these soon passed.[44] The real turning point in Eleanor Roosevelt's relationship with her mother-in-law evidently developed during her husband's illness. Eleanor Roosevelt was then close to forty; she had begun tentative excursions into civic activity; her husband's affliction had forced responsibility on her. She was gaining in poise and self-confidence; and, with FDR's decision against retirement at Hyde Park, Sara Delano's influence thereafter waned. Franklin, previously unsympathetic to his wife's unhappiness about his mother's overbearing family role, now appeared both to understand and to share it. In 1927 Mrs. Roosevelt stated: "I have seen a strong man struggle half his life for emancipation from the gentle but narrowing control of his mother and achieve it in the end only through what seemed heartlessness and entire lack of consideration." [45]

The forceful part played by Mrs. Sara Delano Roosevelt in the early years of the young couple's marriage was doubtless a source of friction — and even unhappiness. But both Eleanor Roosevelt and her husband appear to have outgrown and overcome this influence even before Franklin became Governor of New York. Rather than driving a wedge between the two, Mrs. Roosevelt, Sr., unconsciously became a kind of cement. For both knew her well and could frankly exchange mutual opinions about her. Both were aware of her shortcomings but both understood her. And both seemed to realize, by the time of the White House years, that she had become no longer a threat as much as what might be called a comfortably traditional family nuisance.

In her letters to her mother-in-law, Eleanor Roosevelt had in her younger years frequently resorted to belittling herself and her own abilities. Her narratives were punctuated with such profuse declarations of modesty as, "You must forgive me dear if my letters are long and dull, for I can't write like Franklin and I'm really quite ashamed to send you such stupid epistles after his amusing ones"; or, apropos of the house Mrs. Roosevelt, Sr., had taken for the young couple, "I am looking forward so much to getting it in order with you to help us. I am afraid my unaided efforts would not be very successful." [46] Much of this self-denigration, this extreme humility and want of confidence in her own abilities, could be traced to the young wife's utter certainty that she was physically unattractive. Because she had not been endowed with good looks, she felt, others were not drawn to her. Hence, within her there grew the beliefs that she must defer to the wishes of others, must compensate for her lack of physical charms by "being useful," must needs try "to make life pleasant — both for herself and her loved ones and all those who [came] into contact with her." [47] Carried to an extreme, as they were in Eleanor Roosevelt's case, these convictions resulted in habits of the most excessive diffidence and a timidity which at times verged upon mousiness.

Convinced of her own plainness, she must have considered herself fortunate indeed to have won the affections of her handsome Dutchess County cousin. But it is not true that Franklin D. Roosevelt was her first sweetheart. She herself has said as much.[48] Nor, as a matter of fact, was it true that she was physically unprepossessing. Contemporary photographs of the youthful Eleanor Roosevelt disclose a young woman with a well-molded figure, a willowy grace, and with, in her own description, "a sensitive face with intelligence and quick perception in the brow and eyes." [49] There are, to be sure, the protuberant front teeth (a physiognomic legacy from her Uncle Theodore) and, again in her own words, a "rather poor mouth and chin." [50] Nonetheless, the composite portrait is of a young lady by no means unattractive. Even when she reached middle age and had lost her youthful figure and her demure attractiveness, an interviewer could remark that "in repose she is homely; but when she talks, she is like a magnet." "It was a misfortune that the First Lady was such a poor subject before the camera," recorded presidential secretary Grace Tully. "In actuality, her face is possessed of such life and vitality that she is in person quite an attractive woman." *

Eleanor Roosevelt's conviction that she was homely stemmed almost entirely from the callous remarks made about her looks by her mother. Anna Hall Roosevelt was an exquisite beauty, and she greatly resented the fact that her daughter did not inherit her rare physical gifts. This circumstance thus forced the young Eleanor Roosevelt to make the essentially unfair comparison of her own looks with those of her mother; and the result, as might have been expected, was that Eleanor always overstressed her plainness. That she did come to hold this belief was important; for, as has been noted, it obviously influenced her patterns of thought and of action. But objectively such a belief was untrue; and the best argument for its untruth lies in the fact that she was able to charm and to win an exceptionally handsome young man like Franklin D. Roosevelt. Perhaps Gerald W. Johnson summarized the whole issue best when he wrote that Eleanor Roosevelt's picture of her own physical limitations, though sincere in itself, "must be accepted with a certain reserve." For, in his opinion, "a cynical world does not sustain that belief. Girls

---

* The Unofficial Observer (John Franklin Carter), *The New Dealers* (New York, The Literary Guild, 1934), p. 209; Grace Tully, *F.D.R. My Boss* (New York, Charles Scribner's Sons, 1949), p. 118. Several years after Mrs. Roosevelt left the White House she had an automobile accident which necessitated the removal of her front teeth and the substitution of false ones. The improvement in her appearance was striking.

who are utterly graceless," Johnson concluded, simply "do not captivate well-to-do, good-looking and popular young bachelors." [51]

This captivation, according to some sources, was not of lasting duration. In 1966 Jonathan Daniels, a North Carolina journalist and the son of Franklin Roosevelt's former boss in the Navy Department, asserted in a potpourri of observations on U.S. life and culture between the two World Wars that both Roosevelt's political future and his marriage came near to being destroyed until, *circa* 1918, he "supposedly . . . ended forever his relations with Lucy Mercer to whom actually he was to be attached by ties of deep and unbroken affection to the day he died." Though "Eleanor made no record of the situation," stated Daniels, she was "bitter and jealous of Lucy during all the years until the last when at Franklin's death in 1945 she found that Lucy, on one of her several trips to Warm Springs, had been with her husband when he died." [52]

The Daniels allegations raised an immense furor; and newspapers, magazines and eminent commentators and historians devoted considerable space both to reporting the story and announcing their interpretations of it. Some well-known observers like Raymond Moley called it "An Old Wives' Tale"; others, such as the columnist Drew Pearson, agreed with and expanded upon it. Yet others, among them historian Arthur M. Schlesinger, Jr., assumed a middle ground, averring that although there was some basis of truth in Daniels' position, he was guilty of overstatement and had gone beyond the facts in drawing his conclusions.[53] Whatever their reaction, however, it is evident that many reputable men took the story seriously enough to comment at some length about it.

That this should be so is strange, and even astonishing, for the rumor of young Franklin Roosevelt's infatuation with Lucy Mercer had certainly not escaped the attention of memoirists or historians in the years previous to the publication of Daniels' book. The first printed report of it, insofar as this writer is aware, occurred in *Washington Tapestry*, a gossipy little account of the Roosevelt years in Washington published in 1946 and written by Olive Clapper, the wife of a then recently deceased newspaperman. Mrs. Clapper's book did not enjoy a wide circulation, and the matter does not appear to have been mentioned again until Roosevelt's secretary Grace Tully disclosed that the former Miss Mercer had been a guest of the President's at Warm Springs, Georgia, when he had suffered his terminal stroke on April 12, 1945. Westbrook Pegler, by this time a vitriolic enemy of all things Rooseveltian, thereupon released the information in his column; but because of the recognizedly intemperate spirit of his writings, the public at large tended to ignore much of what he had to say.*

The decade of the 1950's saw the story dealt with by more responsible hands. John Gunther's *Roosevelt in Retrospect* (1950) seemed to accept the Clapper account completely. On the other hand, two years later Frank Freidel — in the course of one of his superbly scholarly biographical volumes on FDR — dismissed it as "preposterous." Yet other historians were more guarded. James MacGregor Burns was of the opinion that "At best the long separations [between Eleanor and Franklin in 1917–18] were the source of difficulty," while Arthur M. Schlesinger, Jr., believed the romance existed but amounted only to "the enchantment of summer, later fading away." Even Jonathan

---

* Olive Clapper, *Washington Tapestry* (New York, Whittlesey House, 1946), pp. 238–39; Tully, *F.D.R. My Boss*, p. 360. Although Pegler alluded to the story on several occasions, the best summary of his use of it may be found in his article, "Eleanor Roosevelt," in *American Opinion*, VI (Feb., 1963), pp. 2–10. The incredible tastelessness of and distortions in this article were so gross that even a few readers of *American Opinion*, the official publication of the extreme-rightest John Birch Society, were moved to protest. See "Letters to the Editor," *American Opinion*, VI (Sept., 1963), p. 78.

Daniels, writing in 1954, presented much more tentative views on the whole matter at that time than he would set forth some twelve years later. ". . . that their friendship then ever came to a point where Franklin seriously contemplated divorce in order to marry her," concluded Daniels, "I do not believe." [54]

Lucy Page Mercer first met the Roosevelts in Washington, D.C., in 1913. She was then a strikingly beautiful girl of twenty-two and, although poor, was descended from a socially impeccable family. She became Eleanor Roosevelt's social secretary and, as such, was on close terms with the entire Roosevelt household. According to one source, Miss Mercer "hero-worshiped" the handsome young Assistant Secretary of the Navy from the first;[55] and their friendship was supposed to have ripened into romance by the summer of 1917. Letters of that time, some of them highly circumstantial at best, are cited as evidence for this belief. Franklin Roosevelt's mother is depicted as having obscurely referred to the matter in a 1917 missive to her son and daughter-in-law in which she expressed her concern "that Franklin *is* tired and that my views are not his. . . ." But the context of this reference plainly indicates that the differences between mother and son were over social theories (Sara Delano inferentially derogating being too "democratic" and "the *trend* to 'shirt sleeves' ") rather than something more immediately personal. Nor is it likely that, should any romantic complication have been the subject under discussion, Sara Roosevelt would have addressed the letter to Eleanor as well as Franklin.[56]

Of perhaps more direct bearing on the whole imbroglio was a letter from FDR to his wife in which he chided her for being such "a goosy girl to think or even pretend to think that I don't want you here *all* the summer, because you know I do!" Eleanor Roosevelt seems to have had the idea that her husband was over-anxious for her to leave Washington, D.C., and go to the Roosevelt summer place at Campobello.[57] She was possibly disturbed about this, for she appears to have been easily moved to jealousy and possessiveness. She had, for example, been "jealous beyond description" when during her honeymoon FDR had taken off on a mountain-climbing hike with Kitty Gandy, an attractive New York hat designer. And her wish to be constantly at her husband's side was reflected by such sentiments on her part as "Since the 'Titanic' . . . I don't think I shall ever let you go away again alone" and "I hate your leaving any time." [58] Evidently this mood of worry and insecurity assailed Eleanor Roosevelt once again in the summer of 1917.

Contemporaries of Miss Mercer incline to the belief that there may have been some cause for the future First Lady's unhappiness. Mrs. Eulalie Sallie of Aiken, South Carolina, although heatedly denying that there was "anything scandalous" in Miss Mercer's relationship with Franklin D. Roosevelt, admitted that "of course he was in love with her. So was every man who knew Lucy." Mrs. Sallie's opinion is that FDR would have sought a divorce to marry her, "but Lucy was such a staunch Catholic [that she] would have never married a divorced man." A relative of Miss Mercer's, preferring to remain anonymous, told United Press International that Roosevelt did in fact ask for his freedom, "but Eleanor would not consent to a divorce." The relative's reason for this, that "Franklin was being mentioned in Democratic Party circles for high political office, and Eleanor said she would not let him ruin his career with a divorce," is not, in the light of her comparative disinterest in politics at that time, especially persuasive. Columnist Drew Pearson, after flatly stating that "Eleanor Roosevelt discovered the romance rather abruptly when, driving through Virginia, she saw her husband and Lucy in a parked car," claims that Elsie Cobb Wilson (later Mrs. Louis Little), a friend of both Miss Mercer and Eleanor Roosevelt, told him that she "intervened with Lucy Mercer and helped persuade her to do her part in breaking off the romance." *

Miss Mercer was married to Winthrop Rutherfurd, a descendant of a distinguished Massachusetts family and a man considerably her senior, in February, 1920. Mrs. Barbara Knowles, the only child produced by the Mercer-Rutherfurd union, believes that Roosevelt and her mother saw each other after the marriage at most "perhaps once a year." It is true that FDR sent her inauguration tickets in 1933; it is also true, as Raymond Moley has pointed out, that she was but one of hundreds who received them. Emotional scars on the part of Eleanor Roosevelt, if in fact they had ever been present, seem with the passage of years either to have disappeared or to have been carefully disguised. When her husband sailed for Europe in the spring of 1931 she wrote him:

> . . . I hate so to see you go. . . . We are really very dependent on each other though we do see so little of each other! I feel as lost as I did when I went abroad . . . !
> . . . Dear love to you. . . . I miss you and hate to feel you so far away. . . .[59]

Aside from the expressions of endearment which characterize this letter, its most significant aspect is the remark that "we do

* For the comments of Mrs. Sallie, see *Time*, LXXXVIII (Aug. 19, 1966), p. 23. Mrs. Sallie, at the age of eighty-two still active in the real estate business, was exasperated over the publicity attendant upon the entire matter. "I have had dozens of reporters descend upon me since this thing came up," she declared indignantly, "and I have had the pleasure of telling each of them that Jonathan Daniels is a skunk." *Time*, LXXXVIII (Aug. 26, 1966), p. 13.

The opinions of the "anonymous relative" may be found in *U.S. News and World Report*, LXI (Aug. 22, 1966), p. 13; for an indication of Eleanor Roosevelt's tepid concern with politics in the late 'teens, see Chapter III above. Pearson's observations are in a column he entitled "Eleanor Did Not Give Up Easily," (Butte-Anaconda) Montana *Standard*, Aug. 17, 1966.

Conventional denials of the story were made by both Franklin D. Roosevelt, Jr., and Mrs. Barbara Knowles, the latter Miss Mercer's daughter by a subsequent marriage. Neither statement is particularly relative or convincing. *New York Times*, Aug. 13, 1966.

see so little of each other!" This reflects, of course, the effects of
the growing public duties of Franklin Roosevelt and the increasing "partnership" activities of his wife. As early as 1931, in other
words, Eleanor Roosevelt seemed ruefully aware that their relationship — though affectionate — had begun to have its normal
intimacy marred by the necessities contingent upon official and
semi-official concerns. And certainly this was even more the case
when her husband was elected President and she became mistress
of the White House. Her manifold interests meant ever more
frequent separations from her husband. Even the sometimes do-
mestically imperceptive FDR noticed this, beginning a letter to
the First Lady in 1934: "The Lord only knows when this will
catch up with my Will o' the Wisp wife. . . ." [60] Indeed, the
heavy amount of correspondence which continued to flow between Franklin and Eleanor Roosevelt took on thereafter an increasingly official as opposed to a personal tone. As the Chief
Executive plunged more and more deeply into the intricacies of
the vast domestic and foreign problems which beset the United
States, and as his wife became immersed in her own activities and
a public figure in her own right, there entered into their letters a
formality and a perfunctory note of affection not in evidence
during the pre-presidential years. There was nothing deliberate
about this. Both Roosevelt and his wife were merely suffering
some of the domestic penalties which in any case attach themselves to those who serve in high public capacity.

One accessory irritant, however, appeared. This occurred because of Mrs. Roosevelt's intense concern over certain problems,
her belief that such problems should be attacked head-on, and
her conviction that to compromise about solutions to them was
somehow "wicked." [61] This approach was bound from time to
time to conflict with that of her husband, and there is evidence
that her humorless zeal frequently annoyed the Chief Executive.
Secretary of the Interior Harold L. Ickes relates a conversation

with FDR in late 1940 wherein the latter, "with a feeling he rarely displays," told him:

> The Mrs. came into my room yesterday morning before I was out of bed. She said, "Franklin, I have had a talk with Mr. Straus." I queried her: "Which Mr. Straus?" She said, "Nathan Straus." She went on to tell me that in building his housing projects Nathan Straus had informed her that he never had any difficulty with labor because, before the contract was signed, he always required that there be an agreement with labor. He wanted to build the Army cantonments. "He said that he has not seen you for a month and his feelings are hurt. Can't you give him just five minutes?"
>
> I pulled myself up in bed and said [indicating and speaking very firmly]: "No, I will not see him. And as for building the Army cantonments, they are going to be built by the Army."

Samuel I. Rosenman remembered that Mrs. Roosevelt "never hesitated to express her views to the President, no matter how much she knew he would disagree with them. She was invariably frank in her criticism of him — and of his speeches. Sometimes," Rosenman observed, "I thought that she picked inappropriate times to discuss matters with him. . . . Occasionally I felt that she pressed her point too hard; and sometimes I thought that she used to bring strange company to dinner to meet the President — company we knew he did not relish." Presidential secretary Grace Tully agrees, and recalls FDR complaining to her: "Eleanor had a lot of 'do-gooders' for dinner and you know what that means." [62]

After the United States entered World War II, Mrs. Roosevelt continued to aid her husband loyally and competently. Her trips to various distant points of the globe, made at his behest, were a further fulfillment of her role as "partner" to the President. But her somewhat inflexible seriousness did not make for the moments of ease and relaxation FDR so sorely needed in the midst of his momentous labors. James Roosevelt has put it very well. What his father required in those days, stated he, was

> a little touch of frivolity and sparkling, occasionally aimless conversation. Obviously I do not write this in any derogatory or critical sense, but one of the few things that Mother could never give him — and Mother, who gave him so many things, would be the first to point it out — was that touch of triviality he needed to lighten his burdens.[63]

It was primarily because of this need for lighthearted diversion that Roosevelt must have sought a renewal of his companionship with Lucy Mercer Rutherfurd. He saw her, according to Schlesinger, "at Bernard Baruch's plantation in the spring of 1944 [and] once or twice at Warm Springs." Shortly after Rutherfurd's death that same year* FDR, on the way to Hyde Park, had his private railway car detoured to the Rutherfurd estate at Allamuchy, New Jersey, where he spent several hours with Lucy. Whether or not Mrs. Roosevelt knew of this stopover is conjectural; convenient interpretations to the contrary,[64] the fact that she met her husband's train upon its arrival at Hyde Park is in no way conclusive evidence that she was aware of its route.

Finally, it is now known that Mrs. Rutherfurd was at Warm Springs at the time President Roosevelt suffered his fatal stroke. That she was a guest there is easily explained; she had asked a friend, Elizabeth Shoumatoff, to do a portrait of the President. What appears less plausible is why, if the entire story of the Roosevelt-Lucy Rutherfurd relationship was (as Schlesinger concludes) "a touching and innocent" one, the knowledge of Mrs. Rutherfurd's presence at Warm Springs "shattered, for once, Eleanor Roosevelt's composure."[65] Of additional curiosity is the fact that Mrs. Rutherfurd and Mrs. Shoumatoff were

---

* Lucy Mercer Rutherfurd herself died in 1948.

immediately hustled away from Warm Springs and Mrs. Rutherfurd's having been there at all never mentioned in any of the contemporary accounts of the President's death.

It is this odd set of circumstances which lends a certain credence to the Daniels supposition that Eleanor Roosevelt "was bitter and jealous of Lucy during all the years. . . ." For why else suppress the information that Mrs. Rutherfurd was with the President when he was stricken, that she was a guest at Warm Springs, and that the portrait of Roosevelt had been commissioned at her request? Other individuals in the President's entourage — Margaret Suckley, Laura Delano, William Hassett, even Mrs. Shoumatoff were mentioned prominently. Mrs. Rutherfurd was mentioned not at all; and, again, one wonders why.

The most reasonable reply to these questions seems to be that Mrs. Roosevelt herself must have taken some stock in at least a part of the rumors that associated Lucy Mercer Rutherfurd with her husband. This does not mean that such rumors were true; but the truth or falsity of them is really, within the present context, of secondary consideration. Myth, as is well known, does not depend for its power upon its degree of innate authenticity. Its importance rests instead on how it is viewed in the minds of its adherents. To phrase it somewhat tautologically, if they believe it is true, then it is true — at any rate to them.

Mrs. Roosevelt's apparent reluctance to have published the fact that Lucy Rutherfurd had been at Warm Springs on April 12, 1945, was the result of one of three things. On the one extreme, she may have known, by firsthand experience, that there had indeed been a romance between her husband and her one-time social secretary. The evidence as to whether or not this was so is, however, much too fragmentary. On the other extreme, it is possible to argue that her course of action was determined by practicality; i.e., she saw no reason to add to rumors that she knew were unfounded in the first place.* And yet it is difficult to believe that Mrs. Roosevelt would have become a party to newspaper suppression had her outlook been absolutely clear of suspicion on the point. One feels that, had such been the case, pride in her own certitude and contempt for cheap gossip would have, if anything, led her to insist upon full publication. The third alternative, and the one which seems to make the most sense, is that, whatever the cause, she herself accepted at least a portion of the story. It would have been wholly out of character for her to dissemble otherwise. Once again, this does not establish the veracity of any alleged affair between Franklin Roosevelt and Lucy Mercer Rutherfurd. It does not seem unfair to conclude, on the other hand, that Mrs. Roosevelt was sufficiently sensitive on the subject to allow Mrs. Rutherfurd's presence at Warm Springs to go unreported.

Despite, however, the multitude of obstacles which Franklin and Eleanor Roosevelt faced in their domestic life, their marriage yet appears on the whole to have been a full, satisfactory and contented one. That it occurred in the first place is testimony enough that Eleanor Roosevelt was not the hopelessly plain and dull young lady she thought herself to be; and although she continued to agitate herself with such self-accusations for several years, she obviously outgrew much of the timidity she had in fact possessed. Increased maturity and poise brought also a termination of Sara Delano Roosevelt's dominance over so many aspects of the young couple's lives. The critical years during which Eleanor began to manifest an independent forcefulness of character occurred at the time of her husband's tragic illness; circumstances at that juncture demanded a strength and self-

* This presupposes that Mrs. Roosevelt was aware of the rumors, which she almost certainly was. She was later to cite John Gunther's *Roosevelt in Retrospect* (New York, Harper & Brothers, 1950), which accepted the "romance" story *in toto*, as a singularly well-done "personal picture" of her husband. *The Wisdom of Eleanor Roosevelt*, p. 6.

reliance on her part of which even she hitherto might not have suspected she had command.

It is therefore difficult to agree with the thesis promulgated by sundry commentators to the effect that "Mrs. Roosevelt's restless energy, her travels about the country, [and] her many interests in the New Deal . . . program were dictated in part by the fact that she was a lonely lady." [66] For the beginnings of her ceaseless activities were the result of trying to help her husband rather than of any sense of isolated despair. And it was because of her desire to be "useful," both to her husband and to the countless "underdogs" with whom she came into contact, that she continued and expanded her labors. To "serve" did not connote to her a form of psychic compensation so much as it did the highest fulfillment and completion of her marital relationship.

Eleanor Roosevelt, an emotional and affectionate person, was doubtless at times puzzled and hurt by her husband's self-containment. Rather than sharing his innermost reflections, FDR was a man who steadfastly held that "private, personal matters were a man's own business, not something to be discussed with a second party." He "had no real confidants," finding solace instead in almost total devotion to his public duties. "I don't think I was his confidante, either," Mrs. Roosevelt once confessed to her son James, adding that her husband would seldom even discuss an intimate family matter "unless it was something that had reached the stage at which it just had to be discussed." [67]

Nevertheless, Mrs. Roosevelt was certainly aware that she was as close as it was possible to be to Franklin D. Roosevelt. His reserve concerning intimate matters was a trait which he manifested toward everyone; it was in no sense directed toward her alone, being instead an innate part of FDR's nature. But if she was unable, like everyone else, to penetrate his inner core of reticence, she won — as few other people could have won — his affection and his esteem. The evidence as to this is too plain to dispute.

Some things are mutually exclusive of others. The field of endeavor Roosevelt chose — and the dramatic heights which he reached in his practice of it — precluded, by its very nature, what many people would call a "normal" domestic relationship. Personal characteristics — Franklin's constraint concerning personal matters and Eleanor's lack of light-spiritedness — occasionally made for tension. But the curtailment of certain aspects of domestic life which is enjoined by an active career in public service offers unusual corresponding opportunities to the wife of a man engaged in it. And the want of being perfectly matched in a few attributes of character does not mean a disharmony in the whole relationship of two people. Within the limitations — and there are invariably some limitations to absolute concord in human relationships — imposed by what they were and what they did, Franklin and Eleanor Roosevelt were happy together.

~

Notwithstanding this conclusion, there were — as has been noted — certain areas of friction between the President and his wife, one of which appeared to be the latter's belief that FDR was occasionally prone to move too slowly in the direction of various social reforms. When such was the case the First Lady would often, as Judge Rosenman has phrased it, select "inappropriate times" to discuss her views with her husband, times during which Rosenman felt that she "pressed her point too hard," thus giving rise to a certain irritation on the part of the Chief Executive. Mrs. Roosevelt was in fact questioned about this alleged source of differences between herself and her husband several years subsequent to her departure from the White House, and she candidly replied in the affirmative. Yes, she agreed, "I was much too impatient . . . I wanted to see results much too quickly and therefore would sometimes have accepted the attitude of a benevolent despot rather than have had the patience to wait for democratic forces to work out the problems and solutions far more slowly. With age," she appended, "I have become more patient!" [68]

This frank assessment was on the whole a valid one, and yet it is well to remember that Mrs. Roosevelt did on occasion counsel a course of caution and restraint. As early as 1925 she advised an audience that when pursuing an objective one should "grasp anything which is a step forward [and] not hold out for our particular, ultimate panacea." Though harboring broad, final goals was commendable, she believed that her listeners should nevertheless be reminded that "all big changes in human history have been arrived at slowly and through many compromises." Five years later, commiserating with a friend about the contents of a proposed New York old-age assistance bill, she wrote: "Many of us do not feel that it is a very satisfactory bill but these things come slowly and a little at a time." Mrs. Roosevelt seems to have become especially piqued whenever the more impatient type of reformer accused her husband of lackadaisical leadership. ". . . unless you are Mr. Hitler," she admonished, "you must not lead where your responsible following is not ready to uphold you." To her fellow Democratic activist Mary Dewson, she explained her views on the matter at length:

Please say to everyone who tells you that the President is not giving leadership that he is seeing the [Congressmen] constantly and that he is working with them, but this is a democracy after all and if he once started insisting on having his own way immediately, we would shortly find ourselves in a dictatorship. . . .

The ups and downs in peoples' feelings, particularly on the liberal side, are an old, old story. The liberals always get discouraged when they do not see the measures they are interested in go through immediately. Considering the time we have had to work in the past for almost every slight improvement, I should think they might get over it, but they never do.[69]

It must be admitted, however, that these sentiments, no matter how sincerely meant at the time they were uttered, have a most un-Eleanor Rooseveltian sound. They war with the frequent declarations of contemporaries (and even of herself) to the effect that she was "the agitator" while her husband was "the politician," and that she constantly endeavored to prod him to greater efforts in the matter of reform.[70] This is in no wise to assert that the First Lady did not from time to time advocate a prudent approach toward the solution of certain problems; the case of her activities with respect to Negro Americans, for example, indicates very strongly that she did. But this was unusual — especially after the onset of the Depression and Mrs. Roosevelt's personal contacts with those who suffered most its effects. These contacts, on the contrary, served principally to harden a reformist drive already present within her and to buttress her conviction that either "we solve these problems . . . or else acknowledge that we are beaten and . . . something is wrong with both our government and our economic setup," and that the question of a solution to the economic and social crisis "goes down to the roots of whether civilization goes on or whether civilization dies."[71] The gravity of such statements was hardly reflective of a philosophy hospitable to gradualism and moderation.

But the chief difficulty confronting the First Lady did not, at bottom, involve the pace at which reform should be attempted. Rather, it had to do with the basic shape which reform should take, the proposed contours of which would presumably determine the best *means* through which reform could be effectuated. As was the case in so many of the comparatively peripheral matters with which she concerned herself, Eleanor Roosevelt was of two minds on this most vital of all questions. Her two views, which were in many respects essentially incompatible with one another, dwelt together in an uneasy truce, each trying to break the other's hold upon the allegiance of their mutual owner, and each from time to time evidently succeeding. This internal battle of basic ideas goes far toward explaining the ambiguities which so often seemed to accompany Mrs. Roosevelt's approach to various problems.

One of these two fundamental ideas, and the one to which she most adhered in the early years of her public career, stressed the notion that viable reform must be the product, ultimately, of individual effort. This belief, akin to a sort of secularized regeneration, appears to have stemmed primarily from the influence of her Uncle Theodore. The twenty-sixth President, she pointed out, had emphasized above all else the importance of "character-building"; and in the late 1920's and early 1930's Mrs. Roosevelt reiterated that theme incessantly. "Modern life," she was fond of saying, "tends to make us soft"; history demonstrated that "with the advent of great luxury there is an inevitable softening of the race, and the civilization which reaches the point of great physical comfort is going to die." [72]

There was an oppressively Victorian accent to this doctrine, a dour puritanism which Mrs. Roosevelt would later profess to despise but which she never wholly abandoned. As Professor Schlesinger has aptly put it, she was "a woman sternly devoted to plain living . . . oblivious — and to some . . . it seemed humorlessly, even self-righteously so — to the gaieties of existence." It was this quality which helped turn her against Harry Hopkins' later bent toward high living. It was this part of her makeup which also induced her to tell a foreign dignitary that, with respect to the Depression: "Perhaps it has been a good thing for us that we have had hard times, because so many of us were so complacent about conditions here that we were not willing to face the facts." "For me," she asserted on another occasion, "there is only one answer. Hardships of one kind or another are a necessity to the building of character." [73]

Assuredly, given this outlook, Eleanor Roosevelt could find the 1930's a congenial time in which to build character. Or, perhaps "rebuild" would be a more appropriate word, for the First Lady was decidedly of the opinion that earlier generations of Americans had possessed the virtues of "character." What the contemporary citizen needed, then, was "a little of the stern stuff our ancestors were made of." Like them, "we must voluntarily discipline ourselves and our children . . . in physical ways, learn to harden our bodies, to bear heat and cold, weariness and pain with as little notice as possible and no complaint." "In this country," she remarked, "we do need to be reminded of our antecedents, so as not to allow ourselves to get soft. . . . When the physical world provides you with luxury and ease, you must not deteriorate in inner qualities, and that is one of our dangers." *

It is difficult to ascertain just exactly when Eleanor Roosevelt's reliance on individual capacity for self-improvement as the best vehicle to thoroughgoing reform began to languish. From time to time, it is true, vestiges of her old faith reappeared in her writings. As late as 1939 she expressed the opinion that "I still believe it is the personal and individual thing which is done by one human being for another that is the most valuable assistance which can be rendered in time of trouble," and in the same year she

---

* There is a distinctly familiar halo which hangs over the exhortations of Mrs. Roosevelt as they regard the building of character. Notable in this connection are her frequent use of the words "thrift," "duty," and "self-discipline," and her call "to develop ourselves to the maximum of our ability and our natural endowments." These ideas, as was said about Thomas Jefferson's earlier phrases in the Declaration of Independence, were "in the air" in the middle and latter nineteenth century; but they were most associated with an Englishman by the name of Samuel Smiles. Smiles (1812–1904), although virtually unknown to latter-day audiences, was a man whose books sold phenomenally a century ago. The best known of his writings were *Duty, Character, Thrift,* and *Self-Help.* One wonders whether Mrs. Roosevelt was acquainted with them. ER, *It's Up to the Women,* x, pp. 8–9, 20–21, 137; ER, "Must Success Wear A Hair Shirt?" (June, 1932), "ER, Speeches and Articles," Box 2, FDRL; "My Day," July 4, 1938.

found in Anne Morrow Lindbergh's *Listen the Wind* "a quality
of character involved which takes us right back to our pioneering days and makes us proud to belong to the race which pre-
serves such characteristics." * This kind of pronouncement on
Mrs. Roosevelt's part became, however, increasingly unusual.
Much more typical of her outlook in the latter 1930's was the
view that "our danger today is that we will not outgrow quickly
enough the pioneer idea of each man for himself and the Devil
take the hindmost." No longer was the First Lady wont to de-
clare, as she had during her first year in the White House, that
the sole "new values to replace old values . . . are to be found
in character alone. . . ." And seldom indeed, except for what
appeared to be anachronistic declarations such as those cited
above, was she heard to expound her earlier belief concerning the
efficacy of individual charity or to echo a 1933 conviction like
the following:

> The government cannot support all welfare activities. We must
> try, therefore, to make everybody realize that the help of indi-
> viduals is needed more now, in spite of the present relief by the
> government than it has been for a long time.[74]

For, as the shadows of depression continued to darken the land,
and as Mrs. Roosevelt intensified her interest in those who were
most affected by its baleful shade, she turned more and more to
another method through which to accomplish overall reform —

---

* "My Day," Jan. 4, Oct. 31, 1938. Mrs. Lindbergh's book, which concerned
one of the flights she and her husband had made together, would have been
calculated to exercise an immediate appeal to the First Lady. For Mrs. Roosevelt found a romance in aircraft and those identified with it which she was
never to lose. Flying exploits epitomized to her those virtues of "character"
and "courage" to which she made so great an homage; and she became an invaluable spokesman for air travel. In fact, she wished to learn to fly herself, and
was only dissuaded from doing so by her husband. Amelia Earhart, who disappeared so tragically in 1937, had been her close friend. See Irene Juno, "In
the Air With Our Flying First Lady," *Good Housekeeping*, XCVI (June,
1933), pp. 26–27; ER, "Flying Is Fun," *Collier's*, CIII (April 22, 1939), p. 15.

that of wholesale restructuring of the economic and political system by means of governmental planning and supervision.

Shortly after her husband's election in 1932 Mrs. Roosevelt had announced, in the rhetoric of the day, that there would soon be "a new social and economic order." What form this "new order" would take was, however, far from clear. Not only did the First Lady-to-be not explicate her position, but she continued, as had been seen, to propound the virtues of individual metamorphosis as the high road to a better and more complete life. Nevertheless, a variety of contemporaries bear witness to the fact that she was gradually but inexorably moving toward a more novel position. The British writer H. G. Wells, following a lengthy conversation with both the President and his wife a few months after they had moved into the White House, concluded that both were "*unlimited* people," unawed by the force of traditional American doctrines of government, and instead imbued with the notion that "if it is right we ought to do it." Shortly thereafter, in a gleeful and often penetrating series of comments on New Deal personalities — comments to the effect that they embodied a "laughing revolution" — the so-called "Unofficial Observer" (John Franklin Carter) went a step further. Mrs. Roosevelt knew the direction in which FDR was moving, opined Carter, and though "most of what she says is in harmony with his purposes . . . she is undoubtedly more radical than he is in his public utterances." Oswald Garrison Villard concurred, noting that while the First Lady was muzzled due to the exigencies of her husband's delicate political position, "I cannot but believe that if she were a free agent she would give us some extremely effective criticism of the whole vacillating and dangerous handling of the relief problem . . . [and] about the failure of the housing program and other errors of the Administration." Mrs. Roosevelt's friend Joseph Lash believed "there was much she would like to say to audiences if F.D.R. were not President." [75]

Despite the undoubted fact that the First Lady's public utterances were considerably circumscribed because of the necessities of *Realpolitik*, enough of her private feelings seeped through to friends, fellow workers and even the nation at large to stamp her viewpoint as in some respects markedly innovative. She did not endorse those panaceas which enjoyed much of the public limelight in the 1930's. The schemes of Father Charles Coughlin and Dr. Francis Townsend, for example, received no accolades in her speeches or writings. Of Upton Sinclair's abortive attempt to capture the governorship of California under the banner of his EPIC proposals the First Lady, at her husband's behest, made no mention. She was also — apparently — unsympathetic to the "Share Our Wealth" program put forth by Senator Huey P. Long. The Louisiana "Kingfish" seemed to confirm that such was the case; for, during the course of his remarks preparatory to reading a speech made by the President's wife into the *Congressional Record*, he observed that he was doing so in spite of the fact that she "does not approve of any particular plan that I have offered." *

---

* *Congressional Record*, 74th Congress, 1st Session, Feb. 15, 1935, p. 2002. Long read into the *Record* a reprint by the Washington (D.C.) *Evening Star* of Mrs. Roosevelt's Farm and Home Week speech which the President's wife had delivered at Cornell University on Feb. 14, 1935. The *Star's* version of that portion of the address which referred to the Long scheme was made up of the innocuous phrase: ". . . whether you are a Mr. Townsend, with an old-age plan, or a Senator Huey Long, with a share-the-wealth program," etc. The peculiarity here is that the First Lady's MS of this speech clearly reads: ". . . whether you are Mr. Townsend with his scheme for old age pensions or Huey Long with his *reasonable* [this writer's emphasis] share your wealth [*sic*] program," etc. ER, speech for Farm and Home Week, "ER, Speeches and Articles," Box 6, FDRL.

The inclusion of the word "reasonable" is odd, but it may have been one of the careless insertions not untypical of her original drafts. It must be kept in mind that there was often not only a difference between Mrs. Roosevelt's MSS and the newspaper reports of her speeches but also frequently a dissimilarity be-

Nevertheless, Mrs. Roosevelt generally gravitated toward "planning." She unveiled her public stance in favor of this concept rather slowly at first, her newspaper column's initial laudatory reference to it apparently appearing in 1936 when she obscurely alluded to Old Testament "lesson[s] in planning ahead." With the passage of time she edged toward a more open commitment. Basically, she believed that the State was owed something; there should, in her opinion, be some plan which would compel certain groups of people to work for the good of all. With this in mind in 1938 she saluted as "a very interesting departure in government" a measure "which has just been adopted in Germany, whereby every able-bodied man and woman will be obligated for short-term service to the nation to accomplish nationally urgent tasks. . . ." Still, she was hesitant to endorse publicly a similar scheme for the United States, contenting herself with exhorting U.S. citizens to "voluntarily" participate in "tasks that benefit their communities . . . what Germany has termed 'nationally urgent tasks.' " [76]

The twin specters of continued depression and military threat seem, however, to have overcome her earlier caution. "Stop-gap measures" were no answer; more fundamental solutions must be sought. "I believe that work camps are good for us," she flatly stated to an International Student Service group in 1940: "I believe every young person in this nation should give a year of service to the government. I had no idea when I was growing up that I had an obligation to do something for the country in which I lived. A year is not too long to see how we can be useful." The draft, Mrs. Roosevelt felt, might also be employed as a vehicle for instilling this idea of "service" and "obligation" to

---

tween both of these and the form in which she actually delivered an address. She extemporized with abandon. This habit was confirmed by Mrs. Roosevelt in a letter to Gloria Virginia Ranck in 1952. See Gloria Virginia Ranck, "A Study of Selected Speeches by Mrs. Franklin D. Roosevelt on Human Rights" (unpublished Master's thesis, University of Washington, 1952), p. 34.

one's country. Military training was not, apparently, sufficient; and the First Lady effusively recommended as "excellent" a memorandum sent to her by Morris Ernst which set forth the suggestion that the armed services should stop filling the draftees' leisure time with "the mere process of entertainment a la Eddie Cantor, Fanny Price [sic] and other[s]" but should devote themselves to developing the boys' minds instead. "We need," the memorandum concluded, "an inspired semi-fanatical person who is burning up with the desire to have this mass of men leave the army in a virtual crusade for the re-making of America. I have in mind a man like Robert Sherwood. . . ." [77]

This rather humorless idea is indicative of the fact that Mrs. Roosevelt was able to "cross-breed" certain of her earlier-held notions about "discipline" and "character-building" into her newer enthusiasms about planning. In return for having all boys and girls serve their country for a year, she proclaimed, "they receive training in manual skills, some additional academic training when necessary, and some absolutely vital character training and discipline which can only come with group living." Since the individual had evidently failed under his own power to reach the level of "character" and "discipline" the First Lady considered desirable, the government would accomplish these things for him. Furthermore, "this universal service [to the nation] should, of course, include older people," and although they would be brought in "on a somewhat different basis . . . the idea of fitting them into the service of their country would be stressed." "With a regimented population," she observed brightly, "it would be a simple matter to find twenty-five trained children's workers at a moment's notice." [78]

Such sentiments pointed, of course, to a distinct change of emphasis in Mrs. Roosevelt's outlook regarding the route to and shape of reform. Rexford G. Tugwell, for example, who earlier had felt that the First Lady was convinced he possessed "totalitarian leanings," was subsequently happy to note: "It was evidence of a power of growth in her that she came to understand finally how little good it was possible to do individually and directly, and how necessary it was to sublimate the philanthropic impulses into social programs and permanent systems." [79] But a closer examination of Mrs. Roosevelt's utterances and activities might have indicated to Tugwell that the First Lady had — at least privately — entertained a flirtation with "social programs and permanent systems" as early as 1933. Indeed, in that year, she was to begin a decade-long advocacy of one of the most curious utopian programs promulgated in the entire twentieth century.

This scheme, called "Prohibiting Poverty" or the "National Livelihood Plan," was the work of Mrs. Prestonia Mann Martin, who was a granddaughter of Horace Mann and the wife of a professor at Rollins College in Winter Park, Florida. As outlined in her book, published in 1932, Mrs. Martin's plan embraced the following essentials: (1) all citizens between the ages of eighteen and twenty-six were to be "industrially organized" to produce "Necessaries" for the remainder of the population; (2) the "Necessaries" were food, clothing, shelter, transportation, protection, tools and certain sorts of education; (3) those who produced "Necessaries" were to be called "Commoners"; other members of the population were to be known as "Capitals"; (4) those who "graduated" from the "Commons" (i.e., reached the age of twenty-seven) were then at liberty to join the "Capitals" whose society was to be conducted in accordance with traditional American practices except that "Necessaries" were to be supplied to everyone and the "Capitals" were not to be allowed to compete in any of the fields of activity participated in by the "Commoners." "Yes, Mr. Sociologist," the book declared, "the Plan does envisage a future society which should be dual in character. 'The Commons' is a communistic organization devoted to

Getting-a-Living; 'The Capitals' is the region of society devoted to individualism. . . ." *

Certain rules were to prevail with respect to the "Commons." They would be subject to uniform education "under the direction of a central education board." After service in the "Commons," what Mrs. Martin called "higher ornamental education" might be pursued if desired. Marriage within the group was to be strongly discouraged. ". . . every influence would be brought to bear to persuade young lovers to postpone their conjugal embraces until they had completed their duty to their country and had themselves won their freedom. Most sensible young people," the author concluded smugly, "would undoubtedly see the point." Moreover, no buying and selling was to occur on the part of the "Commons"; money was a low, contemptible thing. "The use of money . . . would be restricted to officials in charge and only the most nominal pocket money [would exist] for the Commoners"; the latters' "*hands must be kept perfectly clean* [original emphasis]." [80]

But the compensations for such petty restrictions were to be infinite. With an ecstatic frenzy characteristic of her prose, Mrs. Martin described some of them:

> In early spring might arrive the great national assembling of recruits, who would come whooping and trooping out of the schools, hastening to join the colors at their several posts all over the country. Towns and villages would celebrate the occasion with rejoicings, cheering the young recruits with bands of music [sic!] and flying banners as they marched away. They are the upholders of the world, the heralds of a new day. Let the drums beat, the bugles sound, the people cheer — youth is on the march!

---

* Prestonia Mann Martin, *Prohibiting Poverty* (New York, Farrar and Rinehart, 1932), pp. 6-13. Mrs. Martin modestly noted that she herself did not evolve the term of eight years for the "Commons." "It was worked out for me by careful statistical investigations made by the New York Labor Bureau, under the direction of Mr. Stuart Chase." *Prohibiting Poverty*, p. 63.

Occasionally the author came perilously close to grief with such odd constructions as "The most expert knowledge on the feeding of human beings would be at the service of the whole people — almost as though they were prize pigs or dogs or blue-ribbon bulls, or sheep or poultry!" But she managed to recover upon contemplating the army-to-be's raiment: "Becoming, inspiring, picturesque and comfortable uniforms for the Young Commoners; cheerful in coloring, simple in cut. Blue jeans for work, white or red for play." Further, "What about rewards, too — medals, citations, crosses, garters — perhaps titles? (happy thought!)" In fact, these fortunate young people, under the absolute direction of hordes of scientists, specialists, experts and researchers for eight years before they received what Mrs. Martin termed their "free papers," were to be "the idols and darlings of society." And, perhaps, America could then "show the world something about genius which it has never yet known. Selah!" [81]

It is distressing — and even disquieting — to find that the First Lady of the Land could subscribe to such a farrago of nonsense, but the unhappy fact is that she did. Possibly the dualism of the "National Livelihood Plan" appealed to the dichotomous approaches concerning reform which were present in her own mind. Both the free play of individualistic self-improvement and the intriguing departures of collectivist planning appeared to enjoy a peaceful and even complementary coexistence in Mrs. Martin's program. In any event, Mrs. Roosevelt was immediately taken with the idea. During her first month in the White House she ordered six copies of the book, and in late 1933 informed the author that she was keeping one of them on her desk.[82]

The President's wife, probably because she recognized the inherent radicalism of the plan and the repercussions which outright public endorsement of it might bring, was reluctant to issue a directly favorable broadside on the subject. Although she oc-

casionally mentioned the scheme in print, she customarily limited
her statements regarding it to oblique approbation.* In the autumn of 1934, for example, Mrs. Martin wrote her that "It
would be a great help if I could say in announcements: 'Mrs.
Roosevelt says that *Everybody Should Read Prohibiting Poverty*. . . .'" The First Lady was agreeable to lending the plan
limited public support of this kind, but at the same time left herself considerable room for defensive maneuver. "My dear Mrs.
Martin," she answered:

> I would be willing to have you say that I think your book should
> be read, if you will qualify it by saying that I am not sure at the
> present time that all of the plans could be put in operation im-
> mediately, but I think it has many things that we should be
> thinking about constantly.[83]

Correspondence between the two languished thereafter, although Mrs. Martin did write the First Lady a lengthy letter in
1936 filled with forebodings about business being "unwilling or
unable — perhaps permanently unable" to keep employment at a
high level. Government, the author of *Prohibiting Poverty* concluded, therefore "*must* take its place," preferably by means of
moving toward a circumscribed version of the "National Livelihood Plan" through an expansion of the CCC. Mrs. Roosevelt
was forced, after having passed the letter on to her husband for
his perusal, to inform Mrs. Martin sadly that "unfortunately,
many of the CCC boys are leaving camp now to take regular
jobs." The First Lady did not, however, forget the plan as an
entirety. In June of 1940 Prestonia Mann Martin wired her as
follows: "HURRAY, HURRAY. SOME OF US THINK THE PRESI-
DENT'S LABOR PROPOSAL FOR YOUTH [universal government — as

---

* Both Caroline Bird, *The Invisible Scar* (New York, David McKay Co.,
Inc., 1966), p. 90, and The Unofficial Observer (*The New Dealers*, p. 210),
confirm that Mrs. Roosevelt boosted the plan privately; she publicly referred
to it in an offhandedly approving manner in "My Day," June 5, 1936.

opposed to military — service] MAY BE A STEP TOWARD THE NA-
TIONAL LIVELIHOOD PLAN FOR PROHIBITING POVERTY." At the
bottom of the telegram, in handwriting plainly discernible as being that of Eleanor Roosevelt, there appears the notation: "I
hope so." [84]

~

What, by way of summary, can be said of the philosophy and
career of Mrs. Roosevelt during the years prior to 1941? Initially, or so it seems to this writer, one is struck by her warmth,
by her deeply sincere humanitarianism, by her genuinely earnest
sense of compassion for human suffering. Of all her personal attributes, this remained the most consistent; indeed, it is virtually
impossible to imagine Eleanor Roosevelt at all without associating this characteristic with her. If at times this humanitarian aspect seemed a trifle severe (as when, in commenting upon a "glorious" winter day, she followed with a stark, "I always think,
however, what this weather means to those who are poorly fed,
poorly housed, and poorly clothed"), it was more often a movingly unadorned plea for sympathy and kindness to one's fellow
man. "In 4½ years," she once said, "386,000,000 school lunches
have been served [under the auspices of the WPA]. But don't
think of figures. Think of boys and girls and milk and soup and
vegetables. . . . Cold figures," she continued,

> reveal that 220,000,000 garments have been made by W.P.A.
> workers in 4½ years — enough for 2 apiece for every man,
> woman, and child in the United States. But think of these things
> in terms of sweaters to keep babies warm, dresses and suits for
> boys and girls who otherwise couldn't go to school for lack of
> clothes to wear, dresses for mothers who haven't known such a
> luxury for years.[85]

For the most part Mrs. Roosevelt, particularly during her
early years of public life, stayed within this tradition, the tradi-

tion of, as she put it, "deal[ing] almost entirely with cases and individuals." This was in accord with the experience of her generation, in which "women were trained to think along certain lines . . . charitable work . . . church work; or finding food and fuel for the needy . . . namely, an approach to social and economic problems via the route of a personal interest in the miseries of humanity." Within such a tradition, which was basically that of a social worker, Mrs. Roosevelt would accomplish much that was good for her fellow man.[86]

At the same time, important as it was in the creation of a certain sphere of understanding, this background was not one calculated to equip Mrs. Roosevelt to deal effectively with the vast and yet intricate problems of high public policy. She was at her best in calling attention to abuses — a role which was exceedingly vital, to be sure — but she was not often responsible for cogent or workable solutions with respect to them. There were simply too many lacunae in her intellectual portfolio. Not that she was not shrewd, for she had a sensitivity for political nuances which was to make her into the most adept female politician in the country. But she did not know economics, she did not know law, and her grasp of history, philosophy and public administration was extremely limited. Of the manifold difficulties which faced business and financial institutions she had no comprehension. Of those which confronted labor and the farmer she had some; but her lack of sustained analysis as to why they existed in the first place rendered her proposals concerning how to alleviate them ephemeral or else fantastic.

Ironically, Mrs. Roosevelt's altruistic interests had a tendency to militate against influences which might have helped fill certain of the gaps in her knowledge. Her activities took her out among people whose intellectual horizons were usually, through no fault of their own, somewhat limited; and when she was in Washington she rarely saw a great deal of anyone except those whose views were similar to those she herself entertained. Her companions were likely to be individuals such as Harry Hopkins or Aubrey Williams; later, she was to cultivate youthful protégés like Joseph Lash and Mayris Chaney. Hopkins and Williams both had backgrounds in social work, Lash was a muddled young leftist when he met Mrs. Roosevelt, and Miss Chaney was a dancer — identified principally with her introduction of a series of gyrations known as the "Eleanor Glide." Perhaps, moreover, the usually well-disposed Dorothy Dunbar Bromley, in commenting that the First Lady's mind "lack[ed] masculine toughness and skepticism," was correct in attributing this to the fact that she "spent too much time with women." In any case, for all her spontaneous generosity, Mrs. Roosevelt remained essentially gullible and disturbingly ignorant.*

If, however, there is anything — in the broad sense — to be learned from a study of Eleanor Roosevelt, it might be this: those who prided themselves on being tough-minded "realists" about the government and its relationship to its citizens, *all* its citizens, and those whose command of legal and financial expertise was infinitely greater than the First Lady's — those people — in the hard, pragmatic test of politics — failed. They failed not because they were contemptuous of the "human" factors involved in suffering — whether that suffering stemmed from poverty, discrimination or sheer ill-fortune — but because they did not consider it an important enough matter to communicate their understanding and concern to their constituents. Mrs. Roosevelt supplied that communication to an unprecedented degree, and the adulation she received in return should be evi-

---

* Dorothy Dunbar Bromley, "The Future of Eleanor Roosevelt," *Harper's Magazine*, CLXXX (Jan., 1940), p. 137. The First Lady's naïveté regarding the complicated functions of government may be indicated by the fact that, when she took over her only official job (in the Office of Civilian Defense) while her husband was President, she picked as her top administrative aides Miss Chaney and movie actor Melvyn Douglas.

dence enough to convince even the most skeptical that those with the competence and experience to best deal with the enormous problems with which we are challenged must never again neglect the "human" factor.

The career of Eleanor Roosevelt provides a singularly pristine example of what Arthur Schlesinger, Jr., once, in another connection, termed "the variety and flexibility and strength, the vanity and the gullibility, the shame and the glory of American liberalism." [87] Her weaknesses were those of many a Depression-generation reformer — self-righteousness, a too-facile division of persons and institutions into categories of "good" and "evil," and a short-sighted view regarding the implications of the schemes she endorsed. But her strong points — points which she perhaps possessed to a more marked degree than almost any other of her like-minded contemporaries — more often than not at least counterbalanced these shortcomings. For Mrs. Roosevelt was the personification of a virtually unblemished kindness, generosity, and — in the best sense of that overused word — goodness.

Her opponents derided her — and this was understandable enough — for her occasional silliness and for her more frequent banalities. But these same critics made their great mistake in failing to look beneath the surface — to the spirit which motivated Mrs. Roosevelt. And in missing this spirit and its meaning — that *somehow* the poor, the downtrodden and the forlorn *must* be given new opportunity and new hope — they missed what will in all likelihood be the most enduring legacy of a truly remarkable woman.

NOTES

BIBLIOGRAPHY

INDEX

~

NOTES

As will be obvious to most readers, the method of footnoting in this work is to allow those footnotes which contain commentary to remain at the bottom of the page of the text itself, while those which are merely for the purpose of reference are contained in the pages which follow the text. This writer has, in both cases, generally used the "cluster" method of footnoting in order to avoid an excessive and possibly distracting number of citations.

Once again, it might be pointed out that all references to Mrs. Roosevelt's column "My Day" indicate (unless otherwise specified) the unedited versions at the Franklin D. Roosevelt Library (FDRL), Hyde Park, New York, while the initials "ER" refer to Eleanor Roosevelt herself.

INTRODUCTION

1. Geneva Kretsinger, "An Analytical Study of Selected Radio Speeches of Eleanor Roosevelt" (unpublished Master's thesis, University of Oklahoma, 1941); Gloria Virginia Ranck, "A Study of Selected Speeches by Mrs. Franklin D. Roosevelt on Human Rights" (unpublished Master's thesis, University of Washington, 1952); Helen Jane Wamboldt, "Anna Eleanor Roosevelt: A Descriptive and Analytical Study of the Speaking Career of AER" (unpublished Ph.D. dissertation, University of Southern California, 1952); Eleanor Janice Bilsborrow, "The Philosophy of Social Reform in the Speeches of Eleanor Roosevelt" (unpublished Ph.D. dissertation, University of Denver, 1957); James R. Kearney, "Mrs. Eleanor Roosevelt and the American Negro" (unpublished Master's thesis, Washington University, 1962); Benjamin A. Spence, "Mrs. Eleanor Roosevelt and Refugee Problems 1938–1952" (unpublished Master's thesis, University of Wisconsin, 1962); Tamara K. Hareven, "The Social Thought of Eleanor Roosevelt" (unpublished Ph.D. dissertation, Ohio State University, 1965).

2. Ruby Black, *Eleanor Roosevelt* (New York, Duell, Sloan and Pearce, 1940); Joseph P. Lash, *Eleanor Roosevelt: A Friend's Memoir* (Garden City, New York, Doubleday and Co., Inc., 1964); Lorena A. Hickok, *Reluctant First Lady* (New York, Dodd, Mead and Co., 1962); Helen Gahagan Douglas, *The Eleanor Roosevelt We Remember* (New York, Hill and Wang, 1963); Alfred Steinberg, *Mrs. R* (New York, G. P. Putnam's Sons, 1958).

1. Mother to a Generation

1. Ruby Black, *Eleanor Roosevelt* (New York, Duell, Sloan and Pearce, 1940), p. 222.

2. Leslie A. Gould, *American Youth Today* (New York, Random House, 1940), p. 25.

3. ER, *This I Remember* (New York, Harper & Brothers, 1949), p. 205.

4. ER, *This Is My Story* (New York, Harper & Brothers, 1937).

5. *Time*, XXIX (March 8, 1937), p. 36; *Newsweek*, X (Nov. 22, 1937), p. 33; *Bakersfield Californian* (Dec. 15, 1937).

6. Arthur M. Schlesinger, Jr., *The Crisis of the Old Order* (Boston, Houghton Mifflin Co., 1957), pp. 325–27; Frank Freidel, *Franklin D. Roosevelt: The Apprenticeship* (Boston, Little, Brown and Co., 1952), pp. 67–69; Rexford G. Tugwell, *The Democratic Roosevelt* (Garden City, New York, Doubleday and Co., Inc., 1957), p. 61.

7. ER, *This Is My Story*, pp. 1–52, *passim*.

8. *Ibid.*, p. 1; *The Wisdom of Eleanor Roosevelt* (a compilation of her columns done for *McCall's Magazine*) (New York, n.d.), p. 44.

9. ER, unpublished article marked only "Vogue" and probably written in 1929, "ER, Speeches and Articles," Box 1, FDRL.

10. ER, *This Is My Story*, pp. 11, 17, 22.

11. Alfred Steinberg, *Mrs. R* (New York, G. P. Putnam's Sons, 1958), p. 18.

12. ER, *This Is My Story*, pp. 6, 20, 34.

13. *Ibid.*, p. 50.

14. ER, "In Defense of Curiosity," *The Saturday Evening Post*, CCVIII (August 24, 1935), p. 9; ER, *This Is My Story*, p. 27.

15. Speech before the Pelham (N.Y.) Parent-Teachers Assn. (October 2, 1931), "ER, Speeches and Articles," Box 1, FDRL.

16. Second in a series of radio broadcasts delivered for the Pond's Co. (undated but probably Dec. 16, 1932), "ER, Speeches and Articles," Box 3, FDRL.

17. Speech at Greensboro, No. Carolina (undated but *circa* 1932), "ER, Speeches and Articles," Box 5, FDRL.

18. ER, "Diary" (entry of Nov. 15, 1899), reproduced in Richard Harrity and Ralph G. Martin, *Eleanor Roosevelt, Her Life in Pictures* (New York, Duell, Sloan and Pearce, 1958), p. 9; second in a series of radio broadcasts for the Pond's Co., see fn. #16.

19. Joseph P. Lash, *Eleanor Roosevelt: A Friend's Memoir* (Garden City, New York, Doubleday and Co., Inc., 1964), p. 48.

20. ER, *This Is My Story*, pp. 109–10.

21. *The Wisdom of Eleanor Roosevelt*, p. 110; ER, *If You Ask Me* (New York, D. Appleton-Century Co., Inc., 1946), p. 54; "My Day" (Feb. 4, 1936); speech before the Pelham Parent-Teachers Assn., see fn., #15; ER, *This Is My Story*, p. 44; "My Day," Seattle *Post-Intelligencer* (July 27, 1948); "Broadcast by Mrs. Eleanor Roosevelt" in Edward P. Morgan and Raymond G. Swing (eds.), *This I Believe* (New York, Simon and Schuster, 1952), p. 30; ER, *It Seems to Me* (New York, W. W. Norton and Co., Inc., 1954), p. 61; speech before the Pelham Parent-Teachers Assn., see fn. #15.

22. *The Wisdom of Eleanor Roosevelt*, p. 110.

23. Freidel, *Franklin D. Roosevelt: The Apprenticeship*, p. 80.

24. ER, "Ethics of Parents," written for *Collier's* but unpublished, "ER, Speeches and Articles," Box 1, FDRL.

25. James Roosevelt and Sidney Shalett, *Affectionately, F.D.R.* (New York, Harcourt, Brace and Co., 1959), p. 24.

26. Harold L. Ickes, *The Secret Diary of Harold L. Ickes*, 3 vols. (New York, Simon and Schuster, 1953–54), I, p. 238; James Roosevelt and Shalett, *Affectionately, F.D.R.*, pp. 81–82, 161.

27. ER, *This I Remember*, pp. 19–20.

28. Frances Perkins, *The Roosevelt I Knew* (New York, The Viking Press, 1946), p. 63; John Gunther, *Roosevelt in Retrospect* (New York, Harper & Brothers, 1950), p. 164.

29. ER to FDR (all n.d.), quoted in James Roosevelt and Shalett, *Affectionately, F.D.R.*, pp. 24, 96–97, 151.

30. ER to FDR (Sept. 2, 1933), quoted in *ibid.*, pp. 24, 96–97.

31. "Mrs. Franklin D. Roosevelt's Speech for Movietone" (undated but apparently made about 1929), "ER, Speeches and Articles," Box 1, FDRL.

32. ER, *This I Remember*, p. 18; "My Day," pilot article #18 (never released), FDRL; Ickes, *Secret Diary*, I, p. 184.

33. ER, *This I Remember*, p. 18.

34. "My Day" (Sept. 9, 1938).

35. Lash, *Eleanor Roosevelt*, pp. 144–45.

36. James Roosevelt and Shalett, *Affectionately, F.D.R.*, p. 266.

37. ER, *This I Remember*, pp. 9, 21.

38. Oswald Garrison Villard, "Issues and Men," *The Nation*, CXLVIII (Dec. 31, 1938), p. 15.

39. Speech to a Mother's Day Breakfast, Brooklyn YWCA, May 11, 1924, quoted in the *New York Times* (May 12, 1924); ER, *It's Up to the Women* (New York, Frederick A. Stokes Co., 1933), pp. 120, 132.

40. Interview with Marion Dickerman (May 25, 1965).

41. ER, MS marked only "Home Education — Books We Should All Read," (n.d., but probably written *ca.* 1929), "ER, Speeches and Articles," Box 1, FDRL.

42. ER, MS marked only "Education — Vocation" (n.d., but early 1930's), "ER, Speeches and Articles," Box 5, FDRL.

43. ER, "In Defense of Curiosity," *op. cit.*, p. 65.

44. ER, "Learning to Teach" (from "Mrs. Roosevelt's Page"), *Woman's Home Companion*, LXI (April, 1934), p. 4; ER, *It's Up to the Women*, p. 155.

45. Kathleen McLaughlin, "The First Lady's View of the First-Lady Role," *New York Times Magazine* (Jan. 21, 1940), p. 20.

46. *The Wisdom of Eleanor Roosevelt*, p. 15.

47. ER, *It's Up to the Women*, p. 158; *Opportunity*, XIV (Jan., 1936), pp. 22–23.

48. ER, "A Message to Parents and Teachers," *Progressive Education*, XI (Jan.–Feb., 1934), p. 38.

49. ER, *It's Up to the Women*, p. 137.

50. George P. Rawick, "The New Deal and Youth: The Civilian Conservation Corps, the National Youth Administration and the American Youth Congress" (unpublished Ph.D. dissertation, University of Wisconsin, 1957), pp. 20–29, *passim*.

51. From a speech by Mrs. Roosevelt, quoted by the *New York Times*, excerpts of which were read by Senator Huey P. Long, Democrat of Louisiana, into the *Congressional Record*, 73rd Congress, 2nd Session (May 8, 1934), p. 8270.

52. Radio broadcast (NBC) by Mrs. Eleanor Roosevelt (April 19, 1933), "ER, Speeches and Articles," Box 5, FDRL.

53. ER, "Camps for Unemployed Women," designed for the *Encyclopaedia Brittanica Bulletin* (n.d. but late 1933), "ER, Speeches and Articles," Box 5, FDRL.

54. Anna Lou Riesch, "Conservation Under Franklin D. Roosevelt" (unpublished Ph.D. dissertation, University of Wisconsin, 1952), *passim.*

55. ER, *This I Remember*, pp. 162–63.

56. Charles W. Taussig to ER (June 28, 1935), "Papers of Charles W. Taussig," Section I, Box 14, Folder Y–134, FDRL.

57. Lash, *Eleanor Roosevelt*, p. 242.

58. See, for example, "My Day" (April 10, Nov. 12–18, 1936; March 10–30, 1938).

59. *Life*, VIII (Feb. 5, 1940), pp. 72–73.

60. ER to Aubrey Williams (Aug. 13, 1936); ER to Williams (n.d. but summer, 1936), "Papers of Aubrey Williams," Group 58, Box, 4, FDRL.

61. Williams to ER (July 7, Aug. 15, 1936), both in *ibid.*

62. Taussig to ER (May 4, 1936); ER to Taussig (Jan. 23, 1936), "Taussig Papers," Section I, Box 14, Folder Y–134, FDRL.

63. Copy of a St. Louis (Mo.) educator (name not in copy) to ER (Jan. 28, 1936), *ibid.*

64. New York *Herald Tribune* (Feb. 6, 1940).

65. ER, speech at a youth dinner in her honor, Murray Hill Hotel, New York City (Feb. 22, 1939), quoted in Gould, *American Youth Today*, p. 98.

66. Rawick, "The New Deal and Youth," p. 217.

67. *Ibid.*, pp. 289–95; *Time*, XXXIV (Dec. 11, 1939), p. 16.

68. "My Day" (Jan. 27, 1936).

69. *Ibid.* (Aug. 9, 1938).

70. Speech before the New York State Conference of the NYA Advisory Committee, Albany, New York (Nov., 1938), quoted in *Youth Digest* (published by the New York City Council, American Youth Congress), I (Dec., 1938), p. 6.

71. "My Day" (Feb. 23, 1939); Joseph Cadden to Taussig (Dec. 19, 1938), "Taussig Papers," Section I, Box 1, Folder Y–12, FDRL.

72. *Hearings Before a Special Committee on Un-American Activities*, House of Representatives, 76th Congress, 1st Session (Nov. 30, 1939), p. 6994.

73. *Time*, XXXIV (Dec. 11, 1939), p. 17.

74. "My Day" (Dec. 2, 1939).

75. New York *Sun*, quoted in *Time*, XXXIV (Dec. 11, 1939), p. 17; Heywood Broun, "It Seems to Me," New York *World-Telegram* (Dec. 6, 1939); New York *World-Telegram* (Dec. 2, 1939); New York *Herald Tribune* (Dec. 2, 1939).

76. "My Day" (Dec. 5, 1939).

77. Quoted in Gould, *American Youth Today*, p. 8.

78. Samuel I. Rosenman (compiler and collator), *The Public Papers and Addresses of Franklin D. Roosevelt*, 13 vols., (New York, The Macmillan Co. [vols. VI through IX only], 1938–50), IX, pp. 85–94.

79. *Washington* (D.C.) *Post* (Feb. 11, 1940).

80. *This Is Youth Speaking*, pamphlet (New York, American Youth Congress, 1940), pp. 26–27.

81. Salt Lake City *Tribune* (Feb. 14, 1940); Walter Lippmann, "Today and Tomorrow," New York *Herald Tribune* (Feb. 17, 1940); Detroit *Free Press* (Feb. 14, 1940); Ernest K. Lindley in the Richmond (Va.) *Times-Dispatch* (Feb. 14, 1940).

82. Foreword by Eleanor Roosevelt in Gould, *American Youth Today*, p. vii.

83. "My Day" (June 15, July 11, 1940).

84. (Madison) *Wisconsin State Journal* (July 6–8, 1940).

85. Lash, *Eleanor Roosevelt*, p. 234.

86. Speech of Eleanor Roosevelt read by Caroline O'Day (June 23, 1930), "ER, Speeches and Articles," Box 1, FDRL.

87. Lash, *Eleanor Roosevelt*, p. 76.

88. Walter Lippmann, "Today and Tomorrow," New York *Herald Tribune* (Feb. 17, 1940).

89. "My Day" (Feb. 13, 1940).

90. Ernest K. Lindley, *The Roosevelt Revolution* (New York, The Viking Press, 1933), p. 283; Miss Thompson quoted in *Life*, VIII (Feb. 5, 1940), p. 76.

91. Rawick, "The New Deal and Youth," p. 343; ER, speech before the New York State Conference of the NYA Advisory committee, see fn. #70; Gould, *American Youth Today*, pp. 100–105; "My Day" (July 5, 1939); (Madison) *Wisconsin State Journal* (July 5, 1940); *New York Times* (Aug. 2, 1940).

92. ER, *This I Remember*, pp. 200–205.

93. "My Day" (Dec. 5, 1939).

94. ER to Harry H. Nagle (n.d. but 1939), quoted in Gould, *American Youth Today*, pp. 150–51.

95. ER, *This I Remember*, p. 203.

96. Rawick, "The New Deal and Youth," fn., p. 337; James Wechsler, *The Age of Suspicion* (New York, Random House, 1953), p. 71; Murray

Kempton, *Part of Our Time* (New York, Simon and Schuster, 1955), pp. 1–11, 300–334, *passim;* Lash, *Eleanor Roosevelt, passim.*

97. ER, Speech before the New York State Conference of the NYA Advisory Committee, see fn. #70; "My Day" (Jan. 25, 1940).

98. (Boston) *Christian Science Monitor* (Feb. 12, 1940). For an opinion maintaining that the provisions of the Youth Bill were "not the American way," see the St. Louis *Globe-Democrat* (Feb. 13, 1940).

99. ER, Speech before the New York State Conference of the NYA Advisory Committee, se fn. #70.

100. "A gal who likes you for yourself" to ER (n.d.), filed with "ER, Speeches and Articles," Box 5, FDRL; "My Day" (Jan. 17, 1940); New York *Herald Tribune* (Feb. 6, 1940); Rawick, "The New Deal and Youth," pp. 370–71; Lash, *Eleanor Roosevelt,* pp. 109, 183.

101. *This Is Youth Speaking,* p. 27; Lash, *Eleanor Roosevelt,* pp. 10–12, 88.

102. (New York) *Daily Worker* (May 26, 1938); Gil Green quoted in the same source (Dec. 9, 1936).

103. Quoted in Lash, *Eleanor Roosevelt,* p. 117.

11. Friend to a Neglected Promise

1. W. W. Rostow, *The Stages of Economic Growth* (Cambridge, The University Press, 1961), pp. 6–9.

2. ER, "Some of My Best Friends Are Negro," *Ebony,* IX (Feb., 1953), pp. 17–18.

3. ER to Sara Delano Roosevelt (Aug. 1, 1905), quoted in Elliott Roosevelt (ed.) and James Rosenau (asst.), *F.D.R. His Personal Letters 1905–1928* (New York, Duell, Sloan and Pearce, 1948), p. 52.

4. ER, "Jeffersonian Principles the Issue in 1928," *Current History,* XXVIII (June, 1928), 354–57.

5. ER, untitled MS fragment (dated 1928), "ER, Speeches and Articles," Box 1, FDRL.

6. ER, untitled MS (1928), "ER, Speeches and Articles," Box 1, FDRL; *New York Times* (Nov. 1, 1925).

7. ER, "Democratic Plank on Law Enforcement" (dated 1928), "ER, Speeches and Articles," Box 1, FDRL; Richard L. Watson, Jr., "A Political Leader Bolts — F. M. Simmons in the Presidential Election of 1928," *North Carolina Historical Review,* XXXVII (October, 1960), p. 530.

8. See for numerous examples of this Edmund A. Moore, *A Catholic Runs for President* (New York, Ronald Press Co., 1956).

9. W. E. B. Du Bois, "Is Al Smith Afraid of the South?" *The Nation*, CXXVII (October 17, 1928), pp. 393–94.

10. Watson, "A Political Leader Bolts — F. M. Simmons in the Presidential Election of 1928," *op. cit.*, pp. 535–38.

11. *New York Times* (Jan. 30, July 10, 1928); ER, "Servants," *The Forum*, LXXXIII (Jan., 1930), p. 24; *The Wisdom of Eleanor Roosevelt* (a compilation of her columns done for *McCall's Magazine*) (New York, n.d.), p. 89; ER, *This I Remember* (New York, Harper & Brothers, 1949), p. 40.

12. ER, *This Is My Story* (New York, Harper & Brothers, 1937), pp. 149–50; Frances Perkins, *The Roosevelt I Knew* (New York, The Viking Press, 1946), p. 141.

13. ER, "What Religion Means to Me," *The Forum*, LXXXVIII (Dec., 1932), p. 322; ER, "I Answer Two Questions" (from "Mrs. Roosevelt's Page"), *Woman's Home Companion*, LX (Dec., 1933), p. 24.

14. ER, *The Moral Basis of Democracy* (New York, Howell, Soskin & Co., 1940), p. 57.

15. For a brief discussion relating to Mrs. Roosevelt's concern with Indian problems and especially her correspondence with Secretary of the Interior Harold L. Ickes in this regard, see Tamara K. Hareven, "The Social Thought of Eleanor Roosevelt" (unpublished Ph.D. dissertation, Ohio State University, 1965), pp. 168–70.

16. "My Day" (March 7, 1938); ER, speech to a Jewish women's group, Bellevue-Stratford Hotel, Philadelphia (spring, 1934), quoted in an unidentified newspaper clipping in "President's Personal File #2," Box 1, FDRL.

17. Florence Rothchild, "The Mistress of the White House," (Milwaukee) *Wisconsin Jewish Chronicle* (March 9, 1934).

18. *Opportunity*, XIV (Jan., 1936), p. 22; *The Crisis*, XLVI (Aug., 1939), p. 243 and (Sept., 1939), p. 284; Chicago *Defender* (July 15, 1939); *New York Times* (May 27, 1936).

19. ER, "What Religion Means to Me," *op. cit.*, p. 324.

20. ER, "Some of My Best Friends Are Negro," *op. cit.*, p. 18.

21. Thomas Mathews, *Puerto Rican Politics and the New Deal* (Gainsville, Fla., University of Florida Press, 1960), pp. 154–58; Rackham Holt, *Mary McLeod Bethune* (Garden City, New York, Doubleday and Co., Inc., 1964), p. 178; Cleo Moultry to "Mrs. Franklin Roosevelt" (May 9, 1934), quoted in Allen Kifer, "The Negro Under the New Deal 1933–1941" (unpublished Ph.D. dissertation, University of Wisconsin, 1961), p. 215.

22. *Opportunity*, XII (June, 1934), p. 167.

23. *Congressional Record*, 73rd Congress, 2nd Session (June 18, 1934), p. 12607.

24. Clarence E. Pickett, *For More Than Bread* (Boston, Little, Brown and Co., 1953), pp. 48–49; Walter White, *A Man Called White* (New York, The Viking Press, 1948), pp. 168–69.

25. Kifer, "The Negro Under the New Deal," p. 89.

26. Martin quoted in White, *A Man Called White*, p. 22. See also the *New York Times* (Jan. 30, 1936); Arthur M. Schlesinger, Jr., *The Politics of Upheaval* (Boston, Houghton Mifflin Co., 1960), p. 522; and ER, "Some of My Best Friends Are Negro," *op. cit.*, p. 25.

27. Paul W. Ward, "Wooing the Negro Vote," *The Nation*, CXLIII (Aug. 1, 1936), p. 120; William E. Leuchtenburg, *Franklin D. Roosevelt and the New Deal 1932–1940* (New York, Harper & Row, 1963), p. 186.

28. *The Crisis*, XLII (Dec., 1935), p. 371.

29. Frank Freidel, *Franklin D. Roosevelt: The Apprenticeship* (Boston, Little, Brown and Co., 1952), fn., p. 322.

30. *New York Times* (May 23, 1932); Henry Lee Moon, *Balance of Power: The Negro Vote* (Garden City, New York, Doubleday and Co., Inc., 1948), p. 17.

31. *The Crisis*, XLI (Jan., 1934), p. 5; Donald Porter Geddes (ed.), *Franklin D. Roosevelt, A Memorial* (New York, The Dial Press, 1945), pp. 140–47; *The Crisis*, XLI (March, 1934), p. 61.

32. Leslie H. Fishel, Jr., "The Negro in the New Deal Era," *Wisconsin Magazine of History*, XLVIII (Winter, 1964–65), p. 113; "Just a Colored Mother" to FDR (June 16, 1935), quoted in John R. Salmond, "The Civilian Conservation Corps and the Negro," *Journal of American History*, LXX (June, 1965), p. 81.

33. *New York Times* (Aug. 27, 1933; March 4, 1934; Jan. 8, 1935); Hoey's speech was delivered Dec. 31, 1933, excerpts of which are in the *Congressional Record*, 73rd Congress, 2nd Session (Jan. 11, 1934), 432; *The Crisis*, XLI (Nov., 1934), pp. 332–33.

34. *Pittsburgh Courier* (Oct. 17, 1936); Robert C. Weaver, "The New Deal and the Negro," *Opportunity*, XII (July, 1935), p. 202; *New York Times* (April 15, 1934).

35. Fishel, "The Negro in the New Deal Era," *op. cit.*, p. 111; Kifer, "The Negro Under the New Deal," p. 277; Mrs. Bethune quoted in George P. Rawick, "The New Deal and Youth: The Civilian Conservation Corps, the National Youth Administration and the American Youth Congress" (unpublished Ph.D. dissertation, University of Wisconsin, 1957), p. 242.

36. *Opportunity*, XIV (Jan., 1936), p. 5.

37. Memo from ER to FDR, James A. Farley, *et al.* (July 16, 1936), "Papers of Mary W. Dewson," Group 37, Box 3, FDRL; *New York Times* (Sept. 3, 1936).

38. Louis Harris, *Is There A Republican Majority?* (New York, Harper & Brothers, 1954), p. 160.

39. *New York Times* (April 26, 1931); "A White House Tea-Party Tempest," *Literary Digest,* CI (June 29, 1929), p. 10.

40. *New York Times* (Oct. 2, 1932); Arthur Krock, "Did the Negro Revolt?" *Opportunity,* XI (Jan., 1933), p. 19.

41. Schlesinger, *The Politics of Upheaval,* p. 430; John G. VanDeusen, "The Negro in Politics," *Journal of Negro History,* XXI (July, 1936), p. 273.

42. *New Republic,* LXXI (Nov. 14, 1934), p. 1.

43. *New York Times* (June 10, 1936).

44. Lawrence Sullivan, "The Negro Vote," *Atlantic Monthly,* CLXVI (Oct., 1940), pp. 477–84; Leuchtenburg, *Franklin D. Roosevelt and the New Deal,* p. 187.

45. George W. Robinson, "Right of Roosevelt: Negativism and the New Deal 1933–1937" (unpublished Ph.D. dissertation, University of Wisconsin, 1956), p. 56.

46. *The Crisis,* XLIII (Dec., 1936), p. 369.

47. *Literary Digest,* CXXIII (March 6, 1937), pp. 8–9.

48. ER, *This I Remember,* p. 162.

49. *Congressional Record,* 76th Congress, 1st Session (Aug. 5, 1939), p. A4042.

50. *Ibid.,* 76th Congress, 3rd Session (March 18, 1940), p. 3026.

51. *New York Times* (Dec. 19, 1937); *Opportunity,* XVI (Jan., 1938), p. 28 and (March, 1938), p. 89; *The Crisis,* XLVII (March, 1940), p. 84.

52. *Opportunity,* XIV (Jan., 1936), p. 23; *The Crisis,* XLVI (Feb., 1939), p. 54; XLVII (Nov., 1940), p. 343; Moon, *Balance of Power,* p. 36.

53. ER and Lorena Hickok, *Ladies of Courage* (New York, G. P. Putnam's Sons, 1954), p. 286.

54. ER, *This I Remember,* p. 164.

55. Joseph P. Lash, *Eleanor Roosevelt: A Friend's Memoir* (Garden City, New York: Doubleday and Co., Inc., 1964), p. 44.

56. Quoted in *Opportunity,* XVIII (Dec., 1940), pp. 356–57.

57. ER, *This I Remember,* pp. 173–74; *Life,* VIII (Feb. 5, 1940), p. 63.

58. *New York Times* (March 1, 1939).

59. *Ibid.* (March 5, 1939); excerpts of Taft's speech, delivered March 2,

1939, were read by Senator Charles McNary into the *Congressional Record*, 76th Congress, 1st Session (March 13, 1939), p. A950.

60. *New York Times* (March 19, 1939).

61. *Opportunity*, XVII (March, 1949), p. 67.

62. Minneapolis *Spokesman* (March 4, 1939).

63. *The Crisis*, XLVI (Sept., 1939), p. 285; Chicago *Defender* (July 15, 1939).

64. *Opportunity*, XIV (Jan., 1936), pp. 22–23; ER, "Race, Religion and Prejudice," *New Republic*, CVI (May 11, 1942), p. 630; "My Day" (March 12, 1937; Aug. 5, 1938; March 9, 1939).

65. Clipping, Montgomery (name unknown) newspaper (with date "1939" noted on it) and Hopson Owen Murfee to FDR (Oct. 29, 1939), both items in "President's Personal File #2," Box 2, FDRL.

66. Excerpts of a speech by Mrs. Roosevelt (May 9, 1936) read by Representative James L. Quinn, Democrat of Pennsylvania, into the *Congressional Record*, 74th Congress, 2nd Session (June 20, 1935), pp. 10839–40.

67. *Opportunity*, XIV (Jan., 1936), pp. 22–23; *The Crisis*, XLVI (Sept., 1939), p. 284.

68. *Opportunity*, XLVII (Dec., 1940), p. 357.

69. ER, *If You Ask Me* (New York, D. Appleton-Century Co., Inc., 1946), p. 120.

III. Partner in a Champion Political Combination

1. Andrew Sinclair, *The Available Man* (New York, The Macmillan Co., 1965), pp. 33–56.

2. Joseph P. Lash, *Eleanor Roosevelt: A Friend's Memoir* (Garden City, New York, Doubleday and Co., Inc., 1964), p. 134; ER, *This I Remember* (New York: Harper & Brothers, 1949), pp. 6–7.

3. James R. Farley, *Behind the Ballots* (New York, Harcourt, Brace and Co., 1938), p. 354.

4. ER, "Wives of Great Men," *Liberty*, IX (Oct. 1, 1932), p. 12.

5. ER, untitled MS labeled only "Reader Questions and ER Answers" (undated but probably 1933), "ER, Speeches and Articles," Box 4, FDRL; *The Wisdom of Eleanor Roosevelt* (a compilation of her columns done for *McCall's Magazine*) (New York, n.d.), p. 16.

6. *New York Times* (July 17, 1917); FDR to ER (July 18, 1917), quoted in Elliott Roosevelt (ed.) and James Rosenau (asst.), *F.D.R. His Personal Letters 1905–1928* (New York, Duell, Sloan and Pearce, 1948), p. 349.

7. ER to FDR (July 20, 1917), quoted in Elliott Roosevelt (ed.) and

Rosenau (asst.), *F.D.R. His Personal Letters 1905–1928*, p. 350; ER to FDR (August, 1920); ER to Sara Delano Roosevelt (autumn, 1920), both quoted in James Roosevelt and Sidney Shalett, *Affectionately, F.D.R.* (New York, Harcourt, Brace and Co., 1959), pp. 133–34; Frank Freidel, *Franklin D. Roosevelt: The Ordeal* (Boston, Little, Brown and Co., 1954), p. 72.

8. ER, *This Is My Story* (New York, Harper & Brothers, 1937), p. 316.

9. ER, "Women Must Learn to Play the Game as Men Do," *Red Book Magazine*, L (April, 1928), p. 78.

10. ER, *This Is My Story*, p. 347.

11. Interview with Marion Dickerman (May 25, 1965); *New York Times* (Aug. 7, 1922).

12. Flora Merrill, "Mrs. Franklin D. Roosevelt's Opinions On What the Tariff Bill Means In the Home," *Democratic Bulletin*, IV (Oct., 1929), p. 10; *New York Times* (Nov. 2, 1924); Bellamy Partridge, *The Roosevelt Family in America* (New York, Hillman-Curl, Inc., 1936), p. 291; ER, unpublished article entitled "Politics Here and Elsewhere" (undated but 1928), "ER, Speeches and Articles," Box 1, FDRL.

13. ER, *It's Up to the Women* (New York, Frederick A. Stokes Co., 1933), p. 202.

14. ER, untitled MS, "ER, Speeches and Articles," Box 1, FDRL.

15. ER, "In Defense of Curiosity," *The Saturday Evening Post*, CCVIII (Aug. 24, 1935), pp. 8–9.

16. ER, *This Is My Story*, p. 320; copy of radio speech delivered over Station WRNY (Nov. 2, 1927), "ER, Speeches and Articles," Box 1, FDRL.

17. *New York Times* (Nov. 1, 1925); Lash, *Eleanor Roosevelt*, p. 87.

18. Speech before the Democratic Junior League (Jan. 4, 1927), quoted in the *New York Times* (Jan. 5, 1927); ER to FDR (no date but mid-1920's), quoted in Alfred Steinberg, *Mrs. R* (New York, G. P. Putnam's Sons, 1958), p. 144.

19. Mrs. Halsey W. Wilson to editor, *New York Times* (April 7, 1928); ER, memo (undated but 1928), "ER, Speeches and Articles," Box 5, FDRL.

20. See, for example, "My Day" (Feb. 5, May 12, 1936; Feb. 3, 1937; Oct. 26, Dec. 28, 1938).

21. New York *Herald Tribune* (Oct. 26–27, 1934); Dorothy Frooks Peekskill to FDR (Nov. 4, 1934), "President's Personal File #2," Box 1, FDRL; *Newsweek*, IV (Nov. 3, 1934), p. 8.

22. "Papers of Mary W. Dewson," Group 37, Box #3, FDRL.

23. *Newsweek*, IX (April 17, 1937), p. 24; interview with Bess Furman Armstrong (June 11, 1965).

24. *Newsweek*, IX (April 17, 1937), p. 24.

25. Mary W. Dewson, "An Aid to the End," 2 vols. (unpublished MS, FDRL), pp. 8–11.

26. Emma Bugbee in the New York *Herald Tribune* (Jan. 16, 1934).

27. Cf. Chapter II of the present work.

28. ER, MS marked only "Speech, 1928," "ER, Speeches and Articles," Box 1, FDRL.

29. Grace Tully, *F.D.R. My Boss* (New York, Charles Scribner's Sons, 1949), p. 107.

30. ER, *This I Remember*, p. 99.

31. ER, radio speech for the Pond's Co. (March 3, 1933), "ER, Speeches and Articles," Box 3, FDRL.

32. ER, "I Want You to Write to Me" (from Mrs. Roosevelt's Page"), *Woman's Home Companion*, CX (Aug., 1933), p. 4.

33. Lucy E. Curtis to ER (July 15, 1933); Mrs. A. Godfrey to ER (Nov. 24, 1934); Mrs. Nevin E. Grieb to ER (Oct. 17, 1933), all in "Federal Emergency Relief Administration, Old Subject File" (hereinafter "FERA"), Box 84, National Archives, Washington, D.C.

34. Mrs. Gertrude Lee to ER (Jan. 3, 1935); Mrs. Jeanette Beresford to Fulton Oursler (March 22, 1934), forwarded to ER; Mrs. Iola Hancock to ER (Jan. 12, 1934), all in *ibid.*; [?] Olson to ER (autumn, 1933), quoted in James MacGregor Burns, *Roosevelt: The Lion and the Fox* (New York, Harcourt, Brace and Co., 1956), p. 194.

35. Mrs. Olive Winn to ER (Aug. 15, 1934); Mrs. Hazel B. Harcum to ER (Nov. 12, 1934), "FERA," Boxes 84, 85, National Archives.

36. Martha Pressly (FERA District Supervisor, South Carolina) to ER (July 2, 1934), *re* case of Mrs. Ottey M. Perry; ER to Mrs. R. M. Humphreys (Jan. 7, 1935), both in *ibid.*; "My Day" (Nov. 7, 1938).

37. Marian G. Haines to ER (Dec. 3, 1934); Clifford Puckett to ER (Aug. 10, 1934); Gertrude H. Hale to ER (May 11, 1935); John R. Lewis to ER (Jan. 17, 1934); Mrs. Ellison Gilmore to ER (Feb. 18, 1934); Mrs. A. F. deLespinasse to ER (Nov. 19, 1933); Mrs. Lilah Older Bell to ER (March 29, 1934), "FERA," Boxes 84, 85, National Archives.

38. Edith A. Lowell to ER (Nov. 1, 1934); Mrs. Harry Kaplan to ER (March 13, 1934); Marian G. Haines to ER (Dec. 3, 1934), *ibid.*, Box 84, National Archives.

39. Federal Emergency Relief Administration, *Proceedings of the Con-*

ference on Emergency Needs for Women (Nov. 20, 1933), *ibid.*, Box 85, National Archives.

40. Malvina T. Scheider to Ellen Woodward (June 26, Oct. 10, 1934); ER to Ellen Woodward (April 5, Sept. 1, 1934); transcript of long distance telephone conversation, Ellen Woodward and I. J. Steinbach (Head, FERA Bureau of Adjustment, Madison, Wisconsin, April 23, 1934); Chloe Owings to Ellen Woodward (Sept. 11, 1934), *ibid.*, Box 84, National Archives.

41. Katherine Hardy *et al.* to ER (Nov. 15, 1933); Julia Helm to ER (Dec. 28, 1934); Malvina T. Scheider to Chloe Owings (Dec. 2, 1933); memo, Harry Hopkins to Ellen Woodward (Dec. 8, 1933); Ellen Woodward to ER (Dec. 9, 1933), *ibid.*, Boxes 84, 85, National Archives.

42. ER to Louis Howe (April 28, 1933); Ickes to ER (Dec. 18, 1933); Vi Sutton to ER (Oct. 21, 1937), all in "President's Personal File #2," Howe and Ickes, Box 1; Sutton, Box 2, FDRL.

43. ER, unpublished MS entitled "How to Spend Christmas" (Dec. 12, 1932), "ER, Speeches and Articles," Box 2, FDRL.

44. "Diogenes" in the *Literary Digest*, CXIX (Jan. 26, 1935), p. 13.

45. Paul U. Kellogg to ER (April 20, 1934), "Papers of Survey Associates, Inc.," Box 105, Folder 792, Minnesota Social Welfare History Archives Center, Minneapolis; Lash, *Eleanor Roosevelt*, p. 27; Dewson, "An Aid to the End," I, p. 2; for Taussig see Chapter I of the present work; for White see Chapter II of the same.

46. Freidel, *Franklin D. Roosevelt: The Ordeal*, p. 70.

47. ER (as told to Catherine Brody), "What I Want Most Out of Life," *Success Magazine*, XI (May, 1927), p. 70.

48. ER, MS of interview with M. K. Wisehart, "Mrs. Franklin D. Roosevelt Answers A Big Question — What Is A Wife's Job Today?" "ER, Speeches and Articles," Box 1, FDRL. This interview, in somewhat revised form, was published in *Good Housekeeping*, XCI (Aug., 1930).

49. ER, "Wives of Great Men," *op. cit.*, pp. 12–16.

50. Drawing reproduced in Roger Butterfield, *The American Past* (New York, Simon and Schuster, 1947), p. 409; Arthur M. Schlesinger, Jr., *The Crisis of the Old Order* (Boston, Houghton Mifflin Co., 1957), p. 263.

51. Lela Stiles, *The Man Behind Roosevelt* (Cleveland and New York, World Publishing Co., 1954), p. 265; Arthur M. Schlesinger, Jr., *The Coming of the New Deal* (Boston, Houghton Mifflin Co., 1958), p. 15.

52. ER, "It Seems to Me," *McCall's Magazine*, LXXVI (July, 1949), p. 16; Arthur L. Hennessy, "Bonus March of 1932" (unpublished Ph.D. dissertation, Georgetown University, 1957), pp. 333–35.

53. *New York Times* (July 30, 1932).

54. Hennessy, *Bonus March of 1932*, pp. 348–49.

55. *New York Times* (Oct. 20, 1932).

56. Maurice P. Sneller, "The Bonus March of 1932" (unpublished Ph.D. dissertation, University of Virginia, 1960), p. 321.

57. *Ibid.*, pp. 320–21.

58. Stiles, *The Man Behind Roosevelt*, p. 265.

59. James Roosevelt and Shalett, *Affectionately, F.D.R.*, p. 314; ER, *This I Remember*, p. 56; Kathleen McLaughlin, "Mrs. Roosevelt Goes Her Way," *New York Times Magazine* (July 5, 1936), p. 7.

60. Frances Perkins, *The Roosevelt I Knew* (New York, The Viking Press, 1946), p. 70; Tully quoted in Schlesinger. *The Coming of the New Deal*, p. 526; Rexford G. Tugwell, *The Democratic Roosevelt* (Garden City, New York, Doubleday and Co., Inc., 1957), pp. 528–29.

61. Tugwell, *The Democratic Roosevelt*, pp. 527–29.

62. Monte Bourjaily to Steve Early (May 11, 1933); T. V. Ranck to Louis Howe (June 2, 1933), both in "President's Personal File #2," Box 1, FDRL; *Newsweek*, VII (Jan. 4, 1936), p. 32; *Time*, XXVII (Jan. 13, 1936), p. 23; *Time*, XXXIII (April 17, 1939), p. 22.

63. "My Day" (July 7, 1936; March 6, 1937; June 3, 1938).

64. *Ibid.* (July 17, Sept. 29, 1936; July 3, 1937; April 18, 1938).

65. *Ibid.* Dec. 11–15, 1936; Jan. 19, 30, Feb. 2, 1937; Feb. 2, 1938).

66. Oswald Garrison Villard, "Issues and Men," *The Nation*, CXLII (April 15, 1936), p. 482; letter from reader and ER's answer in "My Day" (Jan. 26, 1937); letters of encouragement commented upon (Feb. 1, 1937).

67. ER, untitled MS, "ER, Speeches and Articles," Box 1, FDRL.

68. "My Day" (July 17, Oct. 27 and 28, 1936).

69. *Ibid.* (Oct. 30, 1936).

70. *Ibid.* (Nov. 7, 1938).

71. *Ibid.* (Feb. 10, 13, 1937).

72. *The Saturday Evening Post*, CCXII (Sept. 9, 1939), p. 24; Arthur Krock in the *New York Times* (Aug. 10, 1939).

73. Tully, *F.D.R. My Boss*, p. 110; *Time*, XXXIV (Oct. 9, 1939), p. 12; FDR to ER (Nov. 13, 1940); quoted in Elliott Roosevelt (ed.) and Joseph Lash (asst.), *F.D.R. His Personal Letters 1928–1945*, 2 vols. (New York, Duell, Sloan and Pearce, 1950), II, p. 1077.

74. Bernard F. Donahoe, *Private Plans and Public Dangers* (South Bend, Indiana, University of Notre Dame Press, 1965), *passim*.

75. James A. Farley, *Jim Farley's Story* (New York, McGraw-Hill Book Co., Inc., 1948), pp. 299–300.

76. Perkins, *The Roosevelt I Knew*, p. 133.

77. Lash, *Eleanor Roosevelt*, p. 139.

78. Bernard Bellush, *Franklin D. Roosevelt as Governor of New York* (New York, Columbia University Press, 1955), p. 8; Freidel, *Franklin D. Roosevelt: The Ordeal*, p. 255.

79. Schlesinger, *The Crisis of the Old Order*, p. 422; ER to FDR (n.d. but early 1941), quoted in James Roosevelt and Shalett, *Affectionately, F.D.R.*, pp. 301–02.

80. Tugwell, *The Democratic Roosevelt*, p. 497.

81. Robert E. Sherwood, *Roosevelt and Hopkins* (New York, Harper & Brothers, 1948), p. 117; Farley, *Jim Farley's Story*, p. 314.

82. "My Day" (Jan. 18, 1937); memorandum, ER to FDR (Aug., 1938), quoted in Elliott Roosevelt (ed.) and Lash (asst.), *F.D.R. His Personal Letters 1928–1945*, II, p. 802; Lash, *Eleanor Roosevelt*, p. 243.

83. Quoted in Lash, *Eleanor Roosevelt*, p. 243.

84. B. W. Hill to Elenore [sic] Roosevelt (June 30, 1938); Elmer P. Mooney to FDR (Feb. 14, 1940); "President's Personal File #2," Box 2, FDRL.

85. ER, "Can A Woman Ever Be President of the United States?" *Hearst's International Cosmopolitan*, IC (Oct., 1935), p. 22.

86. Frank Freidel (citing an interview with Frances Perkins), *Franklin D. Roosevelt: The Triumph* (Boston, Little, Brown and Co., 1956), p. 17.

87. ER, "What Do Ten Million Women Want[?]" *The Home Magazine*, V (March, 1932), pp. 19–20.

88. ER "Wives of Great Men," *op. cit.*, p. 16.

89. ER to FDR (October, 1940), quoted in James Roosevelt and Shalett, *Affectionately, F.D.R.*, p. 301.

90. Lash, *Eleanor Roosevelt*, p. 38; Samuel I. Rosenman, *Working With Roosevelt* (New York, Harper & Brothers, 1952), p. 346.

91. Rosenman, *Working With Roosevelt*, p. 346; Sherwood, *Roosevelt and Hopkins*, p. 831; Tugwell, *The Democratic Roosevelt*, pp. 527–29; Jesse H. Jones with Edward Angly, *Fifty Billion Dollars* (New York, The Macmillan Co., 1951), p. 264.

92. Farley, *Behind the Ballots*, p. 354; introduction of Mrs. Roosevelt by Mrs. Thomas F. McAllister, Director of the Women's Division of the Democratic National Committee, before the National Institute of Government, Washington, D.C. (May 4, 1940), quoted by Senator Alben Barkley, Democrat of Kentucky, in the *Congressional Record*, 76th Congress, 3rd Session (May 15, 1940), p. A2959.

93. Herkimer (N.Y.) *Evening Telegram* (Feb. 12, 1934).

94. ER to Steve Early (July 22, 1936); ER to Marvin McIntyre (Aug. 28, 1936), copies of both in "President's Personal File #2," Box 1, FDRL.

95. Taussig to FDR (Feb. 14, 1938), "Papers of Charles W. Taussig," Section I, Box 14, FDRL.

IV. ADVISER TO A NATION

1. Harold L. Ickes, *The Secret Diary of Harold L. Ickes*, 3 vols. (New York, Simon and Schuster, 1953–54), I, p. 218.

2. Allen F. Kifer, "The Negro Under the New Deal 1933–1941" (unpublished Ph.D. dissertation, University of Wisconsin, 1961), pp. 156–57.

3. "My Day" (Feb. 7, 1938); ER, speech entitled "The Widening Horizon of the Home" (n.d. but early 1930's), "ER, Speeches and Articles," Box 5, FDRL.

4. ER, copy of a radio speech delivered July 12, 1932; ER, MS entitled "Must Success Wear A Hair Shirt?" typed June 6, 1933, and sent to *Liberty Magazine* but never published, both in "ER, Speeches and Articles," Box 2, FDRL.

5. ER, speech at Cornell University for Farm and Home Week (Feb. 14, 1935), "ER, Speeches and Articles," Box 6, FDRL.

6. Clarence E. Pickett, *For More Than Bread* (Boston, Little, Brown and Co., 1953), p. 45; ER, *This I Remember* (New York, Harper & Brothers, 1949), pp. 129–31; ER, *If You Ask Me* (New York, D. Appleton-Century Co., Inc., 1946), p. 27.

7. Alfred B. Rollins, Jr., *Roosevelt and Howe* (New York, Alfred A. Knopf, 1962), p. 407.

8. Wesley Stout, "The New Homesteaders," *The Saturday Evening Post*, CCVII (Aug. 4, 1934), pp. 5–6; Rollins, *Roosevelt and Howe*, p. 409.

9. Paul K. Conkin, *Tomorrow A New World* (Ithaca, New York, Cornell University Press, 1959), pp. 240–42. See also Millard Milburn Rice, "Footnote on Arthurdale," *Harper's Magazine*, CLXXX (March, 1940), p. 411.

10. Washington (D.C.) *Star* (April 29, 1934); ER, typed MS of an article entitled "Subsistence Homesteads," published in *Forum and Century*, XCI (April, 1934), pp. 199–201, MS in "ER, Speeches and Articles," Box 5, FDRL.

11. Pickett, *For More Than Bread*, pp. 58–59; Conkin, *Tomorrow A New World*, pp. 246–48.

12. *Congressional Record*, 73rd Congress, 2nd Session (Jan. 24–26, 1934), pp. 1272, 1359, 1431–32.

13. *Ibid.* (Feb. 19, 1934), pp. 2753–54.

14. *Ibid.* (Feb. 28, 1934), pp. 3417, 3433–34; (March 7, 1934), p. 3902.

15. Conkin, *Tomorrow A New World*, pp. 251–52; Rollins, *Roosevelt and Howe*, pp. 409–10.

16. Ickes, *Secret Diary*, I, pp. 18, 207, 218, 228.

17. *Ibid.*, pp. 252–54, 260–61, 266, 271, 442.

18. "My Day" (May 24, 1937; June 28, 1938). For other of her favorable references to Arthurdale see columns of Jan. 28, April 8, and Dec. 3, 1936, and June 19, 1937.

19. S. J. Woolf, "Energy," *New York Times Magazine* (May 28, 1939), p. 10.

20. ER, *This I Remember*, p. 133.

21. Conkin, *Tomorrow A New World*, pp. 245, 250, 254.

22. Washington (D.C.) *Post Magazine* (Aug. 12, 1934), pp. 5–6.

23. Conkin, *Tomorrow A New World*, p. 255.

24. ER, "Economic Readjustments Necessary," *Democratic Bulletin*, VII (Aug., 1932), p. 4; ER, speech to the New York State Adult Education Dept. (early 1934), "President's Personal File #2," Box 1, FDRL.

25. ER, MS entitled "Must Success Wear A Hair Shirt?" see fn. #4; ER, speech at Ithaca, New York, for Farm and Home Week (Feb. 14, 1935), "ER, Speeches and Articles," Box 6, FDRL.

26. ER, "Economic Readjustments Necessary," *op. cit.*, p. 5; ER, "Ratify the Child Labor Amendment" (from "Mrs. Roosevelt's Page"), *Woman's Home Companion*, LX (Sept., 1933), p. 4.

27. "My Day" (March 19, 1936).

28. *Ibid.* (March 7, 1938).

29. ER, "Economic Readjustments Necessary," *op. cit.*, pp. 3–4.

30. ER, untitled speech (dated 1928), before a women's group, "ER, Speeches and Articles," Box 1, FDRL.

31. *New York Times* (Oct. 10, 1924); ER, untitled speech before a women's group (dated 1928), "ER, Speeches and Articles," Box 1, FDRL; Flora Merrill, "Mrs. Franklin D. Roosevelt's Opinions on What [the] Tariff Bill Means In the Home," *Democratic Bulletin*, IV (Oct., 1929), p. 11.

32. ER, article (apparently unpublished) entitled "Politics Here and Elsewhere" (dated 1924 but should be 1928), "ER, Speeches and Articles," Box 1, FDRL; ER, "Women in Politics," radio speech delivered over WABC (Sept. 21, 1928), copy in *ibid.*

33. ER, "Women in Politics," see fn. #32.

34. ER, "Economic Readjustments Necessary," *op. cit.*, p. 4; ER, "Pres-

entation of $500 Award in National Smiles Contest" (Dec. 1, 1932), "ER, Speeches and Articles," Box 1, FDRL.

35. "My Day" (Feb. 20, 1936).

36. *Ibid.* (March 1, 1938).

37. *Ibid.* (Dec. 30, 1938; June 24, 1939).

38. *Ibid.* (Aug. 6, 1940).

39. Ralph Robey, "Mrs. Roosevelt on Conscription of Wealth" (from "Business Tides"), *Newsweek*, XVI (Aug. 19, 1940), p. 38.

40. ER, remarks delivered to an American Youth Congress group (February, 1940), quoted in Joseph P. Lash, *Eleanor Roosevelt: A Friend's Memoir* (Garden City, New York, Doubleday and Co., Inc., 1964), p. 67.

41. Quoted in the *New Republic*, XVI (Feb. 9, 1918), p. 43.

42. *New York Times* (Aug. 7, 1922).

43. For Mrs. Roosevelt's ideas on this score see ER, "Servants," *The Forum*, LXXXIII (Jan., 1930); ER, *It's Up To the Women* (New York, Frederick A. Stokes Co., 1933), pp. 27-30; "My Day" (Sept. 14, 1936); *Time Magazine*, XXXIV (Dec. 11, 1939), p. 16.

44. ER, "Setting Our House in Order" (from "Mrs. Roosevelt's Page"), *Woman's Home Companion*, LX (Oct., 1933), p. 4; copies of union publications which featured Mrs. Roosevelt's sponsorship of union-made goods can be found in "President's Personal File #2," Box 2, FDRL.

45. ER, *This I Remember*, p. 200.

46. "My Day" (Feb. 10, 1937).

47. Walter D. Britt to ER (Nov. 4, 1933), "Federal Emergency Relief Administration, Old Subject File," Box 84, National Archives, Washington, D.C.

48. Ellen Woodward to Walter D. Britt (Nov. 25, 1933), *ibid.*

49. Ellen Woodward to Frederick I. Daniels (Nov. 25, 1933), *ibid.*

50. "My Day" (Feb. 7, 1937).

51. *Ibid.* (Sept. 3, 1936; April 4, 1939).

52. *Ibid.* (Feb. 12, 1937; April 7, 1939).

53. *New York Times* (March 20, 1940).

54. *Ibid.*

55. "My Day" (March 23, 1940).

56. See, for example, "My Day" (Jan. 21, June 17, July 7, Nov. 12–18, 1936; Sept. 30, 1937).

57. ER to Sara Delano Roosevelt (July 25, 1905), quoted in Elliott Roosevelt (ed.) and James Rosenau (asst.), *F.D.R. His Personal Letters 1905–1928* (New York, Duell, Sloan and Pearce, 1948), p. 48.

58. Lash, *Eleanor Roosevelt*, pp. 108, 148; "My Day" (Dec. 21, 1938).

59. "My Day" (Jan. 18, 1938); ER, "In Defense of Curiosity," *The Saturday Evening Post*, CCVIII (Aug. 24, 1935), p. 64.

60. ER to Mary (Molly) Dewson (Dec. 23, 1925), "Papers of Mary W. Dewson," Group 37, Box 1, FDRL; "My Day" (May 21, 1937); Lash, *Eleanor Roosevelt*, p. 108.

61. Ray Allen Billington, "Government and the Arts: The WPA Experience," *American Quarterly*, XIII (Winter, 1961), p. 468; "My Day" (Dec. 13, 1936; Oct. 19, 1938); ER, *passim* in "Speeches and Articles," Box 6, FDRL; see also remarks of Edward Bruce, NBC radio broadcast (April 25, 1940), in honor of American artists who contributed to the decoration of federal buildings, read into the *Congressional Record* by Senator Elbert D. Thomas, Democrat of Utah, 76th Congress, 3rd Session (April 29, 1940), p. A2478.

62. "My Day" (May 21, 1936).

63. Gerald Rabkin, *Drama and Commitment: Politics in the American Theatre of the Thirties* (Bloomington, Indiana, University of Indiana Press, 1964), pp. 95–123, *passim;* "My Day" (Feb. 16, 1938).

64. Westbrook Pegler, "Fair Enough," New York *World-Telegram* (June 1, Aug. 6, 9, 16, 1940).

65. Hugh Taylor Lovin, "The American Communist Party and the Spanish Civil War, 1936–1939" (unpublished Ph.D. dissertation, University of Washington, 1963), p. 405; interview with Bess Furman Armstrong (June 11, 1965); "Mrs. Roosevelt and the Newspaper Guild," *Christian Century*, LVII (Aug. 28, 1940), p. 1044.

66. "My Day" (March 21, 1936).

67. *Ibid.* (Jan. 29, 1936; May 6, 1939); Hilda W. Smith to ER (June 29, 1939), "Papers of Hilda W. Smith," Box 33, FDRL.

68. *New York Times* (Dec. 5, 1933); Billington, Government and the Arts: The WPA Experience," *op. cit.*, p. 472; H. Glyn Thomas, "The Highlander Folk School: The Depression Years," *Tennessee Historical Quarterly*, XXIII (Dec., 1964), pp. 363–64.

69. *The Highlander Fling* (Sept., 1939); Thomas, "The Highlander Folk School: The Depression Years," *op. cit.*, p. 366.

70. Thomas, "The Highlander Folk School: The Depression Years," *op. cit.*, p. 368; Oklahoma City *Times* (undated but autumn, 1940), in "President's Personal File #2," Box 2, FDRL.

71. Pueblo (Colo.) *Chieftain* (Nov. 1, 1940); R. T. Blair to FDR (Nov. 7, 1940), "President's Personal File #2," Box 2, FDRL.

72. Malvina Thompson to Hilda W. Smith (Sept. 26, 1940); Smith to

ER (Oct. 10, 1940); Smith to Thompson (Nov. 11, 1941), "Hilda Smith Papers," Box 33, FDRL.

73. Lash, *Eleanor Roosevelt*, pp. 227–30.

74. *Literary Digest*, CXVII (May 12, 1934), p. 12; Dorothy Dunbar Bromley, "The Future of Eleanor Roosevelt," *Harper's Magazine*, CLXXX (Jan., 1940), p. 137.

75. ER, speech entitled "The Next Step" (1925), "ER, Speeches and Articles," Box 1, FDRL.

76. ER, *It's Up to the Women*, p. 158; ER, "The Next Step," "ER, Speeches and Articles," Box 1, FDRL; ER, remarks during a radio broadcast entitled "Women Want Peace" (WJZ, Blue Network, Oct. 9, 1935), copy in "ER, Speeches and Articles," Box 6, FDRL.

77. ER, copy of untitled speech delivered over the NBC radio network (Jan. 27, 1935); ER, remarks during a New York *Herald Tribune* conference on international affairs (Oct. 15, 1935), both in "ER, Speeches and Articles," Box 6, FDRL; John Gunther, *Roosevelt in Retrospect* (New York, Harper & Brothers, 1950), p. 299.

78. Lash, *Eleanor Roosevelt*, p. 198; "My Day" (Feb. 10, April 2, 1939); ER to FDR (April 1, 1939), copy in "President's Personal File #2," Box 2, FDRL; Gunther, *Roosevelt in Retrospect*, p. 191.

79. "My Day" (March 18, 1936).

80. *Ibid.* (June 2, 1937).

81. *Ibid.* (Sept. 14, Oct. 9, 1937).

82. *Ibid.* (June 19, 1937).

83. *Ibid* (April 6, June 14, Sept. 22, 1938).

84. *Ibid.* (May 29, 1937; July 13, 1940); Lash, *Eleanor Roosevelt*, p. 83.

85. *New York Times* (Nov. 21, 1939); Raymond Moley, *27 Masters of Politics* (New York, Funk and Wagnalls Co., 1949), p. 26; *Newsweek*, XIV (Dec. 25, 1939), pp. 12–13.

86. Lash, *Eleanor Roosevelt*, fn., p. 113, fn., p. 133; Gustav Regler, *The Owl of Minerva* (New York, Farrar, Straus and Cudahy, 1960), pp. 363–66.

87. "My Day" (Sept. 17, 29, 1938; May 19, Aug. 1, Sept. 5, 1939).

88. *Ibid.* (Sept. 24, 1938).

89. *Ibid.* (Feb. 3, 14, 1939).

90. *Ibid* (March 24, 1939); *Time*, XXXIII (April 17, 1939), p. 22.

91. "My Day" (Sept. 5, 19, 1939); *Time*, XXXV (April 15, 1940), p. 17; "My Day" (July 17, 1940).

92. *Berliner Nachtusgabe*, quoted in the *New York Times* (Jan. 25, 1939); the (Berlin) *Lokal-Anzeiger* quoted in the same source (Feb. 5, 1939).

93. Lash, *Eleanor Roosevelt*, fn., pp. 88, 92–93; Bromley, "The Future of Eleanor Roosevelt," *op. cit.*, p. 137.

94. Malvina Thompson to Paul French (Nov. 28, 1939), "Hilda Smith Papers," Box 33, FDRL.

95. Lash, *Eleanor Roosevelt*, pp. 38, 47; "My Day" (June 19, 1940); ER, *The Moral Basis of Democracy* (New York, Howell, Soskin & Co., 1940), pp. 13–14.

96. "My Day" (May 18, 22, 1940); ER, *The Moral Basis of Democracy*, p. 50.

97. Harold J. Laski, *Where Do We Go From Here?* (New York, The Viking Press, 1940), Chap. 3, *passim*; Lash, *Eleanor Roosevelt*, pp. 96, 154–59, 201.

v. Reformer at Large

1. *New York Times* (Jan. 16, 1939).

2. *Fortune*, XXI (May, 1940), p. 160.

3. ER, "In Defense of Curiosity," *The Saturday Evening Post*, CCVIII (August 24, 1935), p. 9; ER, *It's Up to the Women* (New York, Frederick A. Stokes Co., 1933), pp. 203–04; ER, "What I Want Most Out of Life," *Success Magazine*, XI (May, 1927), p. 16.

4. Raymond Moley, *27 Masters of Politics* (New York, Funk and Wagnalls Co., 1949), p. 39.

5. "My Day" (May 30, 1936); Joseph P. Lash, *Eleanor Roosevelt: A Friend's Memoir* (Garden City, New York, Doubleday and Co., Inc., 1964), pp. 48, 149.

6. "My Day" (Feb. 5, 1937); Arthur S. Link, *Wilson: The New Freedom* (Princeton, New Jersey, Princeton University Press, 1956), p. 71; Alfred Steinberg, *Mrs. R* (New York, G. P. Putnam's Sons, 1958), p. 206; and see especially Tamara K. Hareven, "The Social Thought of Eleanor Roosevelt" (unpublished Ph.D. dissertation, Ohio State University, 1965), pp. 181–82.

7. *New York Times* (April 7, 1925); ER, radio speech (Dec. 9, 1932), copy in "ER, Speeches and Articles," Box 3, FDRL; The Unofficial Observer (John Franklin Carter), *The New Dealers* (New York, The Literary Guild, 1934), p. 210; Lorena Hickok, *Reluctant First Lady* (New York, Dodd, Mead and Co., 1962), pp. 152–54; Steinberg, *Mrs. R*, pp. 218–19.

8. Alice Rogers Hager, "Candidates For the Post of First Lady," *New York Times Magazine* (Oct. 2, 1932), p. 5.

9. *New York Times Index* (1924–1933).

10. *Ibid.*

11. "ER, Speeches and Articles," Box 3, FDRL; *Time*, XXXV (April 15, 1940), p. 17; *New York Times* (July 4, 1940); Lash, *Eleanor Roosevelt*, p. 83.

12. Dorothy Dunbar Bromley, "The Future of Eleanor Roosevelt," *Harper's Magazine*, CLXXX (Jan., 1940), p. 130.

13. Steve Early to Edward Keating (April 4, 1938), "President's Personal File #2," Box 2, FDRL; *Time*, XXXIX (March 8, 1937), p. 36.

14. "My Day" (March 5, 1937).

15. Bellamy Partridge, *The Roosevelt Family in America* (New York, Hillman-Curl, Inc., 1936), p. 284.

16. A. J. Schob to FDR (Sept. 21, 1934), and attached memorandums (n.d.) which give the feelings of Louis Howe, Steve Early, and FDR, "President's Personal File #2," Box 1, FDRL.

17. ER, *It's Up to the Women*, p. 81; ER, "In Defense of Curiosity," *op. cit.*, pp. 64–65.

18. "My Day" (Jan. 16, 1937; Jan. 28, 1939).

19. ER, broadcasts for the Selby Shoe Co., copies of which are in "ER, Speeches and Articles," Box 6, FDRL.

20. Kathleen McLaughlin, "Mrs. Roosevelt Wants 'Just A Little Job,'" *New York Times Magazine* (Oct. 8, 1944), p. 42.

21. Lela Stiles, *The Man Behind Roosevelt* (Cleveland and New York, World Publishing Co., 1954), p. 105; Grace Tully, *F.D.R. My Boss* (New York, Charles Scribner's Sons, 1949), p. 119.

22. Illegible signature to FDR (Feb. 18, 1935); Al Stentz to FDR (Feb. 16, 1935); "A Friend, A Democrat" to FDR (undated); Margaret Frankland to FDR (Feb. 24, 1935); Anonymous to FDR (Feb. 27, 1935), all in "President's Personal File #2," Box 1, FDRL.

23. New York *Post* (Jan. 23, 1933).

24. Fred Cusimano to Editor, Cleveland *Press* (n.d. but early 1930's); "An American Citizen" to Editor, New York *Herald Tribune* (Feb. 25, 1935); Bess Boultinghouse to FDR (June 16, 1936); Ernest M. Townsend to FDR (Feb. 13, 1938), all in "President's Personal File #2," Boxes 1 and 2, FDRL; for Hildebrandt's remarks see *Congressional Record*, 74th Congress, 1st Session (June 7, 1935), p. 8862.

25. "My Day" (Aug. 13, 1938).

26. See "President's Personal File #2," Box 1, FDRL, and particularly therein the (Springfield) *Illinois State Register* (undated but late 1933).

27. Interview, Helen Jane Wamboldt with Elizabeth von Hesse (Oct. 19,

1951), quoted in Helen Jane Wamboldt, "Anna Eleanor Roosevelt: A Descriptive and Analytical Study of the Speaking Career of AER" (unpublished Ph.D. dissertation, University of Southern California, 1952), pp. 182–84.

28. Geneva Kretsinger, "An Analytical Study of Selected Radio Speeches of Eleanor Roosevelt" (unpublished Master's thesis, University of Oklahoma, 1941), pp. 157–59.

29. ER, untitled radio speech delivered over WRNY (Nov. 2, 1927), copy in "ER, Speeches and Articles," Box 1, FDRL; ER, address to the National Institute of Government, Washington, D.C. (May 4, 1940), excerpts of which were read into the *Congressional Record* by Senator Alben W. Barkley, Democrat of Kentucky, 76th Congress, 3rd Session (May 15, 1940), pp. A2959–60.

30. "My Day" (Jan. 20, 1936); ER, untitled MS (dated 1928), "ER, Speeches and Articles," Box 1, FDRL; ER, "Wives of Great Men," *Liberty*, IX (Oct. 1, 1932), p. 12; ER, "The Seven People Who Shaped My Life," *Look*, XV (June 19, 1951), pp. 54–58.

31. ER, *This Is My Story* (New York, Harper & Brothers, 1937), p. 9; Lash, *Eleanor Roosevelt*, pp. 26, 129.

32. "My Day" (March 13, July 30, 1937).

33. ER, "Ethics of Parents" (1927), never published, MS in "ER, Speeches and Articles," Box 1, FDRL.

34. Searle F. Charles, *Minister of Relief* (Syracuse, New York, Syracuse University Press, 1963), p. 239; New York *Herald Tribune* (Oct. 27, 1934); Robert E. Sherwood, *Roosevelt and Hopkins* (New York, Harper & Brothers, 1948), p. 99.

35. James A. Farley, *Jim Farley's Story* (New York, McGraw-Hill Book Co., Inc., 1948), p. 317; Clarence E. Pickett, *For More Than Bread* (Boston, Little, Brown and Co., 1953), pp. 171–72; Harold L. Ickes, *The Secret Diary of Harold L. Ickes*, 3 vols. (New York, Simon and Schuster, 1953–54), III, p. 371; Lash, *Eleanor Roosevelt*, pp. 127, 212.

36. ER, untitled speech delivered at the Federal Industrial Institution for Women, Alderson, West Virginia (May, 1934), "ER, Speeches and Articles," Box 5, FDRL; "My Day" (Sept. 16, 1938); ER to Bernard Baruch (May 11, 1936), quoted in Margaret L. Coit, *Mr. Baruch* (Boston, Houghton Mifflin Co., 1957), p. 451; Farley, *Jim Farley's Story*, p. 299; interview with James A. Farley (May 14, 1965).

37. Lash, *Eleanor Roosevelt*, pp. 209–11; ER, *This I Remember* (New York, Harper & Brothers, 1949), p. 349.

38. Anonymous to FDR (Feb. 27, 1935), "President's Personal File #2," Box 1, FDRL.

39. Frank Freidel, *Franklin D. Roosevelt: The Apprenticeship* (Boston, Little, Brown and Co., 1952), p. 58.

40. *Ibid.*, pp. 66, 70.

41. Quoted in Rita Halle Kleeman, *Gracious Lady* (New York, D. Appleton-Century Co., Inc., 1935), p. 241. The date of the letter is not given, but its context indicates it was written sometime in 1903 or 1904.

42. Steinberg, *Mrs. R*, pp. 58–63; Farley, *Jim Farley's Story*, p. 315.

43. ER to Sara Delano Roosevelt (Dec. 2, 1903), quoted in Elliott Roosevelt (ed.), *F.D.R. His Personal Letters Early Years* (New York, Duell, Sloan and Pearce, 1947), p. 517; ER to Sara Delano Roosevelt (June 7, Aug. 2, 8, 1905), quoted in Elliott Roosevelt (ed.) and James Rosenau (asst.), *F.D.R. His Personal Letters 1905–1928* (New York, Duell, Sloan and Pearce, 1948) pp. 4, 55, 59.

44. James MacGregor Burns, *Roosevelt: The Lion and the Fox* (New York, Harcourt, Brace and Co., 1956), p. 28; Steinberg, *Mrs. R*, p. 61.

45. ER, "Ethics of Parents," see fn. #33.

46. ER to Sara Delano Roosevelt (July 5, Aug. 8, 1905), quoted in Elliott Roosevelt (ed.) and Rosenau (asst.), *F.D.R. His Personal Letters 1905–1928*, pp. 28, 59.

47. ER, "Grandmothers Can Still Be Young," *Liberty*, IX (Feb. 20, 1932), p. 38.

48. ER, *It Seems To Me* (New York, W. W. Norton & Co., Inc., 1954), p. 176.

49. ER, untitled article written in 1928 or 1929 (but never published) which is composed of thinly veiled autobiographical material. "ER, Speeches and Articles," Box 1, FDRL.

50. ER, *This Is My Story*, p. 173.

51. Gerald W. Johnson, *Roosevelt: Dictator or Democrat?* (New York, Harper & Brothers, 1941), p. 67.

52. Jonathan Daniels, *The Time Between the Wars* (Garden City, New York, Doubleday and Co., Inc., 1966), pp. 208–09.

53. Raymond Moley, "Perspective," *Newsweek*, LXVIII (Aug. 29, 1966), p. 76; Drew Pearson, "Eleanor Did Not Give Up Easily," (Butte-Anaconda) Montana *Standard* (Aug. 17, 1966); Arthur M. Schlesinger, Jr., "F.D.R.'s 'Secret Romance,'" *Ladies' Home Journal*, LXXXIII (Nov., 1966), pp. 66–71.

54. John Gunther, *Roosevelt in Retrospect* (New York, Harper & Brothers, 1950), p. 73; Freidel, *Franklin D. Roosevelt: The Apprenticeship*, fn., p. 320; Burns, *Roosevelt: The Lion and the Fox*, p. 68; Arthur M. Schlesinger, Jr., *The Crisis of the Old Order* (Boston, Houghton Mifflin

Co., 1957), pp. 354–55; Jonathan Daniels, *The End of Innocence* (New York and Philadelphia, J. B. Lippincott Co., 1954), p. 233.

55. *Newsweek*, quoting an unnamed friend of the former Miss Mercer, LXVIII (Aug. 22, 1966), p. 60.

56. Daniels, *The Time Between the Wars*, p. 208; Sara Delano Roosevelt to ER and FDR (Oct. 14, 1917), quoted in Elliott Roosevelt (ed.) and Rosenau (asst.), *F.D.R. His Personal Letters 1905–1928*, pp. 274–75.

57. FDR to ER (July 16, 1917), quoted in Elliott Roosevelt (ed.) and Rosenau (asst.), *F.D.R. His Personal Letters 1905–1928*, p. 347.

58. Elliott Roosevelt (ed.) and Rosenau (asst.), *F.D.R. His Personal Letters 1905–1928*, p. 37; ER to FDR (1913), quoted in James Roosevelt and Sidney Shalett, *Affectionately, F.D.R.* (New York, Harcourt, Brace and Co., 1959), p. 150.

59. *Time*, LXXXVIII (Aug. 26, 1966), p. 13; Raymond Moley, "Perspective," *Newsweek*, LXVIII (Aug. 29, 1966), p. 76; ER to FDR (May, 1931), quoted in James Roosevelt and Shalett, *Affectionately, F.D.R.*, p. 313.

60. FDR to ER (July 5, 1934), quoted in Elliott Roosevelt (ed.) and Joseph Lash (asst.), *F.D.R. His Personal Letters 1928–1945*, 2 vols. (New York, Duell, Sloan and Pearce, 1950), I, p. 404.

61. Rexford G. Tugwell, *The Democratic Roosevelt* (Garden City, New York, Doubleday and Co., Inc., 1957), p. 303.

62. Ickes, *Secret Diary*, III, p. 396; Samuel I. Rosenman, *Working With Roosevelt* (New York, Harper & Brothers, 1952), p. 347; Tully, *F.D.R. My Boss*, p. 78.

63. James Roosevelt and Shalett, *Affectionately, F.D.R.*, p. 317.

64. Arthur M. Schlesinger, Jr., "F.D.R.'s 'Secret Romance,'" *op. cit.*, p. 68.

65. *Ibid.*, p. 71.

66. Pearson, "Eleanor Did Not Give Up Easily," (Butte-Anaconda) *Montana Standard* (Aug. 17, 1966).

67. James Roosevelt and Shalett, *Affectionately, F.D.R.*, p. 317.

68. Rosenman, *Working With Roosevelt*, p. 347; ER, *It Seems To Me*, p. 131.

69. ER, speech entitled "The Next Step," (1925), "ER, Speeches and Articles," Box 1, FDRL; ER to Mrs. Alida Miller (March 22, 1930), quoted in Clarke A. Chambers, *Seedtime of Reform: American Social Service and Social Action 1918–1933* (Minneapolis, University of Minnesota Press, 1963), p. 167; "My Day" (Feb. 2, 1939); ER to Mary Dewson

(March 9, 1934), "Papers of Mary W. Dewson," Group 37, Box 16, FDRL.

70. Lash, *Eleanor Roosevelt*, p. 38.

71. "My Day" (Jan. 11, 1939); ER, speech before an American Youth Congress testimonial dinner in her honor, New York City (Feb., 1939), quoted in Leslie A. Gould, *American Youth Today* (New York, Random House, 1940), p. 98.

72. ER, "Wives of Great Men," *op. cit.*, p. 12; ER, "Building Character," *Parent's Magazine*, VI (June, 1931), p. 17; ER, unpublished article, "Must Success Wear A Hair Shirt?" (June, 1932), "ER, Speeches and Articles," Box 2, FDRL. Cf. John M. Blum, *The Republican Roosevelt* (Cambridge, Massachusetts, Harvard University Press, 1954), p. 33.

73. Schlesinger, "F.D.R.'s 'Secret Romance,'" *op. cit.*, p. 68; ER, speech at Women's Faculty Club, Howard University, Washington, D.C. (Dec. 5, 1935), copy in "ER, Speeches and Articles," Box 6, FDRL; ER, "Must Success Wear A Hair Shirt?" see fn. #72.

74. "My Day" (June 24, 1939); ER "Suggested Draft of [A] Message from Mrs. Roosevelt to [A] YWCA and YMCA Joint Luncheon," New York City (Oct., 1933), "ER, Speeches and Articles," Box 5, FDRL; ER, "Mobilization for Human Needs," *Democratic Digest*, VIII (Nov., 1933), p. 3.

75. ER, "Address by Mrs. Franklin D. Roosevelt at Benefit Concert — Women's Trade Union League" (Nov. 28, 1932), "ER, Speeches and Articles," Box 2, FDRL; H. G. Wells, *Experiment in Autobiography* (New York, The Macmillan Co., 1934), pp. 681–82; The Unofficial Observer (John Franklin Carter), *The New Dealers*, pp. 213–14; Oswald Garrison Villard, "Issues and Men," *The Nation*, CXLII (April 15, 1936), p. 482; Lash, *Eleanor Roosevelt*, p. 201.

76. "My Day" (Aug. 31, 1936; June 25, 1938).

77. ER, quoted in *Time*, XXXIII (March 6, 1939), p. 11; quoted in Lash, *Eleanor Roosevelt*, p. 231; memo, Morris Ernst to ER and ER to FDR, marked only "Received 10/11/40," "President's Personal File #2," Box 2, FDRL.

78. "My Day" (June 24, 1940); ER, address to the Monmouth County (N.J.) Women's Press Club, quoted in the *New York Times* (June 30, 1940).

79. Tugwell, *The Democratic Roosevelt*, pp. 60, 414.

80. Prestonia Mann Martin, *Prohibiting Poverty* (New York, Farrar and Rinehart, 1932), pp. 9, 15, 26.

81. *Ibid.*, pp. 19, 22–23, 35, 81.

82. Caroline Bird, *The Invisible Scar* (New York, David McKay Co.,

Inc., 1966), p. 90; ER to Mrs. Prestonia Mann Martin (hereinafter PMM) (Dec. 4, 1933), "Papers of Eleanor Roosevelt," FDRL.

83. PMM to ER (Oct. 8, 1934); ER to PMM (Oct. 9, 1934), "Eleanor Roosevelt Papers," FDRL.

84. PMM to ER (spring, 1936); ER to PMM (June 4, 1936); PMM to ER (June 21, 1940), all in *ibid*.

85. "My Day" (Jan. 24, 1936); ER, speech for WPA "Open House" Week, excerpts of which were read by Representative Clarence Cannon, Democrat of Missouri, into the *Congressional Record*, 76th Congress, 3rd Session (May 21, 1940), p. 6538.

86. ER, quoted in Dorothy Dunbar Bromley, "The Future of Eleanor Roosevelt," *op. cit.*, p. 137; ER, "Wives of Great Men," *op. cit.*, p. 14.

87. Arthur Schlesinger, Jr., commenting upon Eric Goldman's *Rendezvous With Destiny* (New York, Alfred A. Knopf, Inc., 1952).

BIBLIOGRAPHY

Almost all bibliographies are somewhat selective, and the one which follows makes no pretense of being an exception. The literature pertaining to the Roosevelt era is huge, and the greater portion of it usually touches in some way on Mrs. Roosevelt. Nevertheless, this writer has chosen to limit his citations to only that material of which he made the most direct use. To include further works of a general nature would result in virtually a separate volume.

The most useful source material for a study of Eleanor Roosevelt consists of her own words, and it is fortunate for the student of her career that she left an abundance of these. Copies of them are to be found in a wide variety of places; unquestionably, however, they are in the greatest profusion and are best organized for research purposes in the Franklin D. Roosevelt Library at Hyde Park, New York. Here one finds, first of all, bound volumes of her column "My Day"; and these columns are, furthermore, in unedited form which serves to increase their interest. Although it is true that Mrs. Roosevelt could not, by way of her column, give vent to her innermost thoughts on certain subjects, this diary-like series nevertheless remains a matchlessly valuable barometer of the First Lady's interests and reflections. The columns were often hastily prepared, but for that very reason they contained a spontaneity and insight into her perspective on a variety of matters which might well have been lacking in a more deliberately calculated presentation. Those who would know Eleanor Roosevelt must devote to these columns a careful attention and not be disarmed by their bland exterior.

Of even greater importance, there are at the Roosevelt Library six bulky and immensely rewarding boxes of Mrs. Roosevelt's unedited speeches and articles covering the years from 1924 to 1936.

These boxes add up to over one thousand pages of manuscript, much of which has never been published in any form; and this writer has perhaps relied more on this material than on any other single source. A careful reading of these drafts provides a splendid guide to Eleanor Roosevelt's outlook concerning a vast array of subjects. Finally, with respect to her own words, the Library houses copies of essentially all of Mrs. Roosevelt's published articles, articles of which this writer made considerable use and to which references are made in the following pages.

One section of the "Papers of Franklin D. Roosevelt" is of especial relevance to his wife, that section being the one labeled "Eleanor Roosevelt" in President's Personal File #2. The two boxes (nos. 1 and 2) of which this section is partially comprised yield copies of correspondence between FDR and the First Lady, letters of constituents to the Chief Executive concerning his wife's activities, and a number of newspaper articles pertaining to the same subject. Almost all this material sheds additional light upon the role of Mrs. Roosevelt and how it was viewed by a variety of citizens and spokesmen. The Franklin D. Roosevelt Library also has numerous other collections which bear upon the activities of the First Lady, and these will be cited below.

1. *The Words of Eleanor Roosevelt*

UNPUBLISHED MATERIAL (Franklin D. Roosevelt Library, Hyde Park, New York):

"My Day" (unedited copies). Eighteen pilot articles and December 30, 1935–December 31, 1940.
"Eleanor Roosevelt, Speeches and Articles." Boxes 1 through 6.
"Papers of Mrs. Franklin D. Roosevelt." Correspondence with Mrs. Prestonia Mann Martin.

FURTHER UNPUBLISHED MATERIAL

"Papers of Mary W. Dewson." Group 37, Boxes 1, 3, 16. Franklin D. Roosevelt Library, Hyde Park, New York.
"Papers of the Federal Emergency Relief Administration, Old Subject File, Correspondence with the White House." Boxes 84, 85. National Archives, Washington, D.C.

"Papers of Franklin D. Roosevelt." President's Personal File #2, Boxes 1 and 2. Franklin D. Roosevelt Library, Hyde Park, New York.
"Papers of Hilda W. Smith." Box 33. Franklin D. Roosevelt Library, Hyde Park, New York.
"Papers of Survey Associates, Inc." Box 105, Folder 792. Minnesota Social Welfare History Archives Center, Minneapolis, Minnesota.
"Papers of Charles W. Taussig." Section I, Box 14, Folder Y–134. Franklin D. Roosevelt Library, Hyde Park, New York.
"Papers of Aubrey Williams." Group 58, Box 4. Franklin D. Roosevelt Library, Hyde Park, New York.

PUBLISHED ARTICLES:

Roosevelt, Eleanor, "As A Practical Idealist." *The North American Review*, CCXXIV, November, 1927.
——, "Building Character." *Parent's Magazine*, VI (June, 1931).
——, "Can A Woman Ever Be Elected President of the United States?" *Hearst's International-Cosmopolitan*, IC (October, 1935).
——, "Economic Readjustments Necessary." *Democratic Bulletin*, VII (August, 1932).
——, "Fear Is the Enemy." *The Nation*, CL (February 10, 1940).
——, "Flying Is Fun." *Collier's*, CIII (April 22, 1939).
——, "Grandmothers Can Still Be Young." *Liberty*, IX (February 20, 1932).
——, "Ideal Education." *Woman's Journal*, XV (October, 1930).
——, "In Defense of Curiosity." *The Saturday Evening Post*, CCVIII (August 24, 1935).
——, "Jeffersonian Principles the Issue in 1928." *Current History*, XXVIII (June, 1928).
——, "A Message to Parents and Teachers." *Progressive Education*, XI (January–February, 1934).
——, "Mobilization For Human Needs." *Democratic Digest*, VIII (November, 1933).
——, "Passing Thoughts of Mrs. Franklin D. Roosevelt." *Women's Democratic News*, VIII and IX (February–June, 1933).
——, "Presenting Babies — Just Babies." *Babies, Just Babies*, I (October, 1932).
——, "Race, Religion and Prejudice." *New Republic*, CVI (May 11, 1942).
——, (interview with M. K. Wisehart), "Mrs. Franklin D. Roosevelt Answers A Big Question — What Is A Wife's Job Today?" *Good Housekeeping*, XCI (August, 1930).
——, "Mrs. Roosevelt Believes in Paroles." *The Periscope*, III (October, 1935).

———, "Mrs. Roosevelt's Page." *Woman's Home Companion*, LXLXII (August, 1933–July, 1935).

———, "Servants." *The Forum*, LXXXIII (January, 1930).

———, "The Seven People Who Shaped My Life." *Look*, XV (June 19, 1951).

———, "Some of My Best Friends are Negro." *Ebony*, IX (February, 1953).

———, "Subsistence Homesteads." *Forum and Century*, XCI (April, 1934).

———, "What Do Ten Million Women Want?" *The Home Magazine*, V (March, 1932).

———, (as told to Catherine Brody), "What I Want Most Out of Life." *Success Magazine*, XI (May, 1927).

———, "What Religion Means to Me." *The Forum*, LXXXVIII (December, 1932).

———, "Wives of Great Men." *Liberty*, IX (October 1, 1932).

———, "The Woman's Crusade." *Daughters of the American Revolution Magazine*, LXVIII (January, 1934).

———, "Women Must Learn to Play the Game as Men Do." *Redbook Magazine*, L (April, 1928).

PUBLISHED BOOKS:

Roosevelt, Eleanor, *If You Ask Me*. New York, D. Appleton-Century Co., Inc., 1946.

———, *It Seems to Me*. New York, W. W. Norton & Co., Inc., 1954.

———, *It's Up to the Women*. New York, Frederick A. Stokes Co., 1933.

———, *Ladies of Courage*, with Lorena Hickok. New York, G. P. Putnam's Sons, 1954.

———, *The Moral Basis of Democracy*. New York, Howell, Soskin & Co., 1940.

———, *This I Remember*. New York, Harper & Brothers, 1949.

———, *This Is My Story*. New York, Harper & Brothers, 1937.

———, *The Wisdom of Eleanor Roosevelt* (a compilation of her columns for *McCall's Magazine* from June, 1954, until November, 1962). New York, no date.

II. *Eleanor Roosevelt as Principal Subject:*

UNPUBLISHED MATERIAL:

Bilsborrow, Eleanor Janice, "The Philosophy of Social Reform in the Speeches of Eleanor Roosevelt." Unpublished Ph.D. dissertation, University of Denver, 1957.

Hareven, Tamara Kern, "The Social Philosophy of Eleanor Roosevelt." Unpublished Ph.D. dissertation, Ohio State University, 1965.

Kearney, James R., "Mrs. Eleanor Roosevelt and the American Negro." Unpublished Master's thesis, Washington University, 1962.

Kretsinger, Geneva, "An Analytical Study of Selected Radio Speeches of Eleanor Roosevelt." Unpublished Master's thesis, University of Oklahoma, 1941.

Ranck, Gloria Virginia, "A Study of Selected Speeches by Mrs. Franklin D. Roosevelt on Human Rights." Unpublished Master's thesis, University of Washington, 1952.

Spence, Benjamin A., "Mrs. Eleanor Roosevelt and Refugee Problems 1938–1952." Unpublished Master's thesis, University of Wisconsin, 1962.

Wamboldt, Helen Jane, "Anna Eleanor Roosevelt: A Descriptive and Analytical Study of the Speaking Career of AER." Unpublished Ph.D. dissertation, University of Southern California, 1952.

PUBLISHED ARTICLES:

Bromley, Dorothy Dunbar, "The Future of Eleanor Roosevelt." *Harper's Magazine*, CLXXX (January, 1940).

Hager, Alice Rogers, "Candidates For the Post of First Lady." *New York Times Magazine* (October 2, 1932).

Juno, Irene, "In the Air With Our Flying First Lady." *Good Housekeeping*, XCVI (June, 1933).

Lachman, Seymour P., "The Cardinal, the Congressmen, and the First Lady." *A Journal of Church and State*, VII (Winter, 1965).

McLaughlin, Kathleen, "The First Lady's View of the First Lady Role." *New York Times Magazine* (January 21, 1940).

———, "Mrs. Roosevelt Goes Her Way." *New York Times Magazine* (July 5, 1936).

———, "Mrs. Roosevelt Wants 'Just A Little Job,'" *New York Times Magazine* (October 8, 1944).

Merrill, Flora, "Mrs. Franklin D. Roosevelt's Opinion on What the Tariff Bill Means in the Home." *Democratic Bulletin*, IV (October, 1929).

Pegler, Westbrook, "Eleanor Roosevelt." *American Opinion*, VI (February, 1963).

Rice, Diana, "Mrs. Roosevelt Takes on Another Task." *New York Times Magazine* (December 2, 1928).

Robey, Ralph, "Business Tides." *Newsweek*, XVI (August 19, 1940).

Rothchild, Florence, "The Mistress of the White House." *Wisconsin Jewish Chronicle*, Milwaukee (March 9, 1934).

Schlesinger, Arthur M., Jr., "F.D.R.'s 'Secret Romance.'" *Ladies' Home Journal*, LXXXIII (November, 1966).

Singer, Kurt, "Eleanor Roosevelt." *The Negro*, III (July, 1946).
Woolf, S. J., "Energy." *New York Times Magazine* (May 28, 1939).
———, "A Woman Speaks Her Political Mind." *New York Times Magazine* (April 8, 1928).

NEWSPAPERS AND JOURNALS:

Akron *Beacon-Journal* (undated but probably November, 1937).
American Opinion, VI (September, 1963).
Bakersfield *Californian* (December 15, 1937).
Birmingham *Post* (July 17, 1937).
Boston *Transcript* (February 26, 1935).
Broun, Heywood, "It Seems to Me." New York *World-Telegram* (December 6, 1939).
Buffalo *Express* (November 12, 1939).
Chicago *Defender* (June 17, July 15, 1939).
Christian Century, LVII (August 28, 1940).
Cleveland *Press* (undated but early 1930's).
Detroit *Free Press* (February 14, 1940).
Fort Worth *Star-Telegram* (June 16, 1933).
Herkimer (New York) *Evening Telegram* (February 12, 1934).
Illinois State Register, Springfield (undated but late 1933).
Life, VIII (February 5, 1940).
Lippmann, Walter, "Today and Tomorrow." New York *Herald Tribune* (February 17, 1940).
Literary Digest, CI (June 29, 1929); CXVII (May 12, 1934); CXIX (January 26, 1935); CXXIII (March 6, 1937).
Minneapolis *Spokesman* (March 4, 1939).
New York *Age* (October 21, 1939).
New York *Post* (January 23, 1933).
New York *World* (March 18, 1905).
New York *World-Telegram* (December 2, 1939; February 14–16, 1940).
Oklahoma City *Times* (undated but autumn 1940).
Pearson, Drew, "Eleanor Did Not Give Up Easily." (Butte-Anaconda) Montana *Standard* (August 17, 1966).
Pegler, Westbrook, "Fair Enough." *New York World-Telegram* (June 1, August 2–16, 1940); San Francisco *Daily News* (March 17, 1938).
Pueblo (Colorado) *Chieftain* (November 1, 1940).
Richmond (Virginia) *Times-Dispatch* (February 14, 1940).
The Saturday Evening Post, CCXII (September 9, 1939).
U.S. News and World Report, LXI (August 22, 1966).
Villard, Oswald Garrison, "Issues and Men." *The Nation*, CXLII (April 15, 1936); CXLVIII (December 31, 1938).
Washington (D.C.) *Post* (August 12, 1934; February 11, 1940).
Washington (D.C.) *Star* (April 29, 1934).

PUBLISHED BOOKS:

Black, Ruby, *Eleanor Roosevelt*. New York, Duell, Sloan and Pearce, 1940.
Douglas, Helen Gahagan, *The Eleanor Roosevelt We Remember*. New York, Hill and Wang, 1963.
Harrity, Richard and Martin, Ralph G., *Eleanor Roosevelt: Her Life in Pictures*. New York, Duell, Sloan and Pearce, 1958.
Hickok, Lorena A., *Reluctant First Lady*. New York, Dodd, Mead and Co., 1962.
Lash, Joseph P., *Eleanor Roosevelt: A Friend's Memoir*. Garden City, New York, Doubleday and Co., Inc., 1964.
Steinberg, Alfred, *Mrs. R*. New York, G. P. Putnam's Sons, 1958.

INTERVIEWS:

Rolf Andersen. Emergency Shelter, Inc. New York City, May 15, 1965.
Bess Furman Armstrong. Washington, D.C., June 11, 1965.
Marion Dickerman. New Canaan, Connecticut, May 25, 1965.
James A. Farley. New York City, May 14, 1965.
Raymond Moley. New York City, May 26, 1965.
Harry S Truman. Independence, Missouri, September, 1963.

III. *Newspapers and periodicals upon which general reliance has been placed — either as reporting on Mrs. Roosevelt's speeches, commenting on her activities, or observing and interpreting relevant topics:*

The Crisis, Volumes XXXIX–XLVII (November, 1932–December, 1940).
The Nation, Volumes CXXVII–CL (1928–1940).
New Republic, Volumes XVI–CVI (1918–1942).
Newsweek, Volumes IV–LXVIII (1934–1966).
New York *Herald Tribune* (1934–1940).
New York Times (1917–1966).
Opportunity, Volumes XI–XVIII (1933–1940).
Time, Volumes XXVII–LXXXVIII (1936–1966).

IV. *Official Sources:*

Congressional Record. 73rd Congress, 2nd Session–76th Congress, 3rd Session.

Federal Emergency Relief Administration, *Proceedings of the Conference on Emergency Needs for Women*. Washington, D.C., 1933.
Hearings Before A Special Committee on Un-American Activities. House of Representatives, 76th Congress, 1st Session, November 30, December 1, 1939.

v. *General:*

UNPUBLISHED MATERIAL:

Arnold, Delbert D., "The CIO's Role in American Politics, 1936–1948." Unpublished Ph.D. dissertation, University of Maryland, 1952.
Dewson, Mary W., "An Aid to the End." 2 volumes, unpublished, Franklin D. Roosevelt Library, Hyde Park, New York.
Hennessy, Arthur L., "The Bonus March of 1932." Unpublished Ph.D. dissertation, Georgetown University, 1957.
Kifer, Allen F., "The Negro Under the New Deal 1933–1941." Unpublished Ph.D. dissertation, University of Wisconsin, 1961.
Lovin, Hugh Taylor, "The American Communist Party and the Spanish Civil War, 1936–1939." Unpublished Ph.D. dissertation, University of Washington, 1963.
Rawick, George P., "The New Deal and Youth: The Civilian Conservation Corps, the National Youth Administration, and the American Youth Congress." Unpublished Ph.D. dissertation, University of Wisconsin, 1957.
Riesch, Anna Lou, "Conservation Under Franklin D. Roosevelt." Unpublished Ph.D. dissertation, University of Wisconsin, 1952.
Robinson, George W., "Right of Roosevelt: Negativism and the New Deal." Unpublished Ph.D. dissertation, University of Wisconsin, 1956.
Sneller, Maurice P., "The Bonus March of 1932." Unpublished Ph.D. dissertation, University of Virginia, 1960.

ARTICLES:

Anderson, Clifford B., "The Metamorphosis of American Agrarian Idealism in the 1920's and 1930's." *Agricultural History*, XXXV (October, 1961).
Billington, Ray Allen, "Government and the Arts: The WPA Experience." *American Quarterly*, XIII (Winter, 1961).
Clapper, Raymond, "The Ten Most Powerful People in Washington." *Reader's Digest*, CLXXX (May, 1941).
Collins, Ernest M., "Cincinnati Negroes and Presidential Politics." *Journal of Negro History*, XLI (April, 1956).

Dubois, W. E. B., "Is Al Smith Afraid of the South?" *The Nation*, CXXVII (October 17, 1928).

Fishel, Leslie H., Jr., "The Negro in the New Deal Era." *Wisconsin Magazine of History*, XLVIII (Winter, 1964–65).

Krock, Arthur, "Did the Negro Revolt?" *Opportunity*, XI (January, 1933).

Lazarsfeld, Paul N., "The Negro Vote." *The Nation*, CLXIX (September 30, 1944).

Moley, Raymond, "Perspective." *Newsweek*, XIV (July 22, 1940); LXVIII (August 29, 1966).

Rice, Millard Milburn, "Footnote On Arthurdale." *Harper's Magazine*, CLXXX (March, 1940).

Salmond, John A., "The Civilian Conservation Corps and the Negro." *Journal of American History*, LII (June, 1965).

Stout, Wesley, "The New Homesteaders." *The Saturday Evening Post*, CCVII (August 4, 1934).

Sullivan, Lawrence, "The Negro Vote." *Atlantic Monthly*, CLXVI (October, 1940).

Thomas, H. Glyn, "The Highlander Folk School: The Depression Years." *Tennessee Historical Quarterly*, XXIII (December, 1964).

VanDeusen, John G., "The Negro in Politics." *Journal of Negro History*, XXI (July, 1936).

Ward, Paul W., "Wooing the Negro Vote." *The Nation*, CXLIII (August 1, 1936).

Watson, Richard L., Jr., "A Political Leader Bolts — F. M. Simmons in the Presidential Election of 1928." *North Carolina Historical Review*, XXXVII (October, 1960).

Weaver, Robert C., "The New Deal and the Negro." *Opportunity*, XII (July, 1935).

NEWSPAPERS AND JOURNALS:

Chicago *Tribune* (July 19, 1940).

Christian Science Monitor, Boston (February 12, 13, 1940).

New York *Daily Worker* (December 9, 1936; May 26, 1938).

Fortune, XXI (May, 1940).

The Highlander (Folk School, Tenn.) *Fling* (September, 1939).

Pittsburgh *Courier* (October 17, 1936; February 4, 1939).

St. Louis *Globe-Democrat* (February 13, 1940).

Salt Lake City *Tribune* (February 14, 1940).

Thompson, Dorothy, "On the Record." New York *Herald Tribune* (February 16, 1940).

Madison *Wisconsin State Journal* (December 26–30, 1939; July 5–8, 1940).

Youth Digest, I (December, 1938).

BOOKS:

Adams, Samuel Hopkins, *Incredible Era*. Boston, Houghton Mifflin Co., 1939.

Bellush, Bernard, *Franklin D. Roosevelt as Governor of New York*. New York, Columbia University Press, 1955.

Bird, Caroline, *The Invisible Scar*. New York, David McKay Co., Inc., 1966.

Blum, John M., *From the Morgenthau Diaries: Years of Crisis*. Boston, Houghton Mifflin Co., 1959.

——, *The Republican Roosevelt*. Cambridge, Massachusetts, Harvard University Press, 1954.

Burns, James MacGregor, *Roosevelt: The Lion and the Fox*. New York, Harcourt, Brace and Co., 1956.

Butterfield, Roger, *The American Past*. New York, Simon and Schuster, 1947.

Chambers, Clarke A., *Seedtime of Reform: American Social Service and Social Action 1918–1933*. Minneapolis, University of Minnesota Press, 1963.

Charles, Searle F., *Minister of Relief: Harry Hopkins and the Depression*. Syracuse, New York, Syracuse University Press, 1963.

Clapper, Olive, *Washington Tapestry*. New York, Whittlesey House, 1945.

Coit, Margaret L., *Mr. Baruch*. Boston, Houghton Mifflin Co., 1957.

Conkin, Paul K., *Tomorrow A New World*. Ithaca, New York, Cornell University Press, 1959.

Daniels, Jonathan, *The End of Innocence*. New York and Philadelphia, J. D. Lippincott Co., 1954.

——, *The Time Between the Wars*. Garden City, New York, Doubleday and Co., Inc., 1966.

Davies, Joseph E., *Mission to Moscow*. New York, Simon and Schuster, 1941.

Donahoe, Bernard F., *Private Plans and Public Dangers*. South Bend, Indiana, University of Notre Dame Press, 1965.

Dos Passos, John, *Midcentury*. Boston, Houghton Mifflin Co., 1961.

Farley, James A., *Behind the Ballots*. New York, Harcourt, Brace and Co., 1938.

——, *Jim Farley's Story*. New York, McGraw-Hill Book Co., 1948.

Flanagan, Hallie, *Arena*. New York, Duell, Sloan and Pearce, 1945.

Flynn, Edward J., *You're the Boss*. New York, The Viking Press, 1947.

Freidel, Frank, *Franklin D. Roosevelt: The Apprenticeship*. Boston, Little, Brown and Co., 1952.

——, *Franklin D. Roosevelt: The Ordeal*. Boston, Little, Brown and Co., 1954.

——, *Franklin D. Roosevelt: The Triumph*. Boston, Little, Brown and Co., 1956.

Geddes, Donald Porter, ed., *Franklin D. Roosevelt, A Memorial.* New York, The Dial Press, 1945.

Gould, Leslie, *American Youth Today.* New York, Random House, 1940.

Greer, Thomas H., *What Roosevelt Thought.* East Lansing, Michigan, Michigan State University Press, 1958.

Gunther, John, *Roosevelt In Retrospect.* New York, Harper & Brothers, 1950.

Harris, Louis, *Is There A Republican Majority?* New York, Harper & Brothers, 1954.

Holt, Rackham, *Mary McLeod Bethune.* Garden City, New York, Doubleday and Co., Inc., 1964.

Ickes, Harold L., *The Secret Diary of Harold L. Ickes,* 3 volumes. New York, Simon and Schuster, 1953–54.

Johnson, Gerald W., *Roosevelt: Dictator or Democrat?* New York, Harper & Brothers, 1941.

Jones, Jesse H., with Angly, Edward, *Fifty Billion Dollars.* New York, The Macmillan Co., 1951.

Kempton, Murray, *Part of Our Time.* New York, Simon and Schuster, 1955.

Kleeman, Rita Halle, *Gracious Lady.* New York, D. Appleton-Century Co., Inc., 1935.

Koenig, Louis W., *The Invisible Presidency.* New York, Rinehart and Co., Inc., 1960.

Laski, Harold J., *Where Do We Go From Here?* New York, The Viking Press, 1940.

Lasky, Victor, *J.F.K., The Man and the Myth.* New York, The Macmillan Co., 1963.

Leuchtenburg, William E., *Franklin D. Roosevelt and the New Deal 1932–1940.* New York, Harper & Row, 1963.

Lindley, Ernest K., *The Roosevelt Revolution.* New York, The Viking Press, 1933.

Link, Arthur S., *Wilson: The New Freedom.* Princeton, New Jersey, Princeton University Press, 1956.

Martin, Prestonia Mann, *Prohibiting Poverty.* New York, Farrar and Rinehart, 1932.

Mathews, Thomas, *Puerto Rican Politics and the New Deal.* Gainesville, Florida, University of Florida Press, 1960.

Moley, Raymond, *After Seven Years.* New York, Harper & Brothers, 1939.

—— (with the assistance of Elliot A. Rosen), *The First New Deal.* New York, Harcourt, Brace & World, 1966.

——, *27 Masters of Politics.* New York, Funk and Wagnalls Co., 1949.

Moon, Henry Lee, *Balance of Power: The Negro Vote.* Garden City, New York, Doubleday and Co., Inc., 1948.

Moore, Edmund A., *A Catholic Runs For President*. New York, Ronald Press Co., 1956.

Morgan, Edward P., and Swing, Raymond G., eds., *This I Believe*. New York, Simon and Schuster, 1952.

Partridge, Bellamy, *The Roosevelt Family in America*. New York, Hillman-Curl, Inc., 1936.

Perkins, Frances, *The Roosevelt I Knew*. New York, The Viking Press, 1946.

Pickett, Clarence E., *For More Than Bread*. Boston, Little, Brown and Co., 1953.

Pringle, Henry F., *The Life and Times of William Howard Taft*, 2 volumes. New York, Farrar and Rinehart, Inc., 1939.

Rabkin, Gerald, *Drama and Commitment: Politics in the American Theatre of the Thirties*. Bloomington, Indiana, University of Indiana Press, 1964.

Regler, Gustav, *The Owl of Minerva*. New York, Farrar, Straus and Cudahy, 1959.

Robinson, Edgar Eugene, *The Roosevelt Leadership 1933–1945*. Philadelphia and New York, J. B. Lippincott Co., 1955.

Rollins, Alfred B., Jr., *Roosevelt and Howe*. New York, Alfred A. Knopf, 1962.

Roosevelt, Elliott, ed., *F.D.R. His Personal Letters Early Years*. New York, Duell, Sloan and Pearce, 1947.

———, and Rosenau, James N. (asst.), *F.D.R. His Personal Letters 1905–1928*. New York, Duell, Sloan and Pearce, 1948.

———, and Lash, Joseph (asst.), *F.D.R. His Personal Letters 1928–1945*, 2 volumes. New York, Duell, Sloan and Pearce, 1950.

Roosevelt, James, and Shalett, Sidney, *Affectionately, F.D.R.* New York, Harcourt, Brace and Co., 1959.

Rosenman, Samuel I., (compiler and collator), *The Public Papers and Addresses of Franklin D. Roosevelt*, Volume IX. New York, The Macmillan Co., 1941.

———, *Working With Roosevelt*. New York, Harper & Brothers, 1952.

Rostow, W. W., *The Stages of Economic Growth*. Cambridge, The University Press, 1961.

Schlesinger, Arthur M., Jr., *The Coming of the New Deal*. Boston, Houghton Mifflin Co., 1958.

———, *The Crisis of the Old Order*. Boston, Houghton Mifflin Co., 1957.

———, *The Politics of Upheaval*. Boston, Houghton Mifflin Co., 1960.

Sheean, Vincent, *Dorothy and Red*. Boston, Houghton Mifflin Co., 1963.

Sherwood, Robert E., *Roosevelt and Hopkins*. New York, Harper & Brothers, 1948.

Sinclair, Andrew, *The Available Man*. New York, The Macmillan Co., 1965.

Smith, Gene, *When the Cheering Stopped*. New York, William Morrow & Co., Inc., 1964.

Stiles, Lela, *The Man Behind Roosevelt*. Cleveland and New York, World Publishing Co., 1954.

This Is Youth Speaking (transcript of the February, 1940, Citizenship Institute in Washington, D.C.). New York, The American Youth Congress, 1940.

Tugwell, Rexford G., *The Democratic Roosevelt*. Garden City, New York, Doubleday and Co., Inc., 1957.

Tully, Grace, *F.D.R. My Boss*. New York, Charles Scribner's Sons, 1949.

The Unofficial Observer (John Franklin Carter), *The New Dealers*. New York, The Literary Guild, 1934.

Wechsler, James A., *The Age of Suspicion*. New York, Random House, 1953.

Wells, H. G., *Experiment in Autobiography*. New York, The Macmillan Co., 1934.

White, Walter, *A Man Called White*. New York, The Viking Press, 1948.

Wolfskill, George, *The Revolt of the Conservatives: A History of the American Liberty League*. Boston, Houghton Mifflin Co., 1962.

INDEX